C

PART THREE: Her Son

For my beautiful wife Michelle, who passed away in September, 2024, and to our wonderful children, Mickey, Jazmin and Savannah, not forgetting my little granddaughter Grace who met Michelle and shines a bright light on us through such difficult times. A huge thank-you goes out to all the family and friends who have also been so supportive.

– David Gardner

To the amazing and kind-hearted Michelle and to my ever-supportive wife Katherine and children Joanna, Louise and Sophia for listening to me recounting this story for decades. And to my rumbustious grandchildren Luke, Monica, Grace, Esme, Robyn, Toby and Phoebe who make every day so joyful.

– Paul Henderson

A SPY IN
THE FAMILY

MIRROR BOOKS

1

First published in hardback in Great Britain and Ireland in 2025 by Mirror Books, a Reach PLC business.

www.mirrorbooks.co.uk
@TheMirrorBooks

Paperback ISBN: 9781917439534
Hardback ISBN: 9781915306975
eBook ISBN: 9781917439244

Photographic acknowledgements:
Johanna van Haarlem personal collection, Radek
Family personal collection, Pavel Horejsi

Every effort has been made to trace copyright.
Any oversights will be rectified in future editions.

Editing and Production: Christine Costello, Lauren McKeon, Chris Collins, Nick Loughlin

Printed and bound by CPI Group (UK) Ltd, Croydon, CR0 4YY.

A SPY IN THE FAMILY

PAUL HENDERSON DAVID GARDNER

mB

MIRROR BOOKS

CONTENTS

AUTHORS' NOTE

London, 14 December 2024

Some events stay with us forever. Family achievements, stories of love and loss, heartache and joy. They could even be all of these. They may cut so deep they haunt us, burning into our consciousness and cajoling us to do something about them.

Journalists witness snapshots in time that can be inspiring, lifting us up, or violent and deeply dehumanising, stopping the world in its otherwise largely comfortable tracks. Between us, we have covered wars in the Middle East, disasters from 9/11 to Lockerbie, unimaginable tragedies in Sandy Hook, Columbine, and Dunblane, serial killers, and presidential elections. We've covered a pandemic and parades and unique moments in history, including the Good Friday Agreement, which ended Northern Ireland's 30-year conflict, and the fall of the Berlin Wall, which ended the Cold War and opened up the possibility for this book.

As journalists and now authors, our minds keep returning to experiences at the ringside of history in the 100-plus countries, and still counting, from which we have filed reports as foreign correspondents. David was based in New York and Los Angeles for 26 years, and Paul in New York and Miami for five years. When Paul was in London as an editor during the last decade we collaborated on stories on a transatlantic basis.

But, throughout the years, there has always been one story that stood out as unfinished business. It wasn't globally momentous, but it was uniquely resonant of the great human qualities of perseverance, resilience, refusal to surrender, and downright dogged tenacity to get to the truth.

In April 1988, news broke that a Cold War spy had been arrested. David, then a *Daily Mail* crime correspondent, heard from his sources that armed Special Branch officers caught a suspected Soviet Bloc agent red-handed in his north London flat sending coded radio messages to his spymasters. David began working his police and security service contacts for background on the story for months leading up to the agent's trial. The spy was an illegal operative in the shadows, a sleeper ready to be activated for missions drawn up by his spymasters. Some spies work under the auspices of a foreign embassy with a certain level of protection. Others – the "illegals" – are on their own, controlled by their home intelligence masters and separate from the diplomatic service, who will deny any knowledge of them.

David was at London's Old Bailey in 1989 when the agent stood before a judge and jury to face charges of espionage against the state. No one, other than his Czech bosses, knew his real identity. In the Old Bailey, the judge, the prosecutor and the defence team all called him Erwin van Haarlem, even though they knew this name was false.

The newspapers labelled him "The Spy With No Name".

David listened enthralled as Johanna van Haarlem, the prosecution's star witness, told how she had been duped into believing the man in the dock was the son she'd left in a Czechoslovakian children's home during World War Two. In Pitman's shorthand, David took down Johanna's every word as he listened to her testimony from the crowded press benches.

It was already late afternoon when he got to a phone to file his story. The press room in the bowels of the Old Bailey sounded like the frenetic stock exchange just up the road in the City of London. The cacophony was not about financial transactions; this noise came from national paper and agency journalists close to the deadline, filing their pieces about the cruel deception of a spy.

David's report that Johanna was on her way home to the Netherlands meant a reporter had to be sent to Europe to track her down and then try to interview her. *Daily Mail*'s brilliant editor David English drummed into us that stories of great human and public interest were the most important. The Van Haarlem case was now top of his list and we were called into English's office and instructed to tag team the story. We were told in no uncertain terms that the Mail must have every angle covered. It was an extremely competitive environment and it was our job to beat the rest of Fleet Street.

Paul rushed to Heathrow Airport to catch the next flight to Amsterdam. Outside Schiphol's arrivals terminal, he found a taxi driver who spoke reasonable English and, most importantly, had some new technology; a mobile phone fitted into his car. Paul could call London on the move and David could call Paul with any developments. Even better, this cabbie could work late into the night. By going through the country's telephone directories, we found a few Van Haarlem numbers and addresses in The Hague. These Van Haarlems turned out to be Johanna's relatives and one told Paul she was living in a small town called Schaijk in southern Holland. Three hours later, he was at the door but there was no answer at Johanna's woodland bungalow. Paul left a letter; hours later, Johanna called and consented to be interviewed later the next morning.

She opened up about her astonishing life of rejection and hurt. With the deadline approaching for the bigger Saturday edition print run, there was no time to type the story. Paul filed from his notebook around 2,000 words to a copytaker from the new-fangled car phone, telling Johanna's account of the spy story gripping Britain.

The revelations made the front page splash, bylined by David and Paul, and ran into a two-page inside spread. But, there was still work to be done. Johanna was determined to find the real Erwin and Paul was determined to help her follow the story to the end. Czechoslovakia had to be our starting point. Paul and Johanna made their first joint trip there in 1990, along with the masterful photographer Clive Limpkin. Over the years, there were more trips to Czechoslovakia but it wasn't until three-and-a-half decades later that the circle was finally closed and we learned the full truth about the story we started working on together all the way back in 1989.

During that time, the secrecy that defined Czechoslovakia under Soviet rule was replaced by a more transparent democracy and clues to Erwin's life and his ultimate plight were revealed in top secret documents we could never have dreamed of seeing during the Cold War years.

In The Hague, the Van Haarlem family's intriguing World War Two story unfolded through the National Archives; and in Prague, we tracked down 10,800 pages of intelligence service documents charting the work of the spy in the West. Over the last three years, we interviewed dozens of people, including lawyers from the Old Bailey trial, Special Branch officers, and many other victims of the spy's deceit. Woven together, their accounts present an intriguing story of intelligence services battling for control in the shadows of the Cold War at the expense of a mother who just wanted to find her son. This is a story of how a spy operated in deep cover in the UK for more than a decade, but it's also the story of one mother's incredible tenacity and perseverance.

In these pages, you will read how Paul travelled back in time with Johanna to piece together the jigsaw puzzle of what happened to the wartime baby that she was forced to give up.

We sincerely hope you enjoy our story as much as we have enjoyed writing about the memorable events that have stayed in our minds' eyes for 35 years.

PROLOGUE

Hainault Forest, Chigwell, Essex, May, 1977

He felt ridiculous. He'd caught the tube all the way across London and then waited 45 minutes in the rain to catch the bus to Hainault Forest, assuming there would be hardly anyone there. But the woods were teeming with red-faced ramblers all dressed in flapping cagoules in every colour of the rainbow.

He considered himself a snappy dresser, and sneered at the hardy folks with their shapeless camper store shorts, gnarly, rope-veiny legs, and evangelistic bonhomie. His shoulder-length dark brown hair and sharp Slavic features were shrouded in a shapeless hat, and he wore an oversized green anorak zipped to the neck over his smart shirt and slacks. He carried an old bag and a guide to wild mushrooms, showing which ones were good to eat and which were poisonous. As much as he detested the expensively careless zips and toggle clothing of his fellow naturalists, he fitted right in.

He looked at his watch. He'd allowed an extra 30 minutes to cater for the habitual lateness of the London Underground and now he was cutting it fine. He ignored the tea shop and its long, patient line of hungry pensioners and hurried to the park's notice board where he pretended to study the scraps of paper. He searched in his jacket pocket for a poster he'd printed off at the library the previous day. It was advertising a dog for sale. He pinned it on the board and headed for the woods.

The spy had used this dead letter drop since arriving in London. There was another one by the Old Bull and Bush pub in Hampstead which he preferred; it wasn't as far and you could get a glass of wine while you were there. But the forest's seclusion made it his preferred location for his most important drop-offs. He followed the trail to the fork and went right. About one-third of a mile down was a sharp left and there it was, a crooked old tree with branches showering down in an umbrella, offering some respite from the spitting rain. Walking around to the back of the trunk, he made sure no one was watching him before quickly placing a plastic shopping bag into a knotted hole in the bark. There was some other old trash in there; he didn't like to know what, but he wasn't worried. They'd be there soon to pick it up. He just needed a few minutes to get back on the bus.

On the way back, he saw a familiar shape of mushrooms sprouting from a muddy bank. He double-checked with his guide and picked a dozen or so. They were good for his cover and tasted great with rice.

The dog ad would let them know he'd been there. The arrangement was that he had 30 minutes to scarper. Then they'd make the collect. He didn't know who was doing it and he didn't want to know. More to the point, he didn't want them to know who he was. That was the deal.

The noticeboard was checked at the same time each week on a Tuesday so it didn't interfere with work. He tightened the anorak hood around his throat, peered at the bus stop timetable and waited with his mushrooms.

It took him nearly two hours to get back to his cozy, one-bedroom flat in Queen's Gate Gardens in South Kensington and he didn't have much time. He had to get to work. It was one of the drawbacks of working as a spy. He needed his job as a waiter as cover, but he had to work such long hours that there was barely enough time for spying.

In truth, it had been much harder than he'd expected after arriving in Britain with a new name and instructions from his bosses in Prague and Moscow to lie low. He was told to keep busy seeking connections with the Royal Family and the British Government and to report back on anything he could uncover about the West's nuclear arsenal, prime currency at the height of the Cold War. But his real mission was to be ready for anything.

A series of successful MI5 operations had all but emptied London of Soviet and Czech spooks and his superiors had earmarked him as the perfect "sleeper". They'd studied and tested his personality and profile, and found him to have the right ideological upbringing and ruthless confidence to work abroad alone.

Then they wiped his past clean. His history no longer existed. His parents, his childhood, and his friends were all gone. He was given a whole new identity. He had a new life. He learned to lie until it no longer felt like a lie but the truth. He'd been trained in everything from reading Morse code to killing with his bare hands to using unbreakable one-time cipher pads.

There would be a time when he would be called upon.

Until then, his most important assignment was to blend in and not get caught. His identity must be protected above all else. His trainers left him in no doubt that was his biggest secret – the one worth killing for.

Arriving back in South Kensington, he had time to decode the messages from his radio transmission the previous day. One approved his request for a new, small second-hand car and another reported that his parents had been visited by members of the agency's support staff and were well. His parents from another life.

A third message contained a hare-brained scheme to fit electronic bugs into the furniture at Buckingham Palace. He cursed under his breath. They had no idea. The closest he'd got to the royals so far had been in the crowd at the Trooping of the Colour.

He was more concerned about the piece of mail he'd received in the post the previous day – the very same document he'd just rushed to leave at the dead letter drop in Hainault Forest. He had no friends in his new country and none from his old life. His correspondence consisted almost entirely of bills. So he'd been shocked to discover a letter from the International Tracing Service of the Red Cross addressed to Erwin van Haarlem. That was him. The spy had been assured that his new name and stolen identity had come from an orphan. The real Erwin van Haarlem was one of the forgotten children of World War Two who were abandoned in orphanages across Europe. They had no parents and no need for a name or a past. Their only hope was to look forward.

The spy was now Erwin van Haarlem and the boy's history belonged to him. His adopted life story was so drilled into him that he almost believed it himself. It was a well-worn, foolproof tactic used by intelligence services on both sides of the Berlin Wall to hide the true identities of their illegal agents. But now he needed some advice from his spymasters in Prague. The Red Cross said it had been contacted by Erwin van Haarlem's mother.

And she wanted to meet her son.

PART ONE

THE MOTHER

CHAPTER ONE

The Hague, Holland, 19 November 1943

An icy wind whipped through the empty streets around the Van Haarlem family home in the old Hague. The few locals who dared to be out rushed through the shadows, heads down, desperate for the safety of their own walls. The short days and the long nights ran into one another, the relentless grey a welcome refuge from the harsh realities of life under occupation. The beach was just a tram or a cycle ride away, but nobody went there anymore.

Johanna van Haarlem was born on Tuesday, 19 November 1924. Her father, Izaak, ran a thriving home renovation firm, specialising in upholstery. Johanna Hendrika Hanegraaff, her mother, was dedicated to the wellbeing of her seven children, ranging in age from 25 to 11. They were staunch church members and considered pillars of the community. Izaak had become wealthy through inheriting property which he then sold. He lived with his wife and children in the house left to him by his parents in the sought-after district of The Hague.

In 1943, 19-year-old Johanna had no idea about the existence of the gas chambers, even as her Jewish neighbours were being trucked away for extermination. She knew nothing about the

Dutch resistance to the Nazi occupation of her country. She still believed the war was being fought somewhere else. That night in November, the curtains of her neighbours twitched along the road as Johanna walked arm in arm with an equally young man in a German military uniform. Her house was noisy with guests. The couple embraced briefly before Johanna pulled away and ran towards the light. The soldier pulled up his collar and shivered down into his overcoat with a last look at her as she slipped in the front door, her bowed head hiding an excited smile.

Nobody would have noticed her ghosting past the front room as men in distinctive field-grey jackets, swastikas on their arms, lounged in comfortable chairs drinking glasses of fine wine.

Johanna climbed the stairs to her room wondering if she would ever see the handsome serviceman again. She would not have been surprised at the noise going on downstairs late into the night, nor at the German guests her father invited into their home. In Izaak van Haarlem's front parlour the occupiers found a rare welcome from the occupied. Collaborators and occupiers alike drank in the van Haarlem's two connected houses at numbers 34-34a Soendastraat in the well-to-do, leafy suburb. Walther PPKs, bayonets and rifles were always set aside for drinking and the van Haarlems and their German guests ate at a dinner table full of the best food available – the type of food the family's neighbours now lacked. Johanna, naively innocent from a sheltered upbringing, didn't pay much attention to how the neighbours would view these gatherings. After all, she was following her father's example of being friendly with the Germans.

But the neighbours noticed the parties – what they didn't know, and what Johanna didn't even know, was that Izaak had a dangerous secret.

While Anne Frank, a German-born Jewish girl who became famous for her war-time diaries, was hiding in concealed rooms behind a bookcase across the country in Amsterdam fearing exposure with every inadvertent movement, Izaak, whose mother had been a Jew, was hiding his family's Jewish background in plain sight. While he had been raised as a Christian in the fundamentalist Gereformeerde Kerken, which practised strict Protestantism, he feared that one slip of the tongue about even a historic connection to the Jewish faith would lead to catastrophe for his family.

As it became increasingly clear that Germany had designs on Holland and the rest of Europe, Izaak showed his support for the Nazi cause. In 1937, he voted for the Dutch fascist party, the National Socialist Movement (Nationaal-Socialistische Beweging in Nederland, or NSB), which had developed a philosophy based on Italian fascism and German Nazism. His gamble appeared to pay off as the Nazis drew closer and the NSB began winning seats in the Senate, its populist support growing. Like so many others across Holland, the Van Haarlem family would have been glued to the radio when Dutch Prime Minister Hendrik Colijn insisted in a broadcast that everyone should sleep safely in their beds and there was no great cause for concern as war clouds gathered in 1938. But few Dutch were under any illusions. German military aggression could easily be turned on Holland.

Amidst the growing danger, Izaak might have tried to stay under the radar and hope his Jewish ancestry remained buried in the past, but he was too proud of his position in the community to fade into the background. He was also too greedy. He convinced himself cooperating with the Nazis was no bad thing, especially if it could protect his family from the worst abuses of an occupying force – and help him turn a profit in the process.

~

After the German invasion of Poland on 1 September 1939, betting on the Nazi's ultimate victory might have seemed like a safe enough wager. Two days later, Great Britain and France declared war on Germany. The Netherlands had mobilised its army, yet vowed to stay neutral. It was of no use. On 10 May 1940, Hitler ran roughshod over Holland's doomed attempts at neutrality and invaded. The Dutch military resistance lasted just one bombing in Rotterdam and five days of fighting before the capitulation was total. The government and the Dutch royal family fled to London. Dr Arthur Seyss-Inquart, the German Reichskommissar, moved into Plein 4 at the Logement van Rotterdam.

Not long after, the German military set up camp in Izaak's street, erecting tents and open-air kitchens where the occupying forces slept and ate in full view of the petrified locals. They'd been there ever since, using Izaak's upholstery shop as a command centre. Within a year of Holland's surrender to the Wehrmacht, Izaak voluntarily became a full member of the NSB. By November 1943, Izaak had ensured his wife was always busy in the kitchen and that his doors were always open to the Nazis.

The strategy appealed to the German occupiers and they returned his hospitality with lucrative upholstery and decorating contracts. Izaak's long-ago hatched plan had worked but it did not make him popular among friends and neighbours. He made no secret of his collaboration. German cars were always parked outside his two houses which were connected in the middle by an office. One house was used for accommodation and the other for storing materials, tools and other equipment used for renovation contracts. He wanted for nothing and neither did his children, who mixed freely with their guests. Excited conversations in German reverberated across the otherwise blacked-out, sulking neighbourhood as a nightly reminder of what people saw as the family's treachery.

The Germans had set up a telephone exchange in Izaak's office on the ground floor and at times German soldiers were living with the Van Haarlems. In other households across Holland, lodgers in uniform had forced their way in as unwelcome guests. In reality, nobody had the option to say no if a commandant demanded lodgings, whether they were willing collaborators or not. But Izaak never seemed to show any hidden resistance. An NSB flag flew from his house, and he walked the streets selling the party newspaper. He carried a list of his immediate neighbours and families in nearby streets to collect funds for the far-right movement. Some gave out of fear, but others declined even if they were marked out as dissenters.

Izaak became a NSB Block Leader wearing the NSB badge, meaning it was his job to hold meetings and encourage others to join the party. He also worked as a leader at a summer camp in 1942 and 1943 where supporters were indoctrinated in lectures about Nazism, effectively making the camps a form of German brainwashing. His very public political support for the occupiers did not go down well with other members at his Calvinist church, where he was a deacon, and he eventually left for the Reformed Church. The family became more and more isolated as the war went on and many friends and relatives shunned them. Izaak's immediate family had no choice in the matter. They were expected to follow and not to ask questions. His voice in the household was absolute.

Had his old neighbours been aware of his Jewish roots, they would have found it even more difficult to understand how he could betray his own blood. Izaak prided himself on being his own man. He was a decision-maker in business, in family matters and now in politics to ensure survival in torrid and dangerous times no matter what others thought of him. Not only were the opinions of relatives and neighbours of no importance to him, but he also didn't care what his wife and children thought.

Even if he was unaware of the full extent of the German atrocities, Izaak would have been aware of the Nazis' treatment of Jews. The entire Jewish community in The Hague, once the second largest in Holland, was almost entirely decimated during the occupation. He was determined to save his own skin.

CHAPTER TWO

Amsterdam, Holland, 11 November 1943

Johanna had met her handsome German soldier on a train earlier that week on her way home from her office job as a steno typist in The Hague. They had nothing in common but their youth and a desperation to escape from a war that had stolen a carefree youth from an entire generation. Sitting face-fto-face in the packed carriage, the brunette teenager tried her best to ignore the young soldier at first. But he smiled and he made faces and laughter was just one of the many things that were in short supply in wartime Holland. Finally, she relented. If there was something Johanna van Haarlem had learned living under occupation, it was that it was better to smile at the Germans than to scowl. Her father's protection only went so far.

By the time the short journey was over, they had reached an understanding. Life was short and they discovered they did see something in one another, after all; they both just wanted a little fun. He was alone, just back from the Front, based at nearby Wassenaar, an upscale North Sea town about 10 miles north of The Hague, and insistent on walking her home. Funny and sweet, he politely asked to see her again after accompanying her to the bike shed by the station where she would leave her bicycle for the short ride home from the train.

Before the war, she would have asked her father's permission for such a tryst, back in the days when he was a strictly adherent Protestant, and her mother was a devout Catholic. Now Izaak was a card-carrying Dutch Nazi who entertained the Germans. He had no problem with his daughters dating them. Indeed, he encouraged it.

Gregor Kulig was born in Siolkowica, Poland, on 7 June 1922. He had nothing personal against the Dutch, or indeed the British and French soldiers he was pitted against on the battlefield for months at a time. He wasn't even sure why they were fighting. The blond, blue-eyed serviceman had two overriding goals after being drafted from his farm and into action: to survive and to have fun wherever he could find it. His chance meeting with Johanna on the train, at the start of a rare R&R break from the Front, seemed to the 22-year-old Wehrmacht soldier to be a sure sign that his luck was finally changing. Desperate to forget the horrors he had witnessed across the border in France, Kulig had achieved his primary goal of survival, at least for now. The feisty Dutch girl with the sparkling eyes appeared to promise his best chance for some rare frivolity.

Johanna's older siblings were all signed up by their father in the NSB (although his Catholic wife refused to join). Johanna wasn't yet old enough to join the nascent Dutch Nazis, but Izaak settled for making her a member of the National Party youth movement, modelled on Germany's Hitler Youth. Johanna was nearing the end of her teens and insisted later that she joined the youth group for "the sporting activities". She was about to grow up very fast.

Kulig came calling a few times after that initial meeting and

Izaak made no attempt to prevent his daughter from seeing the ardent young soldier. Johanna, who was just 16 when the brief Dutch resistance to Hitler collapsed in 1940, didn't know anything back then about her Jewish grandmother or the threat it held to her. To her, a dalliance with an enemy soldier was nothing to be ashamed of. She followed the example set by her father to be friendly with the invaders. Her sister, Mary, who was three years older than Johanna, courted German soldiers and was allowed to invite them home to meet her parents. Johanna had been taken to a restaurant by Mary and her German beau for her 17th birthday and regularly attended German Lutheran services in The Hague with the soldiers. When she introduced the young soldier to her father, he made no attempt to end the relationship.

Kulig courted Johanna for a couple of weeks and, just before Christmas as the days ticked close to his return to the Front, he invited her to a birthday party for two of his officer friends at his base in Wassenaar. He picked her up from her house and they took the train together. German and Dutch couples were dancing together to a brass band and Johanna felt the troubles of the world slip away with the sway of the music. They toasted the safe return of the German troops from the front line. As the party moved into full swing, Kulig took Johanna's hand for a slow waltz. He was a good dancer and he led her to the edge of the parquet dance floor and opened a small door, quickly pushing her through it into a dimly lit room. There was no one else in the room and tables with covered typewriters surrounded her. Holding his hand across Johanna's mouth to stop her from screaming in surprise, he kept his other hand behind her back.

Fear gripped Johanna as she realised too late what was at stake. She struggled and screamed at her suitor to let go, but Kulig gripped her even tighter. They tripped over a chair leaning against the wall and Kulig fell on top of her. She hurt her hands and back as she fell. Pain and fear paralysed her.

Kulig smiled and then released Johanna, who had been a virgin. Kulig's actions both disgusted and infuriated her. She walked back into the party believing all eyes were on her as if everyone knew what had happened. She insisted on going home, telling Kulig their relationship was over.

The consequences of that night would reverberate through the rest of her life. Kulig was still in The Hague two months later when Johanna realised she was pregnant, and she demanded that he marry her. Coming from a religious household, she had been taught to believe that sex outside of marriage would bring only disgrace, shame, and punishment. Kulig said he would have to speak to his strict Catholic parents before deciding on marriage. Shortly after, he returned to the front line and Johanna never heard from him again.

At first, she tried to hide her condition under loose-fitting dresses and by avoiding her parents. As much as her father flattered and accommodated the Nazis, Johanna was under no illusions about his reaction if she told him she was pregnant with a German's baby. Izaak justified his collaboration by convincing himself that he would do whatever was necessary to protect his family. That would not include having unmarried sex with a German serviceman, whatever the circumstances. Johanna knew that it was one thing to go on dates with the foreign occupiers and quite another to bear one's child. She wasn't going to be given the chance to sit calmly with her parents to explain how it came to this.

As her weight and anxiety grew, Johanna could keep her secret no longer and confided in her sister, Mary. Neither young woman was brave enough to tell their father and so they asked Mary's Dutch fiancé Gerrit Naber to break the news. "I told my (soon to be) brother-in-law so that he would inform my father," recalled Johanna many years later. "When my father heard, he came to me and said, 'You are a sinner. You cannot stay here. You have brought shame on the family. You must get out'."

Izaak was unbending. He dismissed the unborn child as a "war product". He would not hear of her marrying Kulig, even if that was possible, and he insisted Johanna could not keep the baby once it was born. Abortion was not an option either.

The hypocrisy of a Nazi collaborator who welcomed the Germans into his home throwing out the daughter who was victimised by those same soldiers was clearly lost on him. And the wife he domineered made no protest. This was Johanna's shame, not his. "The baby means nothing," he told Johanna.

"They said it would be best if I went somewhere where no one knew me," Johanna later reflected. "My father decided that I had to quit my job immediately. In the end, he said that I couldn't see him anymore. I was afraid and remorseful. I didn't know what to do at all. I felt completely helpless. There was a war, and I didn't even have any savings. Father screamed that he wouldn't give me even a guilder. I gave him half of my low salary every month for the household. For the second half, I got dressed and bought various life necessities. I was completely shocked. I desperately needed my parents to help me. But they made it clear to me that they would not bear any responsibility for me, let alone share my shame. It was extremely cruel of them."

To her horror, Izaak cast Johanna out of the family home. His clever and respectful daughter, once the apple of his eye, had no choice but to go to Scheveningen, a beach suburb and fishing port west of The Hague where her father found a place for her through the social department of the National Socialist Party in a shelter for women such as her: women who had become pregnant through relationships or attacks involving the occupying troops. They were considered fallen women, even if, for many, it was through absolutely no fault of their own. Johanna felt unloved, unprotected, and abandoned at a time when she needed the support and security of her family. The shelter was soulless, barely furnished and full of so much despair. She had no one to trust or ask for advice. For the first time in her young life, she was on her own. She had no idea what childbirth would be like or how she was going to be able to care for a baby without its father. Fear for her and her baby's future tormented her every waking hour. Even though she was a victim, Johanna knew there would be little to no sympathy for a woman carrying a German soldier's child – no matter the circumstances in which she had conceived. She wondered how it had come to this.

She wasn't at the shelter long before Izaak had her moved to the NSB's Boerhaave Kliniek further away in the capital city of Amsterdam where word was less likely to get back home that Izaak's daughter had given birth to a Nazi child. It was another place without hope. All the women in the maternity ward were, like her, having children because of relationships with German soldiers, some of them forced, others consensual, all of them deemed shameful by Dutch communities.

Johanna's "war product" baby began the last part of its journey into the world during a long labour in Amsterdam on 24 August 1944. Once her waters broke, Johanna was put in a room on her own by the clinic staff for delivery of the child. The midwife was run off her feet, looking in on Johanna in between racing to the beds of other women ready to give birth. Gunfire could be heard from outside and several times fire alarms sent both mothers-to-be and staff running to the bomb shelters. Some women were bed-ridden and couldn't move. Others were jealous of Johanna who was soon to have her baby and leave "everything" behind her. It was an excruciating 24-hour labour and, for much of it, she lay in a room alone, screaming out in agony. For Johanna there were no family present, no friends, certainly no neighbours. She felt dead to them all, including her parents, and any dreams she may have had of a life with the child's father were soon to be snuffed out.

Kulig was fighting on the front line at Caen in France as the Allies broke through the German lines to capture the city 26 miles from the Normandy beaches. Caen was in a highly strategic location along the River Orne and Caen Canal. It was also a key road hub for German forces responding to Allied forces landing on the beaches of Normandy in the largest amphibious invasion in the history of warfare, codenamed Operation Overlord, to free the people of north-west Europe from Nazi occupation. Gregor Kulig went missing in action on 8 June 1944, aged 22, in the height of battle. He was presumed dead along with thousands of troops on both sides as the Allies became victorious. Gregor was part of Hitler's waste of youth being thrown into unwinnable battles in his vainglorious campaign for ultimate victory costing at least 5.3 million military lives.

Johanna had no way of learning of the death of her suitor as she preferred to remember him, rather than the villain he was. She desperately wanted a father for her child, not just to save her from what she thought of as a single mother's disgrace, but, more importantly, she felt a husband would keep her child well-cared-for and supported during such uncertain times.

CHAPTER TWO

Sitting in a darkened room, hearing gunshots in the distance, Johanna found solace in her beautiful son, "a helpless baby, radiating warmth and sleeping peacefully at my breast, finally calming me down". She felt unexpected optimism being a mother, feeling positivity flowing through her veins. "I started to feel completely different in body and spirit," she remembered.

The new mum wrestled with what to call the son that was giving her so much hope for a better life even when the world seemed to be trying to tear itself apart in the ghastliest ways. She didn't want to name him after anyone close to her, considering she had become an outcast. Johanna decided on "Erwin".

CHAPTER THREE

Amsterdam, Holland, 30 August 1944

The sound of warfare in all its terrifying forms was getting closer and closer. New mothers fled the hospital, whether to return home or to just get somewhere safer. Safer from bombs and bullets, but not so safe if a street corner vengeance squad discovered a woman had given birth to the baby of a German soldier.

Six days after her son's birth, with beds also becoming scarce in the maternity home, Johanna decided to gather Erwin and her few meagre possessions, to head back to The Hague, praying that her father's resolve to banish them would weaken if he saw that the baby was a healthy boy.

She found herself on the streets of Amsterdam with her babe in arms and walked half an hour through the chaos to the train station, passing the haunted faces of people uncertain about their futures. There was shouting, crying, and hugging as loved ones parted. Johanna felt tears falling down her cheeks. She couldn't stop thinking about how her parents had never visited her at the shelter or the maternity home. She knew Izaak cared more about his reputation than he did for her. She tried to forgive her mother by telling herself that she had only followed

Izaak's lead but, feeling the strong pull of motherhood herself now, she couldn't understand how a woman could forsake her own daughter, no matter how controlling her husband could be. Johanna's own bond to her child already felt unshakeable. Surely, her mother would make a stand.

The train journey from Amsterdam to The Hague was hazardous, especially for a mother and her newborn. Johanna began to think everyone and everything was against her. A few minutes into the trip, the carriages screeched to a halt and all the passengers were ordered to jump from the high steps onto the tracks and lie down in whatever cover they could find on the embankment. Johanna heard the roar of aircraft engines in the distance. The noise got louder as the airborne engines got closer. Allied planes suddenly dropped from the clouds overhead and began to fire at the train. She screamed in terror and covered Erwin from the bullets ripping through carriages. Passengers who'd been sitting patiently next to her a few minutes earlier were now twisted into a terrifying death dance as the tracers sprayed the tracks. She looked at Erwin and survival mode kicked in. She dashed for cover, swaddling the baby. This child didn't deserve an early death. He had a full life in front of him and Johanna wanted to be part of that more than anything else.

In close succession, another attack came, sending them burying their faces back into the stony tracks. Their work done, the planes wheeled around and disappeared into the darkening sky. Pilots, navigators and gunners in another life would have been doing all they could to save this mother and child. But this was war, and they were flying their killing machines in order to stop German advances. It was a means to an end. The train route was often busy with German soldiers on the move. Civilians would be killed.

There was a lingering silence as the train passengers waited for the tell-tale hum of the returning warplanes. Gradually, they dared to believe it was over and stood, brushing themselves down, the relief washing over them with the shame of seeing those so close who were not so lucky. A siren sounded telling passengers the air raid was over. Train guards told everyone to board their bullet-holed compartments and they pulled out again heading for The Hague. The train would not stop for the dead. There was still precious cargo onboard. There were no first and second-class passengers, just the living and the dead.

Arriving in the city she had grown up in and knew as home, Johanna, cuddling her newborn, walked for an hour or more to the Van Haarlem home. Even if her father couldn't forgive his daughter, surely the pitiful sight of Erwin, with dirt streaking his hair and face from the rail embankment, would lead him to take them in. She told herself they were of his own flesh and blood no matter what had happened in the past.

Heart pounding, Johanna knocked on the door. She was desperate for rest in the safety of her home and for kind words from those who once loved her. She wanted to lay her head on her pillow and have her son swaddled in warm clothes at her side in a crib. Maybe, they still did love her, and she and Erwin would be greeted with warm embrace. She wanted it so badly that she almost came to believe it.

But she was mistaken.

Izaak opened the front door and slammed it in her face. The bang of the heavy door against the wooden frame reverberated through her tired body. Unknowing and unwanted, Erwin whimpered in the chill night air.

Johanna, disconsolate, looked up as she walked away. She saw her mother in tears watching her daughter and grandson from the window. She said nothing and disappeared from sight as Izaak entered the room, drawing the curtains on Johanna and her baby.

The young mother stood on the street with a six-day-old newborn in her arms. She had no money, no home, and no means of support. She stayed there for a long while hoping until there was no hope left. Yet still her father's controlling personality held sway and she didn't consider asking close friends or family for help because she didn't want to tell them about the child and risk bringing shame on her parents.

"I'll never understand why my father let me go like I was some kind of beggar," Johanna recalled. "I begged him to at least take us inside for a while and let us breathe a little, but he was adamant. The door remained closed."

~

Exhausted mentally and physically and with Erwin crying uncontrollably, Johanna walked a few streets from her house to the house of the family doctor known for his kindness. When the elderly physician opened the door, Johanna fell into his arms. He took pity on her and showed Johanna and Erwin to a bedroom, carefully tucking in mother and child without judgment.

It wasn't long before word got to Izaak that his daughter was so close to home – the doctor felt it was his duty to let him know she was with him – and he was angry that their family physician had been made aware of the baby. As the Dutch resistance grew, Izaak had begun to fear for his freedom. The resistance was on the hunt for anyone who'd betrayed their country.

Izaak was desperate to bury any knowledge of his daughter's

affair with a German and the resulting child she now held in her arms. His wife had not spoken to Johanna since news of her pregnancy but that didn't stop him from sending her to see their errant daughter. Johanna Hendrika arrived at the doctor's with a bleak and terse message for her daughter: she must leave Holland and find a religious couple to adopt the baby. Or perhaps she could try to find the baby's grandparents in Germany. Maybe they would take in the child. Either way, she could not be allowed to remain in The Hague. She shouldn't even breastfeed Erwin, her mother told her, because that would create a loving bond with her son. The longer she stayed, the more she risked her father's business and his reputation, Johanna's mother warned. Izaak did not want to know how Johanna was coping. On his instruction, her mother delivered the message and then made it clear she'd have nothing else to do with her daughter. It was nothing like the reconciliation that Johanna had been praying for.

"My parents didn't ask what I thought," Johanna remembered. "They didn't care one bit about how I felt. As if Erwin wasn't my flesh and blood and their grandson. I desperately begged them to let me live with them, but they refused."

~

As the tide of the war began to turn and filter through to the Netherlands in late summer of 1944, the whispers about the Van Haarlems being collaborators grew louder and the angry stares in the street became bolder. Izaak pressed with even more urgency for Johanna to leave the country. There were small signs of new life. Some joviality had returned to the neighbourhood where Johanna grew up and people no longer hid in the shadows but started once more to meet one another with a smile. Izaak's bet on the Nazis seemed to have gone sour and everyone now knew Germany's days in the Netherlands were numbered.

The Nazis still gathered at the Van Haarlem home, but their jollities were tinged with desperation. Alcohol and fine food were in short supply and the likes of Izaak van Haarlem were no longer feared in the neighbourhood but treated like pariahs. There would be a judgment day and it felt like it was coming soon.

Hostilities had twisted and turned dramatically across Europe. Allied planes bombarded German cities on an enormous scale and British and American troops had invaded fascist Italy. In the summer of 1944, Allied forces swept back through Nazi-held France, and the Soviets were on the march to overwhelm the Germans in Eastern Europe. The Nazis couldn't prevent news of defeats spreading in Holland and the Dutch people knew their occupiers' days were numbered.

Well-connected as he was with the German officers, Izaak had suspected the Nazi retreat was coming for some months. Holland was heading into what would become known as the "Hunger Winter" – the six months from November 1944 to May 1945 in which retreating Germans cut off food supplies to the western Netherlands in retaliation for the exiled Dutch government's support of the Allies. By the end of it, roughly 20,000 people died from the famine and the consequences of starvation affected many millions more. Already the NSB was in its death throes. Ever the conniving chameleon, Izaak knew he needed to switch sides again to survive and the stain of a German baby in the family could not easily be washed away.

Johanna's stay with the doctor could not last for long. Not

only was it a time of great deprivation, during which feeding two more mouths would have been difficult, the doctor knew the baby had a German father. He knew the problems that could cause. Besides, Izaak had made it clear through his wife's visit that Johanna had to leave for the East. Johanna was so consumed with her own survival and the protection of her child that she hadn't fully understood the dangers she faced from her neighbours and the Dutch authorities. It was her father who had collaborated, not her. Her only crime was that she'd fallen for a German soldier. She had no alternative to her father's instructions to find refuge in the East even though the Russians were overwhelming German forces there. Even now, Johanna was unable to resist her father's wishes. Besides, she had nowhere else to go.

Izaak used his fading connections in the fascist National Socialist Party to get her on a special train taking wounded soldiers and abandoned Dutch women with babies born to German soldiers through Germany and on to Czechoslovakia. He would have been naïve to think that his collaboration could be absolved simply by sending away his second-youngest child, who was still only just 19. He sent Johanna's elder sister, Henriette Maria, 24, to accompany her. His message to Johanna before they left had been heartlessly simple, "If you want to return home, then only come home alone."

It's no wonder that Johanna couldn't help but think her father's help was no act of kindness, but a cruel, calculating way of getting rid of the "war product".

CHAPTER FOUR

Verden, West Germany, 1 October 1944

A little over nine months earlier, Johanna had been on a train, chatting carelessly with a German soldier with scant thought for the future beyond that evening's entertainment and her expectations of a first kiss. Now she was sitting on another train, her hair soaked with sweat, a baby crying in her arms, surrounded by wounded German soldiers and other Dutch women with wounded souls heading east to an uncertain fate. The carriage was thick with the smell of gangrenous limbs, full nappies, and fear. "We slept on seats and took whatever food we were given," remembered Johanna.

If having Jewish blood, even from generations before, was dangerous in The Hague, it could be a death sentence where Johanna was heading. It wasn't something Izaak ever talked about. Having been raised as a protestant by her father, the young single mother was determined to give her son a Christian baptism that he was denied at home.

When the train guard told passengers there would be an extended delay in what would soon become West Germany, Johanna set out with Erwin, determined to find a pastor to carry out the baptism service. Her sister tried to stop her, worried she could get left behind and calling her "crazy". What would she do with Erwin if they were stranded in a city with no friends and under extreme privations? Their only hope, reasoned Henriette, was to complete their journey east to a larger city where they could find work and accommodation. But Johanna wouldn't listen. An elderly, childless German couple gave shelter to the desperate Dutch mother and her baby son, but had no food to offer them. The train was still at the station but Johanna didn't know how long the delay would last and nobody could tell her.

The Third Reich was facing annihilation as winter beckoned in 1944; there was little food, the economy was collapsing, and German towns and cities lay in ruins. The Allies had laid waste to huge swathes of their foe's country. Germany had blitzed London, Coventry, Cardiff, Hull and many more centres of residential areas. The Luftwaffe had bombed the capital for 57 consecutive nights, and sometimes during the day. But the Germans had paid a heavy price. While Johanna could see evidence of the mass retaliatory destruction by the Allies, she could not have known that Britain and her allies were advancing from the West, and the Russians were pushing forward from the East. Johanna was heading towards battle hardened Russian troops whose courage and determination to win was relentless following their victory against highly-trained German forces at the Battle of Stalingrad – the bloodiest battle in World War Two with enormous losses on both sides. The Red Army also carried a reputation for ruthless brutality as it sought vengeance for the millions of Russian lives lost on the Eastern Front.

But there was only one battle that concerned Johanna: to look after her tiny son's welfare. She was able to feed him at her breast even though she was getting hungrier day by day.

They had been in Saxony for two days and the young mother was becoming frantic. If they were to die, she thought, Erwin must be baptised. It was her Christian duty. She finally found a clergyman and told him the whole story. He told her to return to his church the following day and he would baptise her son.

On Sunday, 1 October 1944, Dom Pastor Johann Heinrich Theodore Feise baptised Erwin in the Lutheran church in the Lower Saxony town of Verden, famous for the massacre of 4,500 Saxons by order of Charlemagne in 782. A millennium later it was on the map of war again as a stopping place for the beaten and blooded, the desperate and damned. "I was very ashamed because I had no husband next to me," she said later of her baby's christening. "There were four couples around the font and the priest poured water over the head of each child. I felt so ashamed, but the pastor found me a witness in place of a husband.

"Only God has the right to judge a person, not the rest of us, child," he told Johanna when they first met.

"I felt like an infinite sinner, so I kept my eyes on the priest." It was after the christening that Johanna made the momentous decision to defy her father's demands and keep Erwin rather than seek out his German grandparents or a surrogate family. Her son had not asked to come into the world this way, she reasoned, and the more time she spent with him, the more they bonded. He was a good baby with a happy disposition.

The only issue was money and there were no jobs in Verden. Her best hope was to head further east. She would need to pay for a babysitter but at least Erwin would not be adopted or placed in a children's home. Carrying Erwin, Johanna returned to the train, which luckily was still waiting at the station with Henriette on board. They stayed together until it reached the end of the line in the Czechoslovakian city of Teplice that had been annexed by the Nazis in 1938. Germany was still hanging on, but the writing was on the wall and Johanna knew that staying in Teplice was as unpredictable as moving on, but the train wasn't going any further. The only other direction was back, and she knew there was nothing for her there. There certainly wasn't for Erwin. She'd reached the end of the line in more ways than one. Without transport or money, Teplice would have to be their new home.

~

They rented a small room and Johanna found a job working in a factory producing men's and women's underwear. A neighbour agreed to babysit Erwin, but he was still breastfeeding and couldn't settle without his mother. Johanna expressed her milk every day, but the babysitter soon lost patience with his crying.

After just 10 days, the sisters had no choice but to move out. Desperate, they went to the Red Cross for help, but rather than offering aid, staff instead made Johanna a stark offer: she could leave Erwin in a home and return for him once she had enough money to support them both. The idea horrified her, but she also worried she couldn't refuse it.

Child welfare officers visited Johanna to better understand the circumstances in which she and Erwin lived. They reported that mother, aunt and baby resided in a "furnished room, very cramped living conditions" and that the child should not stay there. Their report gave reasons for placing Erwin in a home: "The child's mother has to go to work, has completely inadequate accommodation in which she cannot keep the child…" It further noted that the child had been born in a maternity hospital in Amsterdam and that a children's home should be found for him as soon as possible.

The Red Cross soon found an orphanage for Erwin in Rumburk, about 70 km from Teplice, and right on Czechoslovakia's border with Germany. Johanna was told half of the fees for caring for Erwin in the orphanage would be paid by the state, the rest would be billed to her when she returned to collect him.

Johanna agonised over the decision for weeks but, once again, ultimately she felt she had no choice. She had no money, no prospects, and the Russians were forcibly repatriating foreigners. Johanna could not bring Erwin back to The Hague. She decided to leave Erwin with one condition – that she could come back for him when she had a more settled life. Weeping, she returned to the Red Cross offices and handed over three-month-old Erwin. They had spent almost every moment of his short life together. At first, she simply couldn't leave.

Finally, the home's sister told her, "You must go now."

Her goodbye to Erwin was the hardest moment of her young life, a life that had already suffered so much cruelty. She couldn't imagine going on without her son and cried bitterly as she kept kissing him. What would she do? She felt like a bad mother, desperately sad and guilty that she had not found a way or the strength to keep her son at her side. Despite this, she decided she had to survive to care for Erwin in the future. She vowed never to return to Holland without her son and to find a way to earn enough money to take care of him in Germany.

About a week later, Johanna found better-paid work in clerical offices at a factory in Neudorf, Germany, about three-and-a-half hour drive from the home where her son was being cared for. She had more responsibilities and was paid a much better salary. Henrietta had returned to the Netherlands and, for a while, Johanna started to believe that she could make it work and go back for Erwin as she'd hoped.

But in early 1945, just as she'd found some stability, the Soviet forces over-ran the country. War would again take away her choices. Russian soldiers swarmed the streets of Neudorf and the Germans surrendered. Weeks later, the Russians ordered all foreign nationals to return home. She was no longer allowed to work in Germany. She wanted to stay – to at least see Erwin one more time – but soon became resigned to defeat. There was no food, no work and the Russians put up posters all over town warning foreigners they were no longer welcome. Johanna tried to get to Rumburk to see Erwin, but was unable to get through the Soviet roadblocks. It gradually dawned on her that she would have to accept leaving Erwin behind. She would not be allowed to stay in Germany and she wouldn't be able to carry him to Holland travelling mainly on foot. She had no idea where they would find food and drink on this perilous journey through the wastelands of Germany. The Russians laughed off her pleas for help. "The boy is taken care of, right?" they told her. "The children's home is responsible for it. We have a lot of more pressing tasks than transporting civilians to where they want to go right now."

~

Hitler's delusion only ended when he took his own life in the Fuhrerbunker in Berlin, on 30 April 1945, shooting himself in the temple rather than face a reckoning. His wife of one day, Eva Braun, used cyanide poisoning to commit suicide. Hitler's remaining loyal staff carried out his last orders to burn and bury their bodies. The dictator was dead, but the suffering continued as Europe came to terms with its new reality. Germany surrendered in Europe on 8 May 1945, with Japan following four months later on 2 September 1945, after the United States dropped atomic bombs on Hiroshima and Nagasaki.

The Allies had been friends in arms. Their leaders Churchill, Stalin and Roosevelt had combined forces to defeat Germany. Now, with Hitler dispatched, Stalin would subjugate Czechoslovakia making it a Stalinist state under the Kremlin's control and a buffer between Germany and Russia. This political move would not only have lasting significance in the balance of power between the world's wrestling superpowers, but also have very personal consequences for Johanna and one day change the course of her life yet again.

In the Netherlands, Izaak van Haarlem's wartime choices were coming back to haunt him. He had chosen to become a Dutch Nazi. Now his family was facing scrutiny as the Germans retreated and millions of displaced people went in search of home, some to return to their own countries and others to settle anew.

Johanna found herself in the middle of this muddled exodus, unable to reach Erwin in Russian-controlled territory. There were no civilian trains, so she walked with her few belongings along with thousands of other foreigners, some hitching the occasional ride in lorries and buses. Hordes of fleeing people slept in the open in bombed-out cities, the roadside piled high with debris and bloodied corpses. Half-naked German soldiers were paraded, heads bowed, through the streets.

At the Dutch border, all Dutch people faced security checks, and if anyone appeared on the list of the security authorities as a collaborator or a member of the National Socialist Party or the SS, they were immediately arrested. Many people who crossed the border at the same time as Johanna ended up in prison in the cities of Hoensbroek and Treebeek in the south, but the frail young Dutchwoman passed through unhindered. Her name was not on the lists. Nobody knew about her son fathered by a Nazi soldier. She was a lone woman, tired and underfed, clearly full of anxiety, just like so many others. She was of no interest to the authorities.

The trains were intermittent. They only ran for two hours in the morning and a few hours in the evening and were packed. After passing through the border, she decided to keep on walking. It was as much as she could do to put one foot in front of the other, all the time grieving the absence of her son. By the time she made it to the family home she was starving, exhausted, and barely able to walk.

Johanna was back in The Hague just as her father had instructed her. Alone.

CHAPTER FIVE

The Hague, 8 May 1945

Izaak van Haarlem was arrested on 8 May 1945. Retribution came within days of the Nazi retreat. In the wake of their occupation, the Dutch had created a specially formed team of political police to investigate NSB members like Izaak who'd colluded with the Germans. Neighbours who had been forced to skulk in the shadows while his family hosted the Germans wasted no time informing on the Van Haarlems. Izaak, who put huge store in his reputation as an influential leader in the community and as a successful businessman, suffered the humiliation of taking himself to a police station, his head hung in shame. He was no longer in a position to call in favours. His Nazi sponsors were long gone; killed on the Front, placed in military prisons, and on the run from the Allies in the West and the Russians in the East. Rather than wait for a knock at the door from the political police, he handed himself over to Dutch interrogators in the hope of getting more lenient treatment.

Izaak was among hundreds of thousands of Dutch people accused of being a collaborator and serving in the German military. Police arrested anyone suspected of betraying members of the Dutch Resistance and also those who'd pointed the finger at their Jewish neighbours. The worst traitors were executed. Many of those investigated were citizens who became members of the NSB as Hitler rose to power in the 1930s and others had joined after the invasion by the Wehrmacht. Like Izaak, they backed the wrong horse in a war that had taken the lives of countless millions and crushed the futures of millions more.

The file on Izaak grew as detectives dug deep. In November 1942, he had begun exchanging correspondence with the German authorities to get contracts for renovating the occupier's administrative offices. He knew his affiliation with the NSB would be more than helpful in getting lucrative war-time work. The Germans considered him a safe pair of hands in their commandeered offices. To them, his active support for the NSB proved his acceptance of Nazi ideology.

The special police's investigation into Izaak revealed that he'd renovated a building in The Hague for the SS, Hitler's feared Aryan bodyguard. During the war the SS ran concentration camps, gathered intelligence and carried out mass shootings. Had they known of Izaak's own "impure" Jewish background, it was likely the businessman and his family would have been shipped off to a concentration camp or murdered on the spot.

Detectives also discovered that the German occupiers had ensured Izaak received supplies of iron and steel, wallpaper and paints, all of which were strictly rationed and almost impossible for other tradesman to secure without paying exorbitant prices on the black market. At Izaak's home and at abandoned Nazi offices, investigators had found supply letters to Izaak stamped with the Nazi Party insignia of an eagle and swastika. The paper trail showed that the Nazis gave Izaak 15 kilos of iron thread to make carpet tacks and other building materials for flooring at a German office in Nassauplein (Nassau Square).

Izaak faced additional accusations of holding parties for his Nazi colleagues, being a leader in a NSB brainwashing summer camp, and trying to recruit Dutchmen to join the German cause. He was told that he faced a stiff prison sentence, depending on the gravity of the evidence against him.

Detectives continued their investigation by speaking to neighbours of the Van Haarlems. Their conflicting accounts reflected the wildly different ways Izaak was seen in the community.

Their first formal interview was good for Izaak. A 45-year-old dentist named Jacques Graftdijk, who lived at 6 Soendastraat, just down from the Van Haarlem's at 34-34a, told investigators he had known Izaak for 20 years as a neighbour and that he was aware Izaak had become a NSB member during the occupation. But Graftdijk said he didn't consider Izaak a fanatic and they never discussed politics. Van Haarlem knew Graftdijk was anti-NSB. Importantly, the two men were also friends. Graftdijk certainly soft-pedalled to help his neighbour. He told detectives, "I have never seen Van Haarlem selling NSB newspapers. There's never been any NSB posters put up at the windows of his house. I have never heard pro-NSB or pro-German comments from him."

Graftdijk went even further, suggesting Izaak didn't have any enemies and was, in fact, apolitical. Then he directly contradicted himself, adding, "Everybody knew he was a NSB member." On the whole, he acted as though it was perfectly normal for the Van Haarlems to play host to the Nazis and said that Izaak wanted to pull away from his right-wing beliefs, but was worried about how that would look to the Germans.

Graftdijk added that Izaak suddenly appeared less positive about the NSB after two of his children returned from Germany, where, the neighbour thought, they'd gone looking for work. In Graftdijk's telling, Izaak was buying time to delicately extricate himself from the NSB, without consequence. But investigators soon unearthed a completely different story – one that wasn't quite so flattering. Another neighbour, Karinus van Leusden, a bicycle salesman, told officers, "I knew Izaak quite well. I saw him multiple times with the NSB pin emblem on his coat. I saw him selling the NSB newspaper more than once. He also circulated other NSB propaganda pamphlets. In 1944, he went from house to house with a list with a German stamp."

Van Leusden said the Van Haarlems clearly benefited from cosying up to the occupiers, recalling that in August 1944, Germans erected a telephone exchange in the Van Haarlem house. He said that the occupiers granted Izaak many special privileges, such as getting to keep his radio while others had to hand over their sets. "During various NSB holidays the NSB flag was flown on Van Haarlem's house. I saw Van Haarlem's son Daan (Daniel) walk around once with a German green uniform." He told the officers of a false rumour that two of Izaak's children had worked in Germany for the East Company, a Dutch organisation aiming to get a foothold in the Baltic states and Ukraine to establish Dutch colonies there to Aryanise Eastern Europe. Another neighbour, bicycle salesman Hans Vrind, 32, told detectives, "He (Izaak) was known as a fanatical NSB member. He was constantly selling the NSB newspaper in the street and from door to door.

"Continuously there were German officers and soldiers at his house. Many times, there were big parties at night and the best food and drink was provided."

For years, Izaak's neighbours had watched from a distance as he flaunted his relationships with the Germans by carousing with them in his home, the shutters left open for everybody to see the power he wielded. Now he was on the outside looking in. And there was no hiding place for the brazen collaborator.

CHAPTER SIX

The Hague, 11 June 1945

Exhausted and heartbroken, Johanna arrived home only to discover The Hague she remembered was now a very different place. The once carefree city of pre-war days was a distant memory and, while the Nazi occupation was over, nothing about it was forgotten. The German soldiers were gone, replaced by the all-conquering Allies. The British, Canadian, American and Polish troops fighting in The Netherlands had paid a terrible price. More than 13,000 soldiers had died to give the Dutch their freedom. So too had more than 200,000 Dutch men, women, and children, the highest per head total of all Nazi-occupied countries, with more than half of them – 107,000 – murdered in the Holocaust. But the fighting was finally over. Laughter was no longer reserved for homes belonging to people like the Van Haarlems; it was everywhere, even as the hardships of war remained. There wasn't enough food, and the occupiers had left devastation in their wake, yet the Netherlands was finally free of its previously ever-tightening Nazi chains and, for many people, there was as much to celebrate as there was to grieve. For others, it was time to pay the price for their collaboration.

Women across the Netherlands were facing the consequences

for fraternising with the enemy. It didn't seem to matter that some of the women had been forced into relationships with Nazis to protect their families and then been raped. They were all denounced as "German whores", who one day would deserve the vilest punishments.

~

As Johanna walked from the train station, she could easily have been confronted by the sight of women and girls standing under guard, their heads crudely shaved, their bodies painted yellow, with placards proclaiming their treachery hung around their necks. Some looking as young as their early teens – in various stages of undress – were placed on the flat beds of trucks. Some were tarred and painted, and others were smeared with excrement. Baying crowds lined streets, shouting insults at slow-moving trucks. On occasions, a woman was singled out and pulled down from a vehicle by a group of men who would beat and kick their victim.

There were far more women "guilty" of the "crime" of having a German soldier's child than the angry vigilantes thirsty for revenge estimated. Dutch institutions did not collate the exact number of children who would carry the stigma of being a "Nazi child." But while Dutch bureaucracy had conveniently failed to account for the number of children in the Netherlands born with German fathers during and after the conflict, the Germans kept detailed birth records where possible as part of the regime's obsession with race. According to the director of the Deutsche Dienststelle WASt, which administers the archives of the German Wehrmacht, as many as 50,000 children were born to Dutch mothers and German soldiers during the war years. After the war, narrative accounts came from the surprisingly high number of Dutch children looking for their German fathers. Some waited 30 to 50 years before seeking their paternal line as their Dutch mothers found it painful to talk about those war-time events they wanted to forget.

Some Dutch mothers also set out to find their children who, because of their purported Aryan purity, had been transported to Germany. Hitler was a great admirer of the Dutch and, along with Nordic countries like Norway, considered them to have a gene pool racially pure enough to boost his quest for an Aryan master race. The Third Reich actively encouraged its soldiers to have sex with Dutch women, who were in turn encouraged, or in some instances, forced, to give birth in maternity hospitals run by the National Socialist People's Health organization (Nationalsozialistische Volkswohlfahrt, NSV), the welfare wing of the German Nazi Party. In the Netherlands, the NSV-run NSB maternity clinic where Erwin's young life began operated under such Aryan principles/motives. At other NSB clinics in The Hague and Rotterdam, the party similarly looked after mothers who provided "racially valuable" children. Once the women proved paternity and presented a reference from the far-right NSDAP (National Socialist German Workers' Party, which created and supported the ideology of Nazism) they were protected and cared for at the clinics by the German authorities.

A veil of secrecy was thrown around pregnancies and births to protect women like Johanna from being ostracised and attacked by their own countrymen and women. Soldiers were also ordered by the Nazi Party to register their children by Dutch women with the German Civil Registry and the NSV. German combatants who fathered children in all occupied countries were under instructions from their superiors to inform the Wehrmacht. Many Dutch mothers were even provided with cash allowances, extra food, and coal to help them live independently. Because of her father's insistence that Erwin's birth remain a secret, and Kulig's subsequent death at the Front, Johanna did not register the birth with the German authorities and consequently received none of the benefits.

Dutch-German babies were placed in dozens of NSV-associated NSB children's homes in The Netherlands, some were sent to the Third Reich and others like Erwin ended up in orphanages in other countries. They were scattered far and wide, many of them oblivious of their parentage. As they grew older and became further institutionalised, many believed they were unwanted and unloved.

~

Back at The Hague, at the end of her long journey, Johanna knocked on her own front door once again, desperate for her bedroom, her father's forgiveness, and a stable family home. Her mother opened the door, with Johanna's 10-year-old sister Alida by her side, and burst into tears. She took her daughter in her arms, but her darting eyes gave her away. She was looking to see if Johanna had defied her father and brought back her son. She needn't have worried. Her daughter was alone.

In her heart, Johanna was determined to go back for Erwin wherever he ended up in the East, but she had come too far and waited too long for this moment to risk her father's wrath once more by telling her family of her plans. It was easier to say he'd been adopted into a loving home. Nobody openly mentioned Erwin, not even her six siblings. It was as if he never existed.

Back in her own bed, her hunger satiated, she vowed to herself to get strong enough to return to the orphanage and make amends for abandoning her child. She had to banish any thoughts in her mind that she wouldn't be reunited with him.

It wasn't until the next morning that Johanna learned that her father and eldest brother were in prison being investigated for collaborating with the German occupiers. The Van Haarlem house was under threat of confiscation by the Dutch authorities as a penalty for the family's treachery. Izaak may have hidden Johanna's pregnancy, but his neighbours had bided their time for long enough. Even without any knowledge of baby Erwin, the list of grievances against Izaak over his relationship with the Nazis was long and damning.

A stench of revenge was in the air. It felt as if people congregated on every street corner, planning how to punish the men and women who had fraternised with German troops. These street corner courts delivered their own sentences. They unleashed their anger on neighbours known to have passed on information about Resistance fighters or given up Jewish families who were sent to the death camps. It didn't seem to matter whether a person had collaborated for greed or survival – there was no mood for forgiveness, whatever the reason.

Not long after her return, Johanna was homeless again. In September 1945, while detectives from the special department probed Izaak's Nazi connections, Dutch government officials arrived at the Van Haarlem home to tell his wife that their house was set to be confiscated. She had 24 hours to prepare for eviction the next morning when a large van would pull up outside. The authorities tossed furniture, kitchen pots and pans, cutlery, and bedding into the vehicle as neighbours looked on. Jewellery had to be handed over and was never seen again. The

CHAPTER SIX

Van Haarlems were paying the price for their treachery. People of their community saw it as just retribution.

The only relatives still speaking to the family took in Johanna's mother and her young sister Alida, a long way from The Hague. An acquaintance gave lodgings to Johanna's older sister Maria and her fiancé Gerrit, and Johanna was given a roof over her head by one of the few neighbours who took pity on her. In return, she looked after the neighbour's house and their five children. Her host family had no idea that Johanna had a son fathered by a German who was now living in an orphanage in Czechoslovakia. She was still following her father's orders for secrecy even while he was in prison. In this situation, it was sound advice. To admit to the relationship, even an abusive one, would have been calamitous.

CHAPTER SEVEN

The Hague, 12 November 1945

Investigators interrogated Izaak van Haarlem several times, but he succeeded in hiding the fact that his daughter had a baby with a German soldier. He wasn't just trying to protect Johanna; he just knew it would be one more damning example of his family collaborating with the Nazis.

Interestingly, he never mentioned any Jewish family connection. Perhaps he feared it would backfire on him because it could be viewed that he had betrayed his own people for financial gain, and he would face harsher punishment. On the other hand, it could be said he collaborated to save his family – hiding in plain sight their part Jewish roots. Whatever it was, Izaak was not going to take the risk of full transparency.

On 12 November 1945, Izaak told his inquisitors, "I have never been in trouble with the police or the justice department. I have never been convicted of any crime. I am not a rich man. I married in 1919 and then started a business as an upholsterer and decorator. I had this business until I was arrested."

He sought to portray himself as a victim, pressured to join the Dutch fascist party against his better instincts. There is no indication that his inquisitors bought his story and they instead presented some of their evidence to prove he was lying. After seeing letters and bills of work he carried out for the Nazis seized from his home and testimony from some of his neighbours, he admitted to his inquisitors that he did sympathise with the NSB's social policies, believing they would be good for the country, and said that he voted for the party in 1937 when they badly lost in the national elections. But he added that he resisted NSB membership even though he was being pressured to join in 1937. He did read the NSB newspaper Volk en Vaderland (People and Fatherland), he admitted, but was not a party activist.

"I sympathised with the NSB programme though, and in January 1941, after repeated pressure, I registered as a member. My interests and work stayed the same for my family and my job as an upholsterer. Nothing changed. Relations between members of my family were always good. We also kept our Christian life."

He confessed to wearing the NSB badge (a triangular brooch with the Dutch flag in red, black and yellow) and to distributing the NSB newspaper.

"I regularly paid my contribution to the NSB and paid a subscription for the paper," he said, adding: "I never influenced my children politically."

The detectives also questioned him about Johanna and her sister's trek east to work in Germany, but Izaak didn't miss a beat. If he was worried someone had squealed and the investigators knew about his illegitimate grandson, he didn't show it. He immediately sought to dispel the suggestion that he was an authoritarian and made all their decisions for them. "I did not object because they were of the age that they could decide for themselves," he said. Rather than try and claim their journey into Germany made him feel uncomfortable, he sought to distance himself from their actions although, in truth, he was directly responsible for them.

His only slip-up occurred when investigators asked about the special treatment his NSB membership bought him when he applied for winter fuel during the five years of the occupation. "I never had any benefit from my NSB membership," he insisted. "I requested coal in 1944 because I didn't have any left. I requested these coals at the Bureau of the East Company (Bureau van de Oostcompagnie) at Laan van Meerdervoort 49 in The Hague."

Investigators then produced Izaak's written fuel request for the winter months, which clearly showed how he leaned on his NSB affiliation to help him. Now on the back foot, he did, however, confess that he renovated houses for the Germans between 1942 and 1943. "I cannot exactly tell you how much I was paid," he said. "The receipts you show me are connected to the payment by the German departments for work I did there."

The receipts totalled thousands of guilders over several years – and that only included what investigators discovered in Izaak's office or in German administration centres. To make himself appear a principled man, he told his interrogators, "I never resigned as a member of the NSB after Germany's surrender because I remained committed to the NSB programme as created by Mussert (Anton Mussert, a fascist politician and NSB co-founder) in the period before the German occupation. When it became clear Germany had lost the war, I didn't want to resign my membership because I didn't want to be a coward. I never realised that the NSB became part of German politics otherwise I would have resigned."

"But wasn't everyone aware that the NSB was collaborating with the Germans?" he was asked.

"I was not in favour of merging Germany and Holland. That's all I can tell you," he replied.

Izaak signed a statement refuting that he was a leader at a NSB camp. He said, "I firmly deny I was ever a 'summer camp' group leader of the NSB. In the summer of 1943, I went for one week to an educational camp where there were lectures about national socialism.

"I was an NSB block leader and vice group leader. Because of that I had a NSB stamp in my possession to use on letters. I admit that a certain person called De Roode came to me in my position as block leader because he needed proof that he was sympathising with the NSB and that there was no objection from me that he could take up service at the NSKK (the National Socialist Motor Corps, a paramilitary organisation within the Nazi party that handled transport)."

Stung by allegations from neighbours that he scouted his Dutch friends to work for the Nazis, he said, "I deny ever recruiting for the German Army. I never did house visits as a NSB member, but I did visit the houses of a few people at their request. I did many times sell the NSB newspaper. I cannot remember that I participated in the spreading of NSB posters. I admit that it happened once or twice that I went with a group of NSB people to fix NSB posters (to buildings). I deny that I ever went from door to door with an NSB list or a list with German stamps."

Detectives presented evidence from his neighbours' depositions that Izaak had distributed posters. Izaak denied he did. He admitted to getting exceptions for people to keep their radios by sending papers to a NSB area office in The Hague.

He tried to wriggle out of the most damaging accusation that he regularly hosted the Germans in his home, but his explanations rang hollow, and it was becoming increasingly clear that his prominent status meant nothing now.

He firmly denied that in mid-1944 he voluntarily made his home available for the German Wehrmacht. "Only my office was taken by them without my permission," he claimed. "After about a week they left my house because this was a group of soldiers in transit. During the German occupation German soldiers who knew me visited me at my home, but I deny I ever threw parties for them at my house."

The NSB, like their German counterparts, were compulsive note-takers and the interrogators had a stack of evidence that contradicted Izaak's testimony. An NSB registration form confirmed Izaak had been a NSB group leader in The Hague and at a NSB camp. Another document revealed when Izaak had requested his NSB uniform of trousers, shirt, and a hat as Block Leader. Put together, the paper trail showed someone who the Germans would have deemed committed to their cause, even as they became increasingly careful about who they trusted. The collaboration had made Izaak rich and the Dutch investigators had the paperwork to prove it. The Van Haarlem family enjoyed boom times while most people were barely surviving on limited rations of food and fuel.

~

Izaak wasn't the only Van Haarlem to come under suspicion for collaborating. Johanna's mother was also arrested at 2pm on Monday, 12 November 1945, for suspected membership of the NSB. Officers brought her into a police station on Langa Voorhout 13 for questioning. She told police she was working as a housemaid at Laan van Meerdervoort 848 in The Hague.

She worked just to survive, there was no pay. The Protestant Veen family provided food and the roof over her head because her home had been seized and she could no longer live with relatives in another city as she wanted to be near her children. Mrs Van Haarlem told officers she had come from Rotterdam to The Hague in 1919 after meeting Izaak. She was currently trying to be the breadwinner for her two youngest children.

Mrs Van Haarlem told detectives, "I'm married to Izaak Van Haarlem. I have no criminal convictions and no money. I married Izaak on 9 July 1919. During the occupation my husband became a member of the NSB in 1941. I never became a member. Politics didn't interest me. I've always tried to keep my children out of politics, but I didn't always succeed in that which made me feel sad.

"I always let my husband lead in everything. And the happiness of my family was the most important thing. I didn't want my children to suffer because of his politics. I never wore a NSB badge."

She said she donated to the "Winterhulp," a Dutch Nazi Party charity providing food and clothing to the disadvantaged in the Netherlands during the winter, adding, "I consider Winterhulp a good social work institution for the poor. I never collected for them as I needed all my time to care for my family.

"When some of my children started to sympathise with the NSB I did not stop it, but I warned them (of the possible outcome). But they were of an age to decide on their politics and have views on the NSB."

Although he had not yet been sentenced, Izaak was being held in a barbed-wire-ringed detention centre where collaborators lived in stark dormitory blocks with few facilities and basic food. There, he had no position of importance among prisoners and no influence on guards. He had to queue like everyone else to get his meagre food rations and shared toilets and washing facilities with hundreds of detainees. It was a grim comedown for a man who had weaseled his way into receiving benefits from the Nazis. While he remained behind bars facing an uncertain future, his wife was released and returned to live with the Veen family. Her freedom was helped by Dr Jan Van Andel, a Protestant church council member, who told officers, "I've known Mrs Van Haarlem for a long time and know her husband was a member of the NSB. I never saw Mrs Van Haarlem with a NSB badge. But I did see her a few times with a Winterhulp badge which meant she had donated. As far as I know she was never a member of the NSB. She's a woman who looked after her family and let her husband lead in everything. She didn't try to stop him from being a NSB member. She thought about her family and did everything to keep them together."

On 4 February 1946, investigators decided no crime had been committed by Mrs Van Haarlem and she was cleared of all charges unconditionally on 27 July 1946. Izaak and Johanna had successfully kept the family's darkest secret. Neither revealed their daughter had been seeing a Wehrmacht soldier who had got her pregnant.

~

As her family fell apart, Johanna tried to scrape a living by taking up whatever office work she could find.

In the end, Izaak's greed helped set him free. After the war, the Dutch judicial system was overloaded with thousands of collaboration cases and to deal with the sheer volume of charges it had set up special tribunal to deal with the likes of

Izaak van Haarlem. The tribunal decided that although he was guilty, Izaak had already spent enough time in jail after 11 months behind bars. To secure his release from the detention centre, authorities set a fine of 2,000 guilders (the equivalent of about 27,500 Euros in 2024) – a large amount considering most families in Holland were just about surviving after the catastrophe inflicted on its economy from the start of the Second World War. But the Van Haarlems weren't most families: Izaak had hidden away thousands of guilders and could easily pay his fine.

Other conditions of his release included behaving like a good Dutchman and staying employed for two years. His release left a bitter taste among his neighbours in The Hague. Incredibly, they said, he had bought his freedom with Nazi blood money – and after having served less than one year in detainment. They kept bringing information about Izaak to the authorities. In a police statement made on 25 October 1946, Cornelia Johanna De Roode, the wife of Pieter De Roode, aged 29, an electrician from The Hague, told police that Van Haarlem tried to recruit her husband to the German Africa Korps during the War. She spoke to police while Pieter was in detention at camp Ronduit in Naarden.

Cornelia, aged 44, said, "I visited my husband in detention, and he told me Van Haarlem had been released for 2,000 guilders. I think it's very unjust that these kinds of people are getting released after they tried to split up families while my husband who went to Germany to earn a living is still imprisoned. Mr Van Kamp and Mr Van Haarlem came to my house many times at the end of 1942 to recruit my husband to the Afrika Korps. Van Haarlem came to my house often as a NSB block leader to see if I had any complaints."

After his release, Izaak moved into a rented house with his wife and four of his children but it wasn't long before he managed to get his properties in Soendstraat returned to him. If nothing else, Izaak was resourceful and it's likely he found more "blood money" to pay for the return of his home and business premises. Although most of his possessions were confiscated while he was behind bars, and he had to undertake to never retrieve them, he'd defied the order and set to work shortly after his release to get everything back. Inside their home in The Hague, it was almost as if none of the Van Haarlem's many ordeals had ever happened.

Now Johanna followed her father back home, prepared to wait silently for the day she could return to pick up her son. Every day she thought about the son she left behind in Czechoslovakia, but she couldn't confide in anyone. It was too dangerous for her to openly speak about Erwin, even at home.

CHAPTER EIGHT

The Hague, 17 January 1947

In January 1947, a Red Cross official tracked the Van Haarlem family down to The Hague and knocked on the family's door. With Europe in the throes of rebuilding after the ravages of a world war, the aid organisation recognised the possibility that calmer heads could fit fractured families back together. A Red Cross aid worker had read in Erwin van Haarlem's case papers that his mother, Johanna, had left him in Czechoslovakia in dire circumstances and that she had done so on condition the agency would keep her apprised of her son's whereabouts so that one day she could bring him home to Holland. War and its indignities had torn mother and child apart.

The official had great news for Johanna. Erwin was alive and well and living in Prague. Izaak had a grandson. Arrangements could be made to bring mother and child back together. Peace would reunite them; good times beckoned again. Arrangements would be made through the Dutch Repatriation Commission in Prague. The only catch was that a married Czech couple were interested in adopting Erwin. If Johanna still wanted him back, she would have to repay 26,000 Czech crowns – more than a year's salary – for his care at the children's home. That payment would be waived if she agreed to the adoption.

The conversation was short and to the point. Whatever indignities Izaak suffered behind bars did nothing to shake his conservative convictions. He turned the Red Cross official away at the front door, telling him the child should be placed with foster parents. "Do not contact us again," he said. "This is the end of the matter."

It wasn't until weeks later that Izaak told his daughter about the visit, and he admitted the Red Cross had also written countless letters to the family home trying to inform her that Erwin was in Prague waiting for his mother to collect him. Johanna felt deeply betrayed. She felt even more burdened by guilt for abandoning Erwin. She imagined him looking forlornly out of a window waiting for his mother, only to be cruelly let down. Johanna's feelings of despair bordered on depression. Somehow, she found the strength to confront her authoritarian father.

Devastated, Johanna demanded to be shown the letters. Her father revealed that he had intercepted and destroyed every one of them. There was to be no further discussion. Showing unprecedented defiance, Johanna peppered him with questions. Had he been shown a picture of the boy? Had he learned of his progress? His health? His character? Where exactly was he? There were no answers. There never would be any. Discussion over.

Johanna never knew exactly what her father had told the official, but she understood the consequences all too well: unless she could stop it, Erwin would soon be adopted. On 26 February 1947, Johanna had one final opportunity to rescue Erwin. Czech social workers arrived at the Van Haarlem house with a document and an ultimatum: either sign an agreement to renounce her hold on Erwin or bring him home. The words on the official paper hit Johanna unbearably hard after all her dreams of being reunited with her son. If she signed the document, it meant Erwin would be lost to her forever.

She fell to her knees and begged her father to allow her to bring his grandson back to The Hague. But he was unbending. Izaak told his daughter she was a bad mother who had to stop thinking about herself and put the child's best interests first. He said she had no husband and the only reasonable course of action was to agree to the adoption. He reminded Johanna that she did not have the money to pay to the Czech authorities for the nearly three years Erwin had been in care so far. Izaak stood over his distressed daughter while pointing at the document to sign, bellowing, "You're going to have to pay a huge amount of money. Can you afford it? I won't give you any money. And remember that your mother and I are disowning the child. We don't even want to see him!"

Although Johanna didn't have any money, she thought there may have been some way of getting Erwin back if she pleaded with the Dutch authorities to forgive the debt, but Izaak was having none of it. He carried on saying that the child wouldn't remember Johanna and a Czech couple would give him a good start in life. Once more, Johanna felt there was no choice. Trembling, she signed away her child forever. Izaak had got his way.

Johanna found the courage to try one more time to change her father's mind. It was hopeless. "You must never have the war product," he told her. The document was produced by a social affairs official. Every word bore into Johanna's heart. It read:

The Hague, 7 May 1947

The undersigned:

JOHANNA HENDRIKA VAN HAARLEM, residing at Scheldestraat (sic) 24 in The Hague, hereby declares that she completely renounces her child ERWIN VAN HAARLEM, born in Amsterdam on 24 August 1944, currently residing in Prague, for the benefit of the foster parents in Czechoslovakia.

She declares that she will not make any further claims on the upbringing of her child and also that she has no objection to her child obtaining another nationality in due course.

Izaak pointed at the line where Johanna must sign. She wrote her name and something broke inside. She would never forgive her parents.

It was a crushing moment for the young mother, both mentally and physically. If only she had been at home when the Red Cross had called or when the letters had arrived earlier in the year, she thought, nothing would have stopped her from getting Erwin. She would have found the money somehow. And yet, her father's insistence that Erwin would be better off with a new family, kept ringing in her head. "Do as you are told," he shouted at her, wagging a finger in her face. "Do as you are told."

The moment she dreamed about had passed.

Johanna resolved to move forward and try and create a new life for herself. She took office jobs and worked as a housemaid for several months. By the late 1940s, Johanna, now in her mid-20s, was still living in the Van Haarlem house but any joy she had once felt in living there was gone. Her relationship with her parents had deteriorated altogether as she struggled to come to terms with losing Erwin. She was angry with them and with herself for being a bad mother.

~

Five years later, Johanna was still at home and still struggling to find her purpose in her life after the war and losing Erwin when she met Henri "Henk" Duffhues in the mid-1950s and began the kind of loving relationship she had yearned for. They were friends who met at work; he'd moved to The Hargue from his hometown of Brabant in the south of the country. He finally plucked up the courage to ask her on a date and they were courting for a while before deciding to get married but again her mother and father intervened, insisting she could not marry Duffhues because he was a Catholic.

It was another life-changing moment for Johanna and, as a result, Duffhues ended his relationship with her and left for his hometown in the south of Holland. Johanna could not dismiss her strong feelings for Duffhues and tracked him down several months later believing she could rekindle their relationship. But she found him in a hospital maternity ward with his new wife, a childhood sweetheart, who had just given birth to a baby son. Johanna was distraught. Not only had she lost the man she wanted to marry, but she was traumatised by her memories of the "house of shame" in Amsterdam where, in heartbreaking contrast to the scene she witnessed with Duffhues, she had given birth alone to Erwin, the son she feared she would never see again.

CHAPTER NINE

Olešovice, Bohemia, Czechoslovakia,
2 April 1949

Little Erwin van Haarlem had experienced enough heartache for a lifetime in his first four years. He knew nothing of the circumstances of his birth, but he knew that he was alone in the world and that his parents had already rejected him. It was a rough start, and the blond tot could have been forgiven for being surly, even at such a young age, but his good humour was infectious, and he was loved by the nurses at Olešovice, the orphanage where he had lived since being moved from the children's home where Johanna left him in Rumburk. He was such a favourite that when a Czech Radio reporter arrived at the home to do a report on the children left behind in the horrors of war, Erwin was sitting on the lap of the staff member being interviewed.

At one point, the reporter broke off and asked the little boy, "What is your name?"

"My name is Erwin."

"And what else can you tell us about yourself?" The reporter kept her recorder running in case she could use the segment in her story.

"My name is Erwin van Haarlem and I'm from Holland," he replied.

"How do you like it here?"

"Very much."

"And do you know a song?"

The little boy was suddenly shy and looked up at his carer. "Well, maybe Little Red Riding Hood?" she asked him.

With an angelic voice, Erwin started singing, "Little Red Riding Hood went through the Black Forest..."

The reporter and her editor were captivated by the song, and it was featured at the end of the report when it aired on the station the next morning.

In a small village in Moravia a couple was listening to the radio when they heard Erwin's song. They were both primary school teachers and unable to have a child of their own. Sitting at the kitchen table, the couple listened to the emotional story about the orphans of World War Two and they heard Erwin's singing, and they knew that they wanted to give the boy with the sad, beautiful voice a home.

~

In the Netherlands, Johanna was still under the thumb of her controlling parents, resigned to being a mother without a child. In Czechoslovakia, her son was about to start a whole new life that didn't include her.

There had been a couple of false starts. Two couples took Erwin home but were unprepared for the ardours of parenthood and returned him to the children's home like a new coat that didn't fit.

On 2 April 1949 Erwin, now four years old, was driven out of the orphanage for the last time. This time for a place unknown. The orphanage was not informed about where he was going or the identity of his foster parents. His nurses packed his few clothes and a couple of toys, praying Erwin would find happiness. Some children did, indeed, find the love they craved but at a time of such disruption it was the most innocent who were often the most forgotten. In almost all cases, the home knew where their children were going when they left Olesovice.

Erwin van Haarlem was the exception. The home kept meticulous records about all its children in a book of heartache. The nurses were deeply concerned about what they saw as a foreboding comment, handwritten in Czech next to the entry of Erwin van Haarlem. There was no name for the foster parents. No forwarding address. The entry read simply, "Chybi Pred. MV."

In English, it meant: "Missing. Hand-over. Home Office."

The boy had been singled out by the authorities, but the staff had no idea why. They had never seen these words used before. They were written by a state official. Any hopes the boy's surrogate mothers had of following his progress were dashed. Any hopes they may have harboured of his biological mother one day returning to bring him home were tempered by the realisation that they would not be able to tell her where he went. Erwin left, never to return. It was as if he was never there.

The teachers who were so enamoured with Erwin's voice on the radio took him home and gave him a new name and a new life with the blessing of the state.

And his real identity, signed away by his mother and wiped clean at the orphanage, was left open for the taking. As the world hurtled toward a Cold War fought not on the battlefields by soldiers, but in the shadows by spies, there was a real value in that.

Children's homes in Czechoslovakia were fertile grounds for spymasters seeking fake identities for agents operating undercover abroad. Having a mother from the Netherlands – offering a possible entré into the West – Erwin's name and background had been flagged to the Czech intelligence services as a potential cover story for an agent sometime in the future. The real Erwin would have a new life with his adopted parents. His name and his traumatic beginnings would be logged by the intelligence section of the Czech Home Office in a classified book listing the possible aliases – with factual accompanying biographies – that could one day be picked out and used by a Czech spy to slip into another person's life.

There could one day be two Erwin van Haarlems – one real, the other an impostor.

CHAPTER TEN

Alkemade, Holland, 25 July 1958

Queen Elizabeth II's state visit to the Netherlands in March 1958 signaled a renewed sense of stability and prosperity. The Dutch royals greeted the Queen and her husband, the Duke of Edinburgh, with glittering pomp and pageantry on the streets and a sumptuous banquet in the Royal Palace of Amsterdam. But Johanna felt none of the nation's post-war optimism. As she walked through the cobbled streets of The Hague to catch a train to work, she cut a lonely figure. She couldn't shake off her guilt over the plight of her son. Johanna felt she had been abandoned too and was trying falteringly to rebuild her life without her son or the man, Henri Duffhues, she thought was the love of her life.

Her simmering anger over her father's ultimatum to get rid of the baby developed into near hatred. But her affectionate feelings for Duffhues endured. The romance had offered the promise of an escape from the family household, suffocating in regrets and divided loyalties. She could be herself with him, although not so much herself that she dared tell him about Erwin. She dated some other men but had no stomach for their frivolities. Any joy she may have found in such things was lost on the road home from Czechoslovakia.

Then, out of the blue, Duffhues contacted Johanna to say he had divorced his wife after just a few years of marriage. He told her that he had made the wrong choice; it had been a big mistake marrying another woman who he never really loved, and he wanted to start afresh with her. Johanna could barely believe her sudden good fortune – she'd been dreaming about a second chance with Duffhues ever since he left. Her life, she thought, was finally starting to turn out how she hoped. They started living together in 1954, in itself a rebellion against her stridently Protestant parents, but Johanna no longer cared much what they thought about her.

Johanna and Henri Duffhues married on 25 July 1958, in the town of Alkemade in southern Holland. It wasn't a white wedding – the spectre of the past still hung over the Van Haarlems. It wasn't just the secret of Johanna's wartime baby; they all had their own very good reasons not to look back. She decided it was better not to invite them at all.

Unable to keep her secret from her new husband, Johanna told him about Erwin and the circumstances surrounding the boy's illegitimate birth. She had hoped for compassion, but she was sorely disappointed. In no uncertain terms, Duffhues made it clear that he also didn't want his wife looking for her first born. He didn't want his wife's scandalous past knocking on his door. For the second time, a man in her life was trying to wipe out all knowledge and acceptance of her baby. Like Izaak van Haarlem, Johanna's husband refused to support her if she tried to trace Erwin and bring him home. It was non-negotiable.

Izaak died two months after Johanna's wedding. His wife lived another eight years.

Without her father's dark presence, Johanna's dream of a stable family life at last appeared to be coming true but there were soon more obstacles to her happiness. Duffhues lost his job at a typewriter factory and he wasn't interested in having another child, while Johanna had been hoping to give up work and focus on starting a family. The divisions between them grew.

They moved to another southern town, Leiden, and, to Duffhues surprise – and Johanna's delight – she fell pregnant. At the age of 40, she gave birth to their son, Henri Johannes, in 1964. Johanna cherished the boy, calling him Hans and giving him all the love and protection that she had not been able to give Erwin.

For a while, Johanna, busy with rearing Hans and still respectful of her husband's wishes, took him at his word and made no attempt to find Erwin. They moved again, and built a home with a large garden in Shaijk. Yet as the years went by, her desire to find Erwin grew and she refused to let the matter drop. Duffhues would not change his mind, considering the entire affair shameful, but neither would she. Johanna's mind was set. In time, she decided her only option was to go behind her husband's back and make her enquiries secretly. If she found Erwin, then she would decide her best course of action. Perhaps, she thought, Henri would come around? But the years passed, and her husband was unbending.

~

Johanna worked hard as an administrator for a local doctor to bring money into the household while raising Hans, who was in elementary school, and juggling household chores with the needs of her small family. She loved Hans deeply and was, not surprisingly, overprotective of the young boy. Hans returned his mother's love and affection, but that year strains began to emerge in her marriage. Johanna was in her mid-40s and wanted to have another child and stay at home caring for the whole family at their house in southern Holland. Henri was not interested in having any more children and insisted they needed the extra income that Johanna's job provided. His continued insistence that she didn't search for Erwin only deepened their rift. Johanna, a strong-minded woman despite, or perhaps because of all her life challenges, ignored him and kept working in secret, writing letters to the authorities asking for information about Erwin. But now hanging over her was the constant fear that Henri would find out and there would be another blistering row. She started to build bridges with her siblings, attending family events and exchanging small gifts, but Johanna could not risk them finding out about her quest in case Henri got wind of it.

After an asthma attack left Johanna seriously ill in hospital for more than a month in 1974, and she felt that her husband didn't show enough empathy, she decided their marriage was over and they started to live apart. She stayed in Schaijk and Duffhues moved east to Arnhem, near the German border. Now that she no longer had to fear Duffhues' reaction, Johanna redoubled her efforts to find her first-born son. Erwin, by then 30 years of age, had not made any choices about how he was brought into the world, she told herself. He was entirely blameless, so how could he be blamed for bringing shame on the family? The shame was Holland's. It was Germany's. It wasn't hers and it certainly wasn't Erwin's. The bloody-mindedness of Izaak and then Duffhues just made Johanna more determined, but she was under no illusions about the task she faced in finding Erwin. Her homeland had put the horrors of a fascist occupation into the past. But the foe she faced now was also implacable. She would be trying to break through hard-line Communist rule and repression. She could expect as much cooperation from Prague and Moscow as she would have received from wartime Berlin.

Post-war Europe posed an altogether new set of obstacles, and they were no less considerable. Since 1948, Soviet communists had controlled what was then Czechoslovakia, imposing the will of Joseph Stalin, leader of the Union of Soviet Socialist Republics (USSR). Stalin may have been an ally against Hitler in World War Two, but he was also another murderous dictator. Johanna didn't know if Erwin was still alive, where he was or how he had been treated. Was he even still in Czechoslovakia? Could he be in a remote region of the USSR? She wondered if he had been abandoned somewhere, like the frozen wastes of Siberia, because his birth father was an enemy soldier? The Russians hated the Germans just as Holland's people did. She had nightmares of Erwin being abused by unloving foster parents.

Not having any of the answers was horrible. She couldn't look at her second son without worrying what became of her first. Johanna's best daytime dreams were of the moment she would find her blond-haired, blue-eyed boy. She didn't like to dwell on the fact that his features would have changed with the years. Her mind's eye image of Erwin was already fading and she struggled to cope with losing her memories of what he looked like. She was a terrible mother, she thought.

Johanna knew there was little chance of travelling to Soviet satellite states. They were becoming more and more insular as Russian leaders, and their thought police, ensured no contact with non-communist influences from the West. But her growing guilt made her restless. She simply couldn't find any peace until she learned the truth. She reached out to everybody she could think of — the Czech authorities, the children's home outside Prague, and the International Red Cross.

The answers to her early inquiries were impersonal and vague. On 8 September 1976, she received a letter from the Czech Embassy in The Hague. It read:

> *Regarding your question of 31 May 1976, we inform you that Mr. Erwin van Haarlem, born 24 August 1944, since 1972 has been staying outside the territory of the Czechoslovak Republic without the permission of the relevant authorities.*

That was it. Another dead end. But at least she knew her son was still alive. It had taken all Johanna's strength to leave her son as a baby and now she was prepared to use everything she had left to get him back. It wouldn't matter how long it took, or how far she had to travel, Johanna would get her reunion and nobody — and no ideology — was going to stop her.

PART TWO

THE SPY

CHAPTER
ELEVEN

Prague, Czechoslovakia, 1960s

The Czech intelligence service, or StB (Státní bezpečnost) first marked Vaclav Jelinek out as a potential candidate while he was in the Czech army, serving his compulsory military service. He had started as a cook's assistant and a waiter in the officer's canteen, rising to the rank of lieutenant. As a rookie soldier, Jelinek's raw ambition had impressed the faceless StB men in Prague trawling military files to find the best candidate for missions in the West. His superiors considered him to be resilient, a potential agent who would be able to blend into communities so well that neighbours would never suspect him, colleagues at work would admire his facade of diligence and good nature, and he would convince new friends he only had good intentions. They thought his single-mindedness and his analytical mind would serve him well while he lived undercover in enemy territory for years, gathering classified intelligence from a government with an opposing ideology.

There was something else, too. So far, Jelinek's life had been boringly normal. His childhood had proved uneventful. When he was four years old, he moved into a new home in Prague where he was popular in school with lots of friends, according to an intelligence report on his background. Apart from a bout of chicken pox, he was a healthy boy. He'd graduated from high school and, before joining the army, had worked in a sugar factory. His bland background, keen ambition, and sharp, friendly nature made him perfect spy material.

When he was 22, two mysterious Czech intelligence officers offered him the opportunity to work for the StB, dangling Richard Sorge's name as an incentive. "We have come to offer you something similar," they told him. Jelenik was fascinated by the Soviet spy, who supplied Moscow with some of Germany's and Japan's most important secrets during World War Two and was said by Bond author Ian Fleming to be the "most formidable spy in history". Jelenik had little interest in working as a diplomat, but he could easily see himself as an Eastern European James Bond on covert missions around the world. Jelenik's curiosity – and vanity – was piqued. He said yes.

Jelinek began training in Czechoslovakia's First Administration of the Ministry of the Interior – the intelligence department – on 1 October 1965. There was nothing glamorous about the Czech intelligence agency's grey, anonymous offices in equally grey, uninspiring Communist-era blocks in Prague. Such was the paranoia levels that doors were encased in leather for soundproofing so that conversations went unheard unless a competitive colleague had bugged the room. Which had happened. The Centre, as it was known, was the operational section of Czech intelligence in Directorate 1 of the Ministry of the Interior. In 1976, it had moved from the building of the Monastery of the Knights of the Cross in Prague 1 to the

"Cottage", a more modern office block on Střelničná Street in Prague's Kobylisy district.

Jelinek's bosses gave him his first pseudonym, Karel Elsner. It was meant to help him get used to the deceptions of living a double life. He was told to dispose of all documents relating to Vaclav Jelinek. He was now someone else. His new passport had his same photo and a similar age. But it said his name was Karel Elsner.

For all intents and purposes, Vaclav Jelinek no longer existed. He cut contact with his biological parents without any explanation other than that he was serving his country and that they should be proud. To his friends and everyone he'd known, he became a ghost.

In training, his first priority was to improve his languages; in his case it was German. And on one point his bosses were emphatic – he could have girlfriends, as many as he liked – but he could not, under any circumstances, get married. A wife could get too close to the truth. Matters would become dangerously complicated.

It was quickly made clear to the pupil spy that his loyalty wasn't just to Czechoslovakia but ultimately to "Mother Russia" – and that any information he managed to secrete back to his spymasters would be forwarded to Moscow.

Following his discharge from the army, Jelinek applied for a job as a waiter at a corporate canteen in Brno, the country's second-largest city after Prague and signed on for a three-year culinary course. By that time, unbeknown to his work colleagues, he was already in training to be a spy. It was a lonely calling. The learning was carried out in isolation with no colleagues. The spy work itself would be the same. As an 'illegal', he would have none of the diplomatic protection afforded to those holding an official diplomatic post with the Czech government. He would be working under false papers and would never report to an espionage station or boss in the country where he was based. He would take orders only from Prague or Moscow. The StB warned him he would not be protected under any diplomatic laws or immunities. As a spy, he would be off-grid and off the books.

~

The StB closely monitored the young agent's progress, noting the early signs were optimistic. He was adjudged to have an IQ of 138, just a few points off being moderately gifted. His lessons in espionage included methods of foiling polygraph lie detector machines that were used to flush out enemy agents. Rather than being taught to remain calm under pressure, the Czech agents were coached to do the exact opposite — to overreact emotionally to the simplest of questions. For instance, asked if water is wet, the subject forced themselves into a state of panic so that while the answer given is "yes" the body's reactions suggest a lie. Jelinek illustrated his ingenuity by hiding a drawing pin in his shoe and pressing his foot down onto it when being asked a question to offer a confused response to the polygrapher.

"He is very persistent, self-motivated, he can control... and he is moderately adaptable," read one early report. "He is very reliable, responsive, less obtrusive, with average awareness and work ethic. He is brave... he can suppress fatigue and sleepiness; he can work at night."

After 12 months, "Elsner" was not deemed ready yet for work in the field. "The examination shows that the personality of the subject is not yet stable — there is a tendency to concentrate on oneself. The hysteric component of the personality with hints of infantile features is evident in the psychological profile," the report continued.

"On the other hand, acquired secondary features are already appearing – self-control, self-reliance, self-confidence."

Nevertheless, it ended, that any assignment would remain "problematic" at that time.

Another psychological examination obtained from Czech intelligence archives reads: "He comes from a business family as the only son, both parents are business people, without political affiliation. He is fit, he is actively interested in sports, boxing and judo. He has a cheerful nature and direct behaviour. His hobbies include theatre, books, and the study of languages."

He was said to be physically and mentally agile and have a sound background for a prospective spy.

"The subject grew up in a working-class environment as an only child, his relationship with his parents is good, his father is more supportive while his mother is permissive," wrote an apparatchik. "I don't know the relationship between his parents. He grew up in a village until he was four years old, later in Prague. He does not report any somatic or psychological illnesses in his immediate family or in his family. He was always good enough for everything at school. He always had a good relationship with his classmates and teachers, he was always 'not the best' in the class, rather he … had a lot of friends both among boys and among the girls.

"He used to be visually mature, and as a result he sometimes imposed a greater distance on himself from others, which he tolerated with great ease. He writes and reads in his spare time, enjoys literature and the theatre, his interests are more technical. He is also a good athlete, he believes that he is in very good physical condition, compared to his friends he appears to be more persistent in this regard. He claims that it is difficult for him to express himself about his character, but others argue that he is more desirable and would be more acceptable to other people. He rates his comprehension and nature as obsessive, and he remembers colourful images and colours the best."

This more impressive assessment helped to have him classed as one of the brightest young agents. By the end of 1966, Jelinek's bosses were grooming him for an elite assignment. They told him he could well end up in London, a renowned hotbed for spies where he would be under the greatest scrutiny. During training, he learned that Britain's counterintelligence service MI5 and the foreign intelligence gathering service MI6 were possibly the most effective in the world at recruiting and exposing spies. In the 70s, the Eastern Bloc was struggling to set up any useful intelligence operations in the UK. The Czech spy would always have to be on his guard. Britain's tough sentencing for convicted agents working for foreign powers was well-documented. Jelinek had read about the most famous case: that of Dutch-born George Blake, original name George Behar, who was born in Rotterdam in 1922. He had been accepted by MI6 as a spy on their side of the Cold War while, in fact, working as a double agent for the Soviet Union's KGB.

Blake became a communist while a prisoner in the Korean War. He betrayed hundreds of Western spies to Moscow and most of his trial was held in secret by the Lord Chief Justice, Lord Parker, who was so disgusted by the level of betrayal and the weight of evidence against Blake that he called then Prime Minister Harold Macmillan on the night before sentencing to consult over the punishment. Lord Parker sentenced Blake to 42 years imprisonment in 1961. Macmillan was so shocked by the eventual sentence he wrote in his diary that night: "The LCJ has passed a savage sentence – 42 years!" Even MI6 was concerned about the draconian sentence deterring any future spies from confessing.

Jelinek was more than impressed when he read about Blake's 1966 escape from London's Wormwood Scrubs jail in a masterly executed operation that was believed at the time to have been orchestrated by the KGB. It later came to light that two radical anti-nuclear campaigners, Michael Randle and Pat Pottle, aided and abetted by Sean Bourke, an Irish petty criminal, sprung the traitor because they believed the prison sentence to be "inhuman". Pottle and Randle faced trial in 1991 for aiding and abetting Blake's escape but were both acquitted.

Jelinek was aware of the risks, but his bosses believed his training would see him through. They also praised his loyalty to the Communist cause. Most important of all, he was confident, bordering on arrogant. He was itching to become the best agent the Czechs had ever produced. He would be playing for high stakes. But first, he would have to prove himself in more benign countries such as Austria and Germany where he could learn the language.

CHAPTER
TWELVE

Halle an der Saale, Saxony,
14 November 1967

At the end of 1967, Jelinek's initial training was complete and his bosses sent him on his first foreign mission to Halle an der Saale, in Saxony, near Leipzig, where he was put up in a STASI East German intelligence safe house and told to work as a technician in a local sugar factory and report back anything he deemed interesting. Quickly tiring of the repetitive work, Jelinek got permission to quit his job to become a waiter, a profession he intended to use once he was secreted into the West. In 1968, he moved on to a nearby hotel, the Continental, and then, in 1969 to a restaurant and hotel in Ostrava, eastern Czechoslovakia.

In the spring of 1971, Jelinek – as Karel Elsner – was working as a waiter in the small Parkhotel in the Alps at Kreuzstein on the border of Bavaria and Bohemia. He was a decent enough waiter, but he was also capable of hand-to-hand close combat; by now, he had been trained as a marksman and acquired surveillance techniques essential to his real line of work. His spymasters had put him through dummy runs on the streets to see if he could spot who was trailing him. The watchers could be a young couple canoodling on a bench, an old man reading the morning paper or two people sitting in a car. He learned to double back to spot faces who had turned with him. There could be more than one team of watchers, too, each peeling off so that new faces populated the streets. Sometimes would-be agents would get so paranoid they would point out virtually everyone in the vicinity. Paranoia is one of the biggest foes for a spy. It leads to extreme anxiety and wrong decisions, especially for those like Jelinek who are expected to stay in the shadows for many years – possibly decades.

There was little intelligence of interest to his Czech bosses in his hotel and restaurant jobs, but that wasn't the point. He was establishing his credentials as an agent to be sent to the West. The need for a Czech agent in London was urgent; recent compromises had left the city of spies spyless. The time came to press the button on Jelinek's mission after Josef Frolik, an 'illegal' working for the StB and loaded with secrets defected to the United States in 1969 and joined the CIA.

To give Jelinek the best possible chance of success, he was given a new identity. Karel Elsner was no more. Now he had a new name and past. His mother was from the Netherlands and his father from Germany. He would be known as Erwin van Haarlem.

He was drilled relentlessly on the details of Erwin's life – both real and manufactured – over and over again, until it was difficult to tell the truth in his own past from the fiction. It was all very well having the appropriate paperwork, but a spy had to believe in the lie. Believe like their life depends upon it. Using his own name and background, Jelinek wouldn't stand a chance in the West. He was a good, if unremarkable, Communist from Prague who'd done his service in the Czech Army and slipped into civilian anonymity.

CHAPTER TWELVE

But with a new name and identity anything was possible. All he had to do was believe.

Being a spy didn't just mean a new name; it meant an entire new life to try for size… and it was up to him to make it fit. His instructors drummed every detail into him until he could answer every question without a moment's hesitation.

The StB wasn't alone in using the identities of orphans, dead or alive, as cover for their spies. It was a convenient source of aliases; partial truths are always preferred to complete fabrications in the spyworld, with no awkward questions asked. But Erwin's history was specifically chosen for Jelinek's mission. The real Erwin had a Dutch mother, allowing for the possibility of a Dutch passport, which would evade the kind of suspicion a Czech passport could bring with it in the UK. The father was dead and it appeared as if his mother had disowned him. The "legend", as the spies called their assumed identities, was watertight. Erwin's identity was tailor-made for Jelinek, and his spymasters had even secured official original documentation from the children's home to help prove his new identity.

He was given the operational name of "Gragert". His intelligence file offered no clues to the reason for his code name, although it is derived from grey or grey monk in North German and might have been a nod to his profession's trademark life in the shadows.

His bosses in Prague gave him the codename "Gragert" but to everyone else, Jelinek was now Erwin van Haarlem.

~

Czech intelligence headquarters decided to appeal directly to the Netherlands' Queen Juliana in order to secure him a coveted

Dutch passport and prepared a letter for Jelinek detailing the tragic story of Erwin's early years, including Johanna's relationship with a Nazi soldier. The experienced and creative constructors of spy legends planned to tell the story of what happened to little Erwin in the hopes of winning the monarch's sympathy.

It worked. The Queen wrote back personally to say Erwin's case was under examination and, three months later, Jelinek was summoned to the Dutch Embassy in Vienna to collect his passport under the name of Erwin van Haarlem.

The passport left the path clear for Jelinek to make plans for London. But first he needed to be knocked down a few pegs. His lingering arrogance concerned his spymasters. They preferred a low-key John Smith approach to a charismatic license-to-kill James Bond.

~

Jelinek was ready for the final major test of his "legend". He was sent on a trial trip to England to see how well his new identity would hold up to scrutiny and see how Jelinek would cope in a country way more challenging for a Soviet Bloc spy than anywhere else in Europe.

His entry into the UK was uneventful, as was his night in the city and he was being closely watched by an StB agent as he checked in at Heathrow Airport for his return flight to Amsterdam using his new Erwin van Haarlem Dutch passport.

He was sharply dressed in a double-breasted dark blue sports jacket, with a striped, open-necked cotton shirt with fashionably large collars open across the lapels. The flares on his beige slacks covered his expensive soft leather calf boots with their high Cuban heels. He smiled at a young woman in front of him in the line and his eyes lingered a moment longer than appropriate, although he thought she didn't appear to mind.

The young spy in training had mastered the use of ciphers, cameras, morse code and radio. He was quick-witted and bold, but they were still worried he was too cocky, too full of himself. And he had just made a serious error on his big test – he had a small knife that he'd bought in London in his hand luggage, drawing attention to himself when it was detected and confiscated. He had botched the number one rule for spies: don't be noticed. The consequences were minimal; he was taken aside by a member of the Heathrow security staff and told that the knife would not be returned. The official was apologetic – this was decades before 9/11 and security checks were perfunctory – but the misstep had effectively made an invisible man visible. There was an asterisk on the record of his entry into the country, even if nobody ever read it. He was pulled back to Prague and told by his spymasters he wasn't ready for his first major mission abroad.

After Heathrow put a black mark on his record, his bosses gave him another chance – only for him to land in hot water again. At an illegal border crossing from Czechoslovakia into Austria he packed too many clothes, drawing attention once more. his colleague wrote, "We went to the station together where Gragert collected his luggage from the storage room, and we left for the bus to the airport. Shortly before half-past-two we left Prague by plane. During the stay abroad, during travel and at the airports and accommodation, there were no violations or other problems."

However, head office was not so impressed.

"Gragert arrived exactly on time," wrote a tutor assigned to Van Haarlem. "He used the identification sign correctly and answered correctly when addressed by the password. He was dressed cleanly and according to the fashion that his peers wear in Austria. However, I have a problem with Gragert that did not correspond at all to the Gragert legend. Gragert made the mistake of taking with him completely unnecessary personal clothing and items with his backpack weighing about 24kg."

The tutor pointed out that the budding spy had too much luggage for his length of time abroad which could alert immigration or intelligence officers.

He'd failed again. But he didn't give up.

~

As the advanced training continued in preparation for London, Jelinek's marks improved accordingly. His final report in 1972 deeming him "fully qualified" denoted his performance as "very good" rather than "excellent" but clearly, from the accompanying comments, he had won over his superiors. It said he had passed "…special training, which places extraordinary demands on the intelligence officer's overall readiness in terms of expertise and morals and politics." Other field work earned him more effusive praise. "His professional readiness was tested in various events, which he completed successfully. He was also entrusted with the implementation of two short-term events abroad, which he fulfilled exactly according to the given instructions. He showed personal courage and responsibility with them," his trainer wrote. "He achieves good results when developing intelligence from a foreign base... His attitude towards work duties is disciplined and proactive and responsible."

Gragert's case for frontline work was further helped by his being deemed a party loyalist. His superiors noted that he presented as a committed communist who believed in joining forces with the USSR and other socialist countries, based on the principles of "proletarian internationalism". Another report continued, "He fully supports the policy of the Communist Party and party congress. From a political point of view, he can correctly navigate the complex phenomena of social development, even if he lives in a hostile environment." The praise put the spy in the making closer to his hoped-for London posting. His controllers described him as honest and tenacious, and they seemed to believe that he no longer had a tendency to be arrogant. A report concluded "that he was politically mature, principled in Marxism-Leninism and proletarian internationalism. In terms of political, professional, character and moral qualities, he has all the prerequisites for the performance of his position in FMV (Intelligence Service of the Federal Ministry of Interior)."

Gragert, as "Erwin van Haarlem", was ready for his big mission. All that was left was to swear an "Oath of Service" – "according to the Minister of the Interior Decree No. 35/1961" for "members of the security forces of the Ministry of the Interior".

Jelinek proudly read the oath, pledging to "always be a brave, honest and disciplined member of the security corps of the Ministry of the Interior".

"I swear that I will always fight decisively against the enemies of my homeland, the enemies of the Soviet Union and other socialist countries," he said, adding, "I promise that I am ready to use all my abilities and risk my life in the fight for the interests of the Czechoslovak Socialist Republic, for the victory of peace and communism."

In June 1975, he was finally on his way to London with just the appropriate amount of luggage and his first assignment – to make connections with the British Royal Family.

CHAPTER THIRTEEN

London, 17 July 1976

Buckingham Palace Road was quiet, and Jelinek pulled up his collar in a vain attempt to keep the driving rain from soaking his expensive new suit. The spy had been in London for a year and he usually enjoyed walking around London at night, sure in the knowledge that when he looked over his shoulder nobody was watching. Counterintelligence operatives need a crowded thoroughfare to hide from their targets. But this July night he felt as empty as the streets.

It was 4am and any high from the alcohol had faded to a whisky melancholy. The Hippodrome in the West End was a good place to meet single women. Tourists and girls from the suburbs looking to party were easy prey for a confident, smartly dressed man with a mysterious charm and money to spend. He never brought them to his flat but was happy to pay for a taxi to their homes as long as they had moved out from their parents and he could share the bed for an hour or two.

A casual one-night stand was not so unusual for a bachelor

living far from home and starved of companionship and sexual gratification. But for Jelinek, it wasn't a matter of choice.

He was under orders to keep any dalliances with the opposite sex, or, indeed, of any sex, to a single meeting. Permission from Prague via coded messages even on his love life was required for any longer relationship. And it would probably be turned down. To disobey the order would be deemed gross insubordination. So, he frequented London's discotheques after work, trying to satisfy his urges with anonymous sex and rejecting any hint of commitment. Romance was not in the job description. Indeed, history had shown it to be kryptonite to a spy.

He had left the Hippodrome at 2am with a determined young psychology student who seemed impressed by his claims of being a stockbroker with a multi-million-pound portfolio. She drunkenly lectured him about the unfairness of a world where the wealth was confined to the top few percent while admiring his expensive watch and then invited him back to her Brick Lane studio flat in London's East End. The sex was perfunctory, and he let himself out as soon as she fell asleep. He wanted to leave her some money but that didn't feel right either. The idea of being a lone lothario had appealed to him in the exciting first few months in one of the world's great capital cities, but nothing had turned out like he had hoped and now he yearned for companionship more than sex. Perhaps he wasn't cut out to be a James Bond after all.

Jelinek had asked if a female partner who knew about his mission could be sent from Czechoslovakia to help alleviate his feelings of alienation. The request was turned down by his bosses because it "could trigger new background checks on him". They dismissed his complaints, saying he was "getting emotional" because of the long-term nature of his position and homesickness.

Prague was nervous about anything that might lead to their man being noticed by the "enemy" authorities, however innocuous. They were already concerned that Gragert had crashed his MG Metro into a London bus. There was no police report, and his insurance company passed on a £750 pay-out to the name on the policy "Van Haarlem", which he used to buy another used blue metallic Metro.

Gragert's stilted personal life would continue to be an issue as his loneliness expanded. A couple of years into his posting he met a scientist at a drawing class in Hampstead and the attraction had been instant and mutual. A Scottish biologist working on new drugs for the treatment of bronchitis and asthma, she was well-educated, beautiful, strong-willed and a committed feminist who had little time for Van Haarlem's old-world charm. Despite this – perhaps because of it – they hit it off and he invited her on a date at a Greek restaurant he regularly frequented in North-West London.

After arguing about who should pay the bill – she was insistent on paying her share – they went back to his flat after dinner, a departure from his usual wariness about female guests. He knew instantly that he couldn't honour the one-night stand rule. He knew his bosses in Prague and Moscow would be furious if they discovered their top operative in the UK was so recklessly risking exposure. He would be deemed to be letting his heart rule his decisions rather than the interests of the Soviet Bloc. A lot of time, training and the building of his legend could be compromised.

Still, the couple saw more of one another, and Jelinek brought her home a gift of gold and diamond earrings after a trip to

Berne in Switzerland to meet with his handlers. But an unlikely issue arose that would doom their relationship: she shared many of his political views and had strong left-wing leanings. The time came when he had to bring the relationship to the notice of his masters. Jelinek was hopeful that the doctor's shared values would make her acceptable as a partner and she would be allowed to move in with him, as he wanted.

He couldn't have been more wrong. Czech intelligence officers wrote in their lovestruck agent's files that "Gragert informed that he knows and is quite attached to the person. He emphasised that she was of the same political views as himself, pro-communist and strongly involved in the … movement in London." The spy wouldn't have known what his bosses were saying about him but he would have been surprised they were no longer altogether against him having a "more permanent acquaintance". "However," they continued, "we cannot allow the fact that she moves in with him and checks the invoices." Further, his involvement with her represented, in their view, a "very serious threat to his security".

Her Communism and interest in the "counter-movement" meant they would move in the wrong kind of circles, with left-leaning people who favoured Soviet ideology, with the potential of bringing the name Van Haarlem to the attention of MI5 watchers, rather than staying under their radar. The romance could compromise him. Had she been a fox-hunting Tory who despised everything Communism stood for, she may have been quite acceptable. He would probably have been encouraged to fast-forward the relationship. Who knows who he would have been introduced to in the upper classes of English society? The balance sheet of risk and advantage would have been in his favour.

His spymasters immediately called him back to Prague for an emergency briefing. The order came through, blunt and unbending: "Terminate the relationship with the person due to the dangers arising and her membership in left-wing organisations."

Jelinek agreed to end the romance within a month.

~

For his first few months after arriving in London in 1975, it seemed to Jelinek that he was quite likely to be sent home in shame without accomplishing anything. Before he left Prague, he was briefed to get as close as possible to the British Royal Family. It was even suggested that once he had infiltrated the privileged world of Western royalty, he could secrete listening bugs in the furniture at Buckingham Palace.

Using his alter ego, he got a position as a waiter at the Hilton Hotel on Park Lane with a view of the royal residence half a mile away. Only a Soviet Bloc spy with no idea about the rarefied upper echelons of the British establishment could imagine even as a very long shot that a Royal would call in for a cocktail at their local bar. The idea was about as realistic as the crowds gathering each day outside the gates of Buckingham Palace expecting to be invited in for afternoon tea served in fine bone china. Gragert was desperate to impress.

After first flying into the UK in 1975, he had rented a room in Denbigh Street, Pimlico, behind Victoria Station, for £7.50 a week, but after getting the Hilton Hotel waiter job he moved into his own flat at 78 Queen's Gate Gardens in South Kensington. It was a fancy address that might have given the impression in Prague that he was in the right place, but after six months without any progress, there were some rumblings of discontent. He had been sent to London with high hopes that his promise in training would bear fruit. But he'd yet to send a single tip back to his bosses.

Things got worse for Jelinek on 5 September 1975 while he was working in the Hilton's Roof Restaurant on the 24th floor when an IRA bomb exploded in the lobby, killing two people and seriously injuring another. Police interviewed him the next day along with all the other employees and took his fingerprints. Scotland Yard had a Czech spy's "dabs" and didn't know it. There was no suspicion that Jelinek was involved in the terrorist attack, but, once again, the attention was making his Czech spymasters nervous.

There was a changing of the guard in Prague and his new boss, Major Karel Přibík, came to meet his supposedly prized spy. It didn't go well. Jelinek was blasted by Přibík for looking like a "hippy" and a "scarecrow" in his western attire. "You haven't done anything during your six-month stay in London," he told Gragert. "Did you get close to the royal family? Have you ever seen the Queen?"

"I've only seen her once waving from a car to subjects near Victoria Station," replied Jelinek.

"And to the other members of the royal family?" continued the spy chief. "You stared at the fence like other tourists, watching the guards change!"

"Yes," replied Jelinek.

Chastened, he went back to work hoping to perhaps find a job as a footman or something similar in a royal residence knowing that his poor English and foreign credentials made such a scheme extremely unlikely. In the meantime, he focused his spying on the Hilton, hoping to pick up royal gossip from the guests.

He passed on the fact that when the then Prime Minister Margaret Thatcher attended a banquet at the Hilton, as she did several times while he worked there, she always had a room supplied for her to relax or take a time out from the event. Jelinek learned that while the room was checked by security, they didn't bother with the room next door nor the ones above and below. Before future visits a wiretap would be easy to plant, he ventured. Or a bomb. But his controllers were unimpressed.

He was soon put out of his misery with a message from headquarters to forget about the royals and concentrate instead on trying to infiltrate the Labour Party. But any relief he might have felt was short-lived. Not long after, he received another communication in the post and it was far more disconcerting. The International Red Cross had traced him through government contacts in the Netherlands and London to his address in the capital and had sent a letter with an urgent request from Johanna van Haarlem. She was looking for Erwin. Johanna was desperately sorry she had given him away all those years ago – and she wanted to meet.

CHAPTER FOURTEEN

Prague, 11 May 1977

The letter sent on behalf of Johanna van Haarlem left Gragert shell-shocked in what he considered to be his London bunker. An official was asking if they could pass on his address so that his mother could make arrangements to meet him. If he refused, she may still find a way. And refusal could lead to questions about why he had decided this was the best course. He feared that more enquiries would unearth something to expose him. This would be the end of a career that he hoped would make him a hero of the motherland. He was unsure he could live his lie well enough in the presence of a woman who had to be convinced that a Czech spy was her long-lost son. She could unknowingly trip him up with otherwise innocent questions. He had learned his Erwin van Haarlem legend to perfection, but this would be the greatest test. Gragert forwarded Johanna's written plea to see him, along with a note asking for his spymasters' guidance, by dropping it at a dead letter box for his bosses in Prague. Gragert also sent "Top Secret" messages to Prague through his short-wave radio at designated times each week for conversations with HQ. The Red Cross missive was top of his agenda as he sent over the hurried high-pitched dots and dashes of morse code to Prague.

Once received, the Red Cross letter immediately sent alarm bells ringing through the corridors of power in the Ministry of the Interior. "We hope you are the above mentioned," the letter to Erwin van Haarlem began. It was on headed notepaper from the International Red Cross. The aid organisation wanted consent to hand over Jelinek's address to the woman who believed herself to be his mother via its International Tracing Service and asked if he wanted her address so he could write directly to her. Much time and money had been spent maintaining Jelinek's anonymity as Van Haarlem in London. Any ripples, however small, that highlighted the spy's presence in the British capital sent the spymasters into panic.

The deputy head of the illegals section, Colonel Mráz, was suspicious about the timing. "Why did she start to care?" he asked in an internal memo questioning if the potential meeting would put the spy at any risk and, if not, how it should be approached. "GRAGERT is not interested in family life or closer contacts with his mother or with the family," his note added. "He has not yet responded."

After much hand-wringing by top-level personnel, always terrified of the consequences for themselves if mistakes were made, the conclusion was that Jelinek should agree to Johanna's request and contact her but should "behave with restraint, even coldly". To shun Johanna, his bosses finally agreed, would only cast more attention on him if she refused to back off. Contact was permitted just so long as it did not "tie his hands for further intelligence activities".

Gragert had his orders: he should tell Johanna that he

was happy to be in touch even after more than 30 years. His spymasters urged him to imagine Erwin's state of mind. "He understands now that he has been wronged in some way," they suggested. "But he himself has already built a certain way of life, he is used to taking care of himself, he has no intention of complicating her life in any way. She has her own family, her own family relationships, and from all of this she has certain obligations, etc. It could therefore happen that he would enter her family today as a person who may unintentionally cause disapproval towards her from the circle of the family or relatives. He does not want to possibly cause relatives to suspect that he sought support or other expressions at the expense of her family."

It took a while for the Red Cross to pass on his home address in London to Johanna but on 22 October 1977 he received an emotion-charged letter from her. It read:

> *My dear son,*
>
> *I finally received your address from the CK. I would like to ask you and tell you many things, but first of all, I want you to know that I loved you with all my motherly heart. Please accept it. Can I hope for further contact with you? I do my best and write to you in English. I assume you know this speech. Please drop me a line or send a postcard. I will write you.*
>
> *Many Loves.*
>
> *JOHANNA HENDRIKA van HAARLEM,*

Jelinek's solitary life in London was about to change. As cautious as he felt about the communication and, perhaps, suspicious about Johanna's motives, she offered the possibility of improving his cover by learning more about his adopted family. After all, he was trained to be curious, and this subject could not be closer to his life. He had become accustomed to leading two lives and was confident about being able to hide the nature of his unusual employment. The longer he spent as Erwin van Haarlem, the harder it was to think of himself as Vaclav Jelinek. The lines in his life were blurring. All that was left in the end was "Gragert".

CHAPTER FIFTEEN

Schaijk, Holland, 8 November 1977

Dear Mother, thank you for your letter of 19th October. It was really a strange feeling to receive a letter from you after so many years!

Johanna's heart almost stopped as she held the letter that she had waited almost her entire life to read. She was afraid to read on, fearing that Erwin was unforgiving for all those lost family years. But she needn't have worried. His reply was all she could have hoped for and more.

You may write to me in German. I speak this language as well. Could you write a few words about yourself, as I don't know practically anything about your life.

I look forward to your letter.
Yours sincerely,
Your son,

Erwin van Haarlem

There was no mention of a reconciliation, but it was a start.

Sitting in her bungalow, reading and rereading the letter with its unfamiliar handwriting, she could finally imagine a meeting with her boy. Only he wasn't a boy anymore and she had no idea whether he would find it in his heart to understand the terrible dilemma she faced as a young mother and how desperately she wanted to make amends. She had tried so many times to imagine what he looked like; now she hoped she could begin to colour in the blank pictures in her mind.

Johanna read the letter over and over again, scarcely able to believe that she'd finally found her long lost son. Her heart pounded with joy. In a quivering hand Johanna put pen to paper. Over the years of emptiness, she had wondered what she would say in her first conversation with Erwin, be it in writing or in person. She knew so much would hang on those words if they were going to have a future as mother and son. "I felt so upset, sad, excited – I had an incredible sense of expectancy. I told him how much I loved him," she recalled years later. "I assured Erwin that I had never forgotten him. Every year on 24 August, I quietly celebrated his birthday with a toast. I emphasised that despite the distance that separated us, he was still present in my heart."

Johanna sent two photographs to Erwin, one showing her aged 18, when she gave birth to him, and the other taken recently.

And then... nothing. Every day she would wait for the mail, expecting his reply, and she would be disappointed. She had been promised Erwin would get back in touch, but the weeks passed by and there was still no word from him. She was beside herself with worry.

She decided to write another letter. She told Erwin she wanted to leave Holland immediately to see him for Christmas. She simply couldn't wait any longer. This time, she included photos of herself when she was 19 with her brother so he could compare their facial features, their chin, their lips, their eyes.

At last, she received a response, post stamped from London. Just opening the envelope sent shivers down her spine. Johanna was fearing the worst.

The letter didn't start well for her. Gragert put her off saying it was a busy time of year for him at work at London's Hilton Hotel in Park Lane. He would be putting in long hours as a barman at the hotel and couldn't contemplate such an emotional get-together.

He continued, "I thought a lot about your letter. It's a very sad story. But such things happen in life and it's over. We must look to the future. I will be very honest. I can't get to Holland; we are the busiest at work on holidays. I could not devote myself to you as I would like. So, you will have to spend Christmas this year only with Hans, but you mustn't be sad about it. We've waited so long that the extra month doesn't matter anymore.

"Although I live alone without a family, I have a girlfriend, so I spend my free time (if I have any at all) with her. I wish you and Hans a merry Christmas and a happy New Year's Eve. I hope the coming year will be a happy one for us all. I think about you a lot. With love, Erwin."

She ignored his entreaties and wrote again with her travel details. She told him about his younger brother Hans. They planned to sail together from the Hook of Holland to Harwich. The pull was too strong for Johanna. She was coming to London with Hans on 1 January. They were booked into the Tudor Hotel in West London and would be there for three days, ample time to get to know Erwin. When Gragert wrote back to ask if she'd seen his letter asking for the visit to be postponed, she told him she never received it.

Johanna decided New Year was a fitting time for a new start with her firstborn. Anxiety overwhelmed her, and she needed to see her son.

Again, Erwin wrote back saying it really wasn't the best time.

"I'm glad you decided to come," he wrote, "but unfortunately, I repeat that you chose the most inconvenient time. This holiday season will be the busiest I've ever seen. One of my colleagues quit his job, so I have to step in for him. It is absolutely out of the question for me to come to Harwich to meet you. The only option is to meet on 3 January 1978 at 9 o'clock in the evening at the Tudor Court Hotel. Think it through. Perhaps it would be wiser to postpone the trip. The decision is yours."

Johanna wasted no time in sending a telegram by return:

I RECEIVED THE LETTER OF 28 STOP PLEASE DON'T WORRY STOP I WILL BE VERY GRATEFUL FOR MEETING AT THE HOTEL STOP I UNDERSTAND YOUR DUTIES AT WORK STOP HANS AND I WILL HAVE FUN IN LONDON STOP WITH LOVE MOTHER STOP

~

It was such a rough crossing from the Hook of Holland to England that Johanna worried for a while that the ferry might capsize, and she would never get to meet her first-born son. Fate, she feared, was keeping them apart. Perhaps it just wasn't meant to be. She prayed that God would keep them safe. It appeared her prayers were answered. The sea was finally calmed. They had arrived in England 10 hours late, but at least they had arrived.

CHAPTER FIFTEEN

Johanna and Hans made it to London in the early hours of 3 January 1978 exhausted from seasickness and shaking with excitement at the prospect of finally meeting Erwin. Later that evening, after trying and failing to get some sleep in her hotel room, Johanna left Hans in the room asleep and walked with nerve-wracked, weakened legs along Piccadilly where a huge and boisterous crowd had seen in the New Year a couple of nights earlier. She crossed the world-famous, neon-lit Piccadilly Circus at the junction of Regent Street. It was nearly midday, but the city was still recovering from the holidays. There were only a few businessmen trudging through the deep snow, which had created a magical white scene around the Eros fountain. The snow muffled the traffic. The eerie silence left her reflecting on the distant past.

Dressed soberly in a twin set under a sensible cream coat for the cold, Johanna saw herself as a lonely trekker venturing into the unknown. She felt numbed, not by the freezing temperature, but by the decades of unknowing that had brought her there. At this time of year in the capital it was seen as polite, caring and uplifting to ask the question of everyone, "What is your New Year's wish?" She had one New Year's wish. That wish consumed her thoughts and she wouldn't be sharing it with strangers.

Johanna could once again feel the pumping of her heart, as if it were outside her body.

She had no idea how the day would turn out. There would be no middle ground, she thought. There were only two outcomes for her. In a short while Johanna would either be elated beyond anything she had ever experienced, or feeling a desperate sense of failure that would end everything she had dreamed about. A desperate sense of failure she knew only too well. Either way, it would be life-defining.

As she headed between Green Park and Hyde Park and past Wellington's Arch, a sense of foreboding made her even weaker, but she had come so far. There was no turning back, she kept repeating to herself. Johanna had much to tell Erwin if she was ever to be given the chance. He would have much to tell his mother.

She turned a corner into the Victorian grandeur of Queen's Gate Gardens. Incredibly, Erwin spotted Johanna in the street. They weren't supposed to meet until later that evening, but chance had intervened.

"Excuse me, but aren't you Mrs. van Haarlem?" he asked.

"I am," said a stunned Johanna.

"My name is Erwin van Haarlem. I am your son. I recognised you from the photos you sent me."

She sobbed as they hugged in the cold. She felt the warmth of a son she had longed to see again since 1944. More importantly, much more importantly, he called her "mother".

It was a practiced lie, of course. It was an important moment for Jelinek too. He needed to know that she believed him. She wasn't to know, but had that first meeting gone differently – had she greeted him with suspicion rather than joy – then she might have paid with her life. His masters had told him that on no account could his 'legend' be compromised and that he should do anything necessary to prevent his cover from being blown.

CHAPTER SIXTEEN

London, England, 3 January 1978

With Hans still sleeping at the hotel, Johanna went alone to Jelinek's home. It wasn't anything glamorous, just a rented room in a house, but he took out two glasses and a bottle of champagne to celebrate. Johanna was weeping and laughing as they chinked glasses and sipped the bubbly.

Several pictures of nude women hung on the wall and there was a small Christmas tree festooned with colourful ornaments on a chest of drawers. He noticed her looking at the provocative pictures but neither of them said anything. Never one to be blinded by sentiment, Johanna asked the man she believed to be her son to provide proof of his identity, and he duly showed her his Dutch passport and any other identification he had. It all added up.

Despite his earlier protestations that he would be too busy to see her and Hans, he took two days off from his work at the Hilton and the three of them spent every moment they could together. He even showed her real pictures of himself as a young boy. They talked in his room and went out to restaurants and all the time he called her "mother".

Johanna could not have foreseen a better reunion. It seemed a perfect meeting for mother and son who had been wrenched apart by conflict, occupation, and uncaring bloody-mindedness by his grandfather. There was just one small thing that gave her pause. She was struck by his brown eyes. So much time had passed and she sometimes had trouble conjuring up the image of her baby son in her head. She never had any photographs of him. But she was always convinced Erwin's eyes were blue. In fact, she was sure of it.

She felt bad about questioning her good fortune. She decided they must have changed colour when he was a toddler. She'd heard that babies with blue eyes sometimes ended up with eyes that were brown. Perhaps that was even the case when both parents had blue eyes, she wondered. It was such a small detail, she thought, deciding to maybe bring it up another time. Everything was so right, she didn't want to give him any reason to question her commitment to him.

Johanna kept telling him how guilty she felt about leaving him at the orphanage and he reassured her, insisting he had a happy upbringing in Czechoslovakia. He even showed her the application for a place in the children's home, which she submitted to the Teplice authorities in October 1944, saying he found it among his adopted parents' papers when he applied for his Dutch passport and had used it as proof of his identity.

Her doubts over his brown eyes disappeared and she once again felt guilty, this time for doubting him. His spy bosses had done a good job creating a legend so infallible that even Erwin's mother was being taken in by it.

Hans took a picture of mother and son, and Johanna snapped a photo of the two half-brothers. She sat watching and marvelling at the accomplished man who felt so familiar to her in his tailored corduroy suit and black shirt, lighting his pipe. Like mothers everywhere, she enquired about his love life and asked when she would be introduced to his girlfriend, who turned out to be French and almost half his age, having only recently turned 18. She didn't care about the age difference. That was his business. He certainly wasn't saying anything about the relationship to his bosses after the debacle over the previous girlfriend.

Johanna was ecstatic. She had found her son and discovered he was a happy young man seeking a career in London in the hotel business and that he'd recently been promoted.

That first trip was a whirlwind of delights and emotions. Johanna and Hans were treated by "Erwin" to lunch at the Hilton Hotel, hard-to-come-by tickets for the Jesus Christ Superstar musical in the West End and a visit to the Tower of London to see the Crown Jewels.

Before she left with Hans to return home to the Netherlands, Johanna asked the one question that had been gnawing at her ever since she learned that he was alive and living in London. He had the names of his biological mother and father, and her address was on the application for him to be cared for at the orphanage. So, why didn't he try to find her?

"When I was working in Austria, a colleague inquired about you through his Dutch friends," he told her. "He found out you gave me up because I was an unwanted child. He also said that your father was a supporter of the party that collaborated with the Germans."

"What about your father? Didn't you try to find out about him?" she persisted.

"No," he replied. "My adoptive parents told me he was probably German. I wanted nothing to do with such a person."

She wanted to know more about his adopted parents and he told her they were good, hard-working people, yet it seemed to her like there was something he was holding back. He showed her some photographs of himself as a boy but when she asked if he had any pictures of his parents, he shrugged his shoulders and said he didn't. Gragert's masters had either failed or just thought it was a step too far to provide pictures of foster parents. That would inevitably lead to questions about their names and where they lived. That just wasn't part of his legend; he had to steal parts from his own childhood.

But if 'Erwin' felt any resentment towards her, he never showed it. She left excited and happy after that first visit and would go back to London to spend time with him at least twice a year for almost a decade. During those visits, he took Johanna to restaurants and pubs; they went to the theatre and museums together. On one occasion, Gragert treated Johanna, along with Hans and one of her sisters, to dinner at the rooftop restaurant at the Hilton Hotel, waited on by him. She would call him every week and he would visit the Netherlands, at least once a year, to see the Van Haarlem relatives, who had finally taken Johanna back into the familial fold after their parents had died. There were dinners and drinks, and happy parties. He posed for pictures in family groups. Everyone was bowled over by the intelligent, ambitious, polite, and respectful new member of the family. He talked about his girlfriends, his work, and an interest he had developed in antiques which could provide a future career. How he loved London and felt blessed to have his own family for the first time.

In the spring of 1978, Gragert even travelled with Johanna and Hans to Luxembourg, paying for everything and buying her presents including a Wedgewood vase, a gold and sapphire ring, a gold coin, an expensive wallet, and a cashmere jumper. While in Luxembourg, he also bought 20 bottles of sparkling wine for a family party in Holland attended by 30 relatives. He was the life and soul of the event, telling everyone how fortunate he felt to have been accepted by his aunts and uncles, nephews and nieces, and especially by his mother and brother.

On one occasion, Jelinek serenaded Johanna at her house in Schaijk with his version of Elvis Presley's 'Love Me Tender.' In a thin accented voice, he sang the classic song with the words, "Love me tender, love me true, all my dreams fulfilled, my darling I love you," and even recorded it, accompanying himself on guitar and drums with Hans playing the organ. He also sang Johanna some Czech songs, asking her if he should continue.

"Yes," said Johanna, clearly enjoying the ad hoc concert. "That's wonderful," she added, clapping.

~

It wasn't all smooth sailing, however. Johanna's forthright manner didn't always fit in with his surliness and she couldn't help but question why he didn't want to spend more time with her. She got angry on one trip because daylight savings time coincided with their time together and robbed her of one hour with her son. When she asked around her friends and found a potential job for him in the Netherlands that would pay more than his hotel work and allow them to be closer, she was enraged when he snubbed the offer.

He couldn't tell her the real reason he couldn't leave London. As it was, he was getting flak from his Czech bosses for becoming too westernised and not paying enough time to his intelligence work. He'd started to receive thinly-veiled threats that some at The Centre thought he was embezzling the state. There were questions about how he could afford to live what seemed like an expensive lifestyle compared with their existence in the East. He was earning a good salary at the Hilton. It didn't help that Gragert was asking for more money from Prague to be dropped off at pre-arranged 'dead letter boxes' so he could afford his Western lifestyle. It didn't seem to matter that, like a businessman living abroad, he meticulously sent his expenses claims to Prague for vetting. They were pored over with some jealousy as well as suspicion. Prague believed that British authorities periodically checked out foreigners after they had settled in Great Britain for five years. This was Eastern Bloc paranoia based on their own suspicions of foreigners. They were concerned that British intelligence would see Jelinek was taking a lot of frequent foreign travel "disproportionate to his financial situation".

Jelinek argued that his spending was needed to keep up the pretence with his 'mother' that he was a success in London. He pointed out that his life in the West didn't even feel like a fabrication any more. Erwin van Haarlem was a real person living a real life. His alias wasn't a complete lie. Jelinek missed his own parents and relatives. As Erwin, he had it all, a mother and a family. As Gragert, he had the perfect cover.

Spies ply their trade for several reasons. There are thrill-seekers, patriots, ambitious high-fliers seeking recognition and promotion. Others are purely in it for the money. It is money that often drives double agents, those who pretend to be spying for one country but are working for another. Jelinek fell primarily into the categories of patriotism, ambition and thrill-seeking. He knew if he was successful then promotions would follow, feeding his ego and greater recognition from his superiors. Despite his occasional homesickness, he also enjoyed the Western lifestyle with all its luxuries and freedoms. He wore smart suits and brogue shoes, ate at fine restaurants, drank cocktails and champagne for special occasions. And, invariably, had a beautiful woman on his arm, albeit not the same one.

In Communist Prague in the 1970s and 1980s, Jelinek would have been lucky to visit a restaurant with basic menus of beef goulash, pork and dumplings twice in a month, and his clothes would have been shabby in comparison to London's high fashion. The food at home in Czechoslovakia was very ordinary compared to the Italian and French restaurants he favoured in London.

In the Cold War 1980s, Jelinek would find himself on the front line, fighting undercover to enable the Soviets to take back the lead in the nuclear race and increase the Kremlin's chances of finding ways to produce even more powerful weapons. The Communist model was collapsing, and its threat of military might was among the last cards it was able to play with any impact.

Prague – and Moscow – needed Jelinek to succeed. His spymasters relented and kept the money flowing.

CHAPTER SEVENTEEN

London, England, 12 May 1982

"I hear you need some help."

Rita Eker remembers these words from the slim, tall man who came into her office and showered the female staff with compliments as an unlikely but enthusiastic supporter.

Unlikely, because Rita ran the Women's Campaign for Soviet Jewry, an organisation seeking permission from the Kremlin to allow Refusenik Jews to leave the USSR for Israel and other countries around the world. Rita and her activist friends were campaigning for Refuseniks to make the public aware of their situation in Soviet states and their sole desire to live normally as Jews. They wanted to openly practice their faith, and some wanted to go to Israel to fulfil lifetime ambitions. But, for this they were thrown into prison, or, even worse, into psychiatric units.

Erwin van Haarlem wasn't a woman, of course, but he seemed eager to get involved and, while not Jewish himself, he told them that his mother was and he felt strongly that Refuseniks should be allowed to leave the Soviet Union.

Jews had been discriminated against in the Soviet Union

throughout the 20th century. Jewish communities date back 1,500 years in Russia and their treatment in recent times has been volatile. In the 1970s, there was just one synagogue in Moscow despite the city's large Jewish population and antisemitism was both rife and officially sanctioned. Yet when Jews sought to leave Russia for Israel or other parts of the world, they were largely denied permission and often harassed by the KGB and forced out of their jobs. Scientists and academics were removed from their laboratories and classrooms and put to work in mines or given menial positions. In some cases, the Kremlin was so determined to dissuade large-scale Jewish migration that it imprisoned community leaders. Moscow did not want Jewish expertise to be exported to unfriendly countries.

The Russian authorities took the view that many Soviet Jews had been part of the Communist state apparatus for so long they had acquired important information that, if given to a foreign enemy, would damage national security. Academics had been educated through the Soviet system and the Kremlin deemed it a betrayal to take such learning and expertise to the West.

It was against this grim backdrop that the Women's Campaign for Soviet Jewry came into being in North-West London, formed by a group of young Jewish housewives with little or no previous experience of activism. At the time, it was unheard of for women in that community to get involved in politics and their unusual, and sometimes daring, approach threw a crucial spotlight on Moscow's human rights abuses.

The group became known as The 35s, in part because that was the average age of its members but also because it was formed in 1971 with Margaret Thatcher's tacit support following the arrest in Odessa of 35-year-old librarian Raiza Palatnik after she applied to emigrate to Israel. The 35s protested outside the Soviet Embassy in London after Palatnik was jailed for two years in 1972 for distributing banned literature and they maintained a tireless campaign pushing for her release. That same year, the formidable 35s celebrated the formation of a parliamentary cross-party Commons Committee for Soviet Jewry with a so-called banquet comprising food doled out to Soviet prisoners of conscience. The menu included 14oz of black bread, a cup of hot water and a 1oz herring for breakfast; cooked cabbage soup and half a potato for lunch; and a whole potato for dinner. "This diet will not sustain an inactive child of three years old," proclaimed a poster advertising the event.

~

The biggest concern at The Centre in Czechoslovakia had been that Johanna van Haarlem would bring undue attention to their agent's role in London and even raise questions over his Dutch citizenship. After all, he had been raised in Prague, solidly behind the Iron Curtain, a fact that was missing from his heavily censored bio.

After it became clear in the late 70s that his attempts to infiltrate the royal family were doomed to failure, Jelinek had moved to a cheaper, but still fashionable part of North London, taking a room in a large house. He was promoted from a waiter to the Hilton Hotel purchasing manager, and became so busy with work that he didn't have time for espionage. His bosses were getting impatient with his excuses and he was becoming increasingly exhausted and frustrated. He tried to explain to Prague that being a member of the hotel staff was not sufficiently well-regarded to break him into rarefied circles with information worth sending.

There was growing pressure for results. Finally, the spymasters relented. They would send him enough money – £45,000 – so he could afford to quit his job. Jelinek fancied himself as an artist and attended life drawing classes. His classmates weren't particularly impressed by his talents, but in 1981 it gave him the idea to set himself up as an antiques dealer specialising in portrait miniatures. It didn't matter that he didn't know a lot about antiques; he decided he could bluff his way through while learning a lot about his new trade, and he liked the way the ladies looked at him when he told them what he did for a living.

As designed, his new profession gave him more time and, to his relief, his controllers came up with a more realistic target. He had sent long lists detailing the Labour Party's make-up – on local and national levels – through to Prague, and made some connections in Parliament, but nothing that really moved the needle or earned him plaudits across the Iron Curtain. Much of his information was readily available and Gragert was too worried about preserving his legend to groom any decent sources. But now he was sent a radio message ordering the penetration of Jewish organisations who were campaigning for Refuseniks and had political connections at the highest levels in the UK and US. He did his research and moved to Golders Green, a London suburb originally developed by American investors and known for a large population of middle-class English Jews. Some of Gragert's new neighbours worked in London's Hatton Garden, a draw for dozens of businesses dealing in gold, silver, platinum, diamonds, and other precious stones; other Jews had factories in London's thriving 'rag trade' in the East End, mass-producing garments for fashion houses in the prosperous shopping districts of Central and West London; and there were those who made it big in the banks and stock exchange in the City.

Jews in the impoverished East End were largely part of the work force and lived alongside Cockney communities surrounding the docks. They tended to live on council estates and in privately rented properties. The less well-off rented damp-ridden slums with outside toilets and just a couple of bedrooms for large families. These slums had blighted the area before, during and after World War Two. Many of the tenants were immigrants who had fled from anti-Jewish persecution across Europe. Local councils and central government funding had largely improved living conditions with the worst slums being bought under Compulsory Purchase Orders for redevelopment. Jews lived next door to families whose ancestors had moved to Limehouse, Bow, Poplar, Wapping, Bethnal Green and Stepney from Ireland, Scotland and continental Europe to find work around the thriving Royal and West India docks. While men toiled loading and unloading ships from around the world, sometimes lifting hundred weight bags of sugar and asbestos throughout the night to get bonuses, women worked long hours in cramped factories as machinists turning out dresses, skirts and blouses.

Jelinek needed to retain as much knowledge as he could about the Jewish communities he would target for information. He needed to learn about antisemitism so that any group he tried to enter would be convinced by his knowledge of their challenges worldwide. Some of London's Jews were survivors of the Holocaust, among them groups of children who arrived in Harwich on England's East coast by ship to escape the worst excesses of Nazi Germany. Now, they were grown up, taking a full part in British society, many were entrepreneurial.

CHAPTER SEVENTEEN

Antisemitism did reveal itself in Britain through the extreme right-wing, white supremacist National Front which campaigned in the 1970s to stop black immigration. Jews were also on its abhorrent agenda. One of its leaders, John Tyndall, as far back as 1963, claimed, "Jewry is a world pest wherever it is found in the world today. The Jews are more clever and more financially powerful than other people and have to be eradicated before they destroy the Aryan peoples."

Jelinek was well-briefed through book research, reading national newspapers and speaking to people. He learned that in the 1970s the NF made clear its stance on Jews by declaring their principles were "anti-Zionist"; that the party was against people who passionately believed in the creation of the Land of Israel as a home state for all Jews. There was even NF support for Nazi doctrine. In Britain, the NF, with its extreme policies, seemed unlikely to become a political force and has never held seats in the British and European parliaments, but its fanatical and violent members did hold sway over a minority.

Jelinek's new neighbourhood was also home to the thriving Golders Green Synagogue, which dated back to World War One and served an active Jewish community. He had chosen the location well for his deception and contacted Rabbis in several synagogues but especially at the Liberal Jewish Synagogue in St John's Wood Road in London. He considered this place of worship easier to penetrate as it wasn't steeped in orthodoxy and, in his view, was likely to be less questioning of an outsider with an Eastern European accent. He knew the well-connected Jewish community would open avenues to Parliament and influential business people.

Moscow wanted to know about the secret and underground

work of any Jewish pressure groups seeking to free Refuseniks. For them, stealing or copying files on activists in Russia, its satellite states and anywhere else in the world, was a top priority. Moscow wanted Gragert to harvest information about Refuseniks and their supporters so that it could gain bargaining chips with the West in their nuclear arms negotiations. The plan was for Gragert to find out who the US, Moscow's biggest adversary, wanted released, either on humanitarian grounds or for scientific expertise. He was also ordered to find out about Israeli-sponsored underground networks plotting against the Soviets.

Many volunteer groups operated from the synagogue and the charming Dutch antique dealer made tentative inroads into the Jewish community and joined several groups as a volunteer. One such organisation was The 35s. Their office was above an old disused laundry in Greville Road in Golders Green and Jelinek lived nearby, off Helenslea Avenue. He had learned about the organisation through an advert in the Jewish Chronicle newspaper asking for help from people, like him, who spoke fluent Russian. From there, he manoeuvered his way to Eker, crafting the first impression she'd remember all those years later: the kind and helpful stranger. At last, the spy could put to use the easy charm that had so impressed the StB. Eker welcomed him into The 35s, asking him to do some translation work and write on her behalf to several Refuseniks in Russia. She liked that he always seemed eager to aid the cause.

"He wanted to know about our campaign and the politicians who were helping us," she recalled. "He was a normal bloke. He was slim, tall, fair-haired and always paid us women compliments."

Jelinek put on all the appearances of prospering from his

new antiques business. His wardrobe was getting sharper with tailored suits, and he always looked dapper. He was a self-assured "ladies' man", often boasting about his latest girlfriend and where they had been socialising in expensive London restaurants. He seemed very happy with himself – the type of man who exuded confidence. But he also had substance.

The 35s noticed his voracious reading. Saying how fascinated he was with their work, he asked to read files and documents to familiarise himself with the organisation. To Eker's group, the man they knew as Erwin van Haarlem appeared to be something of a selfless Good Samaritan. He hosted an afternoon tea reception at a London hotel and presented the women with chocolates to thank them for their tireless campaign work. But he never said he was Jewish. That would be too dangerous: he would have to know every detail of Judaism and explain how he could have practiced it in Soviet-ruled Czechoslovakia.

It didn't seem to change The 35s warm opinion of the spy, nor did it raise any questions. They had several other non-Jewish people working with them and they also worked closely with a lot of the nearby churches. It was encouraging to see so many non-Jewish people getting involved in their cause.

The women did, however, notice that while Erwin wasn't on the volunteer rota they kept, he was always at the office – often at odd times. This didn't bother them either. He made sure he was pleasant to be around. He was living up to the promise he showed his recruiters as a ruthless charmer. "He was always very charming, well-mannered, and polite. He enjoyed being with ladies – whether it was for his ego, I don't know," Eker recalled. "We were young, married women and we thought, 'What the hell'. We didn't place any importance on it when he would say, 'Your hair looks nice' or he'd say he liked what we were wearing."

His calculated charisma paid off. Soon, Gragert had earned the women's trust and had access to all their files. There were activists in Russia and he could see who they were working with, who their contacts were, in the UK and worldwide. He had access to the personal contact details of MPs and members of the House of Lords. He discovered that political giants Greville Janner and Nicholas Bethell had each at one point led the All-Party Parliamentary Committee for Soviet Jewry. Now he knew where they lived, too.

There were also details of American and Canadian activists, most of them with strong views against the Soviet Union. The 35s' contact list included Lynn Singer, an American lobbyist for the rights of Soviet Refuseniks, who went to Capitol Hill once a month to brief congressmen. The 35s had documents containing the names of other US politicians and detailing what Singer was doing with them, describing the conditions of Soviet Jews, those that were being persecuted, those who were standing on trial and those who were being treated subnormally in psychiatric units. He took copious notes and it was easy enough to smuggle files home so he could copy them wholesale. Like many Soviet spies, he almost certainly owned a KGB issue miniature camera capable of reducing and copying documents on one roll of film, ready for drop off at one of his dead letter boxes. The 35s' files were a gold mine for Gragert. He now had the names of dozens of activists against the Soviets from all over the world. They weren't just names; there was also information about their activities and, in many cases, where they could be found.

It wasn't that The 35s were just well-meaning, gullible

activists. They did sometimes question the motives of people who wanted to help, particularly if they came from outside the Jewish community. But Gragert was a professional spy trained to take emotion out of his work. He may have genuinely liked the people he was using, but he wouldn't give a second thought to betraying them – even if he knew they would face persecution in the Soviet Union, flung into a Siberian salt mine or even tortured and murdered for their beliefs. That part had nothing to do with him, he reasoned. He was just doing his job.

Jelinek began to see a change in attitude from his bosses. They clearly liked what he was sending them and, as a result, they became more amenable to his requests. He was sent larger amounts of money for 'expenses' – all detailed in receipts and reports sent to Prague – and the payments were washed through his antique's business bank accounts and other financial instruments. Cash was still being dropped off. Now able to better finance his pretensions, he moved out of his one-room rented accommodation in Golders Green and bought a two-bedroom flat in a smart suburban block called Silver Birch Court in well-to-do Friern Barnet in north London.

Not one person in the Jewish community was pulling together the various strands of Van Haarlem's lifestyle and actions to reveal anything strange about this young man who had so smoothly assimilated himself into their everyday lives. He stuck to his story that he wasn't Jewish but had a knowledge of Judaism, and that he wanted to do all he could to promote the Refusenik debate in the UK. On instruction from his handlers, he started to drop hints on joining The 35s on trips abroad. His spymasters were sure the trips would provide valuable intelligence.

He also told his new friends the incredible story about how

Johanna had tracked him down to London through the Red Cross. He gave the impression that he adored his mother and took great joy from being with her. Johanna was happy, too. He seemed the perfect son. His cover was working beautifully.

Even his lavish lifestyle failed to raise red flags. Neither his friends, the authorities nor Johanna seemed to question his antiques business's lack of trading, despite the recent purchase of his home and his extravagant gift-giving. The truth was that the Kremlin was making him moderately wealthy.

Gragert's upward mobility wasn't lost on Johanna. She knew that since their first meeting in his single room, he had graduated to bigger and more comfortable accommodation around London. She could tell by his suits and shirts, coats and shoes that he was going in the right direction. But she wasn't suspicious; she was proud.

Other red flags did, however, give Johanna pause. While she appreciated his sensitivity and his determination to absolve her guilt over abandoning him all those years ago, she craved every detail of his past and wondered why he was so reticent about discussing his upbringing.. He had been fine, he assured her. She didn't have to keep beating herself up. Yet, even as their relationship blossomed, Gragert still refused to show her any documents relating to his past and only offered the barest of details about his foster parents. He didn't want to speak in detail about his childhood and would only say that he had had a happy one. There was another oddity, too. He made it clear that Johanna was never to delve into his personal belongings in the flat where she stayed with him.

"I felt he was suspicious of me. He was always watching over me, and I realised that I should not open any of his cupboards," she remembered. Her son's strange, controlling behaviour bothered Johanna, but she didn't see anything sinister in it. She couldn't have known that Gragert remained on high alert. Johanna's intense curiosity about her long lost son's past could sometimes shake the spy's certainty that he'd duped her. He wondered at times if she was on to him. His spymasters would have encouraged this suspicion: Johanna might be his mother, but she also might have been a spy for Dutch intelligence. If Johanna showed the slightest sign of not believing the Gragert legend she could have been placed in mortal danger. His masters would tell him to take whatever action was necessary to keep his cover intact, especially if he was in imminent danger of being exposed. The other option, far better for Johanna, was an emergency extraction from enemy territory – but that would only happen if there was time. Johanna's survival largely depended on the legend being believed without question. Fortunately, she did not persist in questioning Erwin.

The more time Jelinek spent with Johanna the more he began to feel she really was his mother. The arguments they sometimes had over trivial things felt real. Her fussing over him was genuine and, when he wasn't showing a son's genuine irritation with it, he loved it too. It was good to have someone to watch out for him again, to care for him and be proud of his achievements, even if it wasn't his real mother.

But he knew he could never trust her.

CHAPTER
EIGHTEEN

London, England, 8 May 1984

Jelinek may have been a devoted communist, but he had to be a chameleon when it came to party politics in the UK. As Erwin van Haarlem, he joined both the Labour Friends of Israel and the Conservative Friends of Israel. Between them, they had more than 100 Members of Parliament as supporters. All the while, Gragert was getting in deeper with The 35s, winning their confidence and trust without a blemish. His training and, by now, years in the field of espionage, were paying off.

When Rita Eker was finally granted a visa to visit Moscow after years of trying, it made sense for Erwin to go along with her and her husband, Moss, and a small campaign group as their Russian translator. Eker was both excited and anxious about the trip. Her visa applications to the Soviet Embassy in London had been turned down many times over the years. At last, she would be meeting the Refuseniks her organisation was trying to help to get to the West.

Eker's small group packed cash, Hebrew books, medication and Stars of David to take with them. At Moscow Airport they

134

went into customs and Eker's husband was allowed through, but she was stopped by officials. She shouted to Moss, insisting he had to remain with her and the officials finally relented, telling her not to make a scene.

"We were ushered into a small room where my pockets were turned inside out, my shoes were taken off, my coat lining was felt, and I was given a body search which was really scary and unpleasant," recalled Eker. "They asked me why I had come and who I was going to visit. They asked what my part was in the campaign. I told them, 'just follow me and see what I am doing'.

"They told me I could be sent back to London. They never searched my husband while I was being interrogated by a woman for half an hour. It seemed a lot longer. It was frightening. I had 100 silver Stars of David around my neck made by a London jeweller to give to the people we met as gifts. They were all on top of each other like a thick necklace – not once did anyone notice it."

Once out of the airport, a sense of foreboding hung over the group as they were followed everywhere. Eker remembered, "We were being tailed by men in long coats – just like a scene from the movies – and when we got to the Refuseniks, they actually said 'good morning' to them. To their own watchers they would say: 'Hello, these are our visitors from England'. It was surreal but also quite scary."

As well as smuggling cash and medicine into Russia, the group took down the details of the Refuseniks they met and listened to their stories. Their fellow Jews told them of their determination to leave for Israel and anywhere else where they could make a better life for their families. On one occasion they were at a bus stop with Refuseniks, and a group of people came up and called them 'dirty Jews' in Russian.

"I felt really intimidated," remembered Eker. "I don't know how they knew they were Jews." The Refuseniks told the group they were used to it. It was nothing compared to being beaten up or losing their jobs, having their kids victimised at school or not being allowed into higher education.

Jelinek kept a low profile and distanced himself from Eker and the rest of the group. Still, the spy in their midst knew who they were seeing and when. It was valuable information to send back to his handlers. He didn't even need dead letter drops or radio hook-ups to pass over his secrets. He met up with his masters on home turf.

~

It wasn't long after his trip with Eker when a doctor associated with The 35s asked if the group could recommend an interpreter to travel with him on a covert mission to meet with Refuseniks in Russia, Van Haarlem's name came up again. Enfield GP Michael Carmi and his wife, Louise, were a Jewish couple who had started working with Refuseniks after learning about the activist group through the Liberal Jewish Synagogue in St John's Wood, London. Determined to help, Dr Carmi wrote to doctors and academics across the Soviet Union who had been denied permission to leave the country and offered his and Louise's support. They connected with one man in particular named Avram Treiger, who was living in Chernivtsi, now located in western Ukraine but then under the auspices of the Soviet Union. Trieger was interested to know if Carmi was related to his uncle in Hull and the GP decided he wanted to go over and see him and see if he could help. There was only one problem: Carmi didn't speak a lick of Russian. To navigate the country during his visit, and to connect with more Refuseniks, he'd need a trusted translator. Erwin and Carmi first met for lunch at the Hilton in Kensington early in 1983. They hit it off so well that Carmi invited his new friend home to meet Louise and their then 10-year-old daughter, Debi, and son, Adam, 13. Jelinek was in his best duplicitous form; turning on the charm and his apparent desire to help the cause. Thanks to Gragert's skilled manipulation, the two men became fast friends. From then on, after Dr Carmi and his family attended the Liberal Jewish Synagogue in St John's Wood on the Sabbath, they'd stop on their way home to visit their new friend in Silver Birch Court in Friern Barnet. Jelinek gave Carmi's two children Coca Cola which their father would never give them. "My daughter Debi loved him because he gave her Cokes," recalled Dr Carmi. "He was quite handsome, charming, and sophisticated, although he did seem a little shy and lonely," said Louise. The Carmis were being entertained in the very place where their friend Erwin became Gragert in secret, sending coded messages to his spymasters about his visitors.

The couple invited him over for dinner. He would always turn up alone and didn't appear to have many friends. He wove his familiar cover story, sketching out all the details of his past from birth to then, saying he was in Czechoslovakia completing some catering courses when his employers sent him to Austria for another course. He embroidered his usual bio, explaining to the Carmis that the Austrians told him, "Well, look, why don't you go to the Dutch Embassy because you are a Dutch national?"

With his new Dutch passport, he was able to come to Britain. The timeline was questionable, but nobody was asking too many questions.

In April 1987, Carmi invited his new friend to a surprise party he was throwing for his wife's 40th birthday. Gragert seemed uncomfortable sitting next to a guest who introduced himself as a high-ranking police officer. When they invited him over for another party later that year, he made his excuses, perhaps concerned the police chief would be there to make more small talk. "We invited him over for Boxing Day and we took the dog out for a walk and when we got back there was a magnum of champagne on the porch and a note saying he couldn't come because he had the flu," recalled Louise.

Around this time, his grey-suited bosses in Prague were concerned about the high number of 'shipments' he was sending through the postal services. They worried that the increased frequency of shipments could have created a high level of interest from the English counterintelligence service. They also acknowledged that the preparation, writing and encryption of documents was very demanding. They were considering what could be done to lighten the load.

~

The plan was for Dr Carmi and his friendly interpreter to fly to Moscow and to then visit Chernivtsi, Kyiv and Odessa by train before flying back to the Russian capital, meeting prominent Refuseniks in every city. For Carmi, it was an opportunity to reach out a hand of friendship to help Jews in need. To Jelinek, it promised a gold mine of firsthand information about the Refusenik cause.

Among the Refuseniks they visited in Moscow were electronics engineer Arkady Mai and his wife Helena. They had been denied permission to emigrate in 1974 because of Mai's supposed knowledge of "state secrets" (they were finally given permission to leave in September 1987). The doctor and the spy also met with leading geneticist David Goldfarb (who was allowed to leave in October 1986). In Chernivtsi, they saw Marat Osnis, who was prevented from leaving for Israel in 1971 because his engineering job – for which he never needed security clearance – was deemed to involve classified secrets (he was finally allowed to leave in March 1988). And in Odessa the two met with Refusenik activists Valery Pevsner and Jakob Mesha. While in the city, they also met with a Refusenik who had been a Soviet Union boxing champion. The boxer knew there were agents following him, so Carmi, Jelinek and the boxer quickly dispersed and met up at a synagogue, where they were greeted with suspicion. There was a strong concern among the locals – entirely accurate, as it turned out – that the outsiders would attract KGB attention. Carmi heard later that the boxer had been arrested by the KGB.

Among all the cities they visited, Moscow proved the most fruitful for Gragert. While he was there, they also met with Refusenik scientist Alex Ioffe. The conversation turned political as they discussed Star Wars and Soviet leader Mikhail Gorbachev's position. Ioffe told Carmi and his interpreter that the USSR was 20 years behind the US and that President Reagan should continue to refuse to negotiate. He and other scientists recommended the Americans should demand an answer from the Soviet authorities in any protests about the Refusenik situation. Jelinek planned to write a detailed reply for the scientific committee – and no doubt send a copy to his controllers in Moscow.

In their luggage, along with a couple of new suits and some shoes for the Refuseniks – and an expensive watch for one of the wives – they hid some medication that was hard to get in the

Soviet Union, especially for those on the authorities' watch lists. At each stop, they turned on the water tap whenever they talked in their rooms in case they were bugged. Sometimes, they even used Etch A Sketch toys to write to their new friends so that they could promptly wipe off everything they had written. For Gragert the careful evasion was, of course, a façade. He was going back to his hotel room and writing everything down in his notebooks to hand over to the Russians.

One Gragert report included details of a meeting Carmi had with mathematician Professor Yuri Rodin. The academic was the Head of the Department of Mathematics at the Institute of Solid State Physics of the USSR Academy of Science in Chernogolovka, near Moscow. He'd recently fallen from grace after he applied for a visa for his family to emigrate in 1979. His application was denied and authorities attempted to get him kicked out of the institute as further punishment. His colleagues rebuffed the move and stood together in solidarity against the campaign to unseat him and, while he was demoted, he continued to work at the college.

Carmi and Yuri developed a strong bond. For the next decade after their meeting, Carmi would coordinate a phone call with Yuri when he knew he was visiting his mother every Sunday morning, and they kept up the connection in part so that the Soviets understood that the academic and his family weren't isolated entirely from the rest of the world. Yuri trusted the doctor. The two men had met before, during a previous visit. During that meeting, he gave Carmi a letter detailing how he'd solved a special equation. He didn't say what the equation was for, but Carmi knew it was important. At Yuri's direction, Carmi tore the letter into 64 pieces to smuggle home. Carmi was terrified that the letter would be found and he would be accused of being a spy.

CHAPTER EIGHTEEN

Once he was back in London, Carmi followed Yuri's directions and mailed copies of the letter to a list of Yuri's friends. There was just one person on the list who lived in England, a Nobel Prize winner who specialised in quantum physics. After his second visit to Yuri with Erwin, Carmi recounted the mysterious story to his new friend.

Gragert duly noted it all down and sent the anecdote in his next spy package, suggesting the incident happened on the trip he made with the doctor and that Carmi had smuggled the letter out for him. Although it wasn't true, information was currency to a spy and he wasn't going to let a good story go to waste.

Gragert would never learn what the equation was for, but years later at a local library, Carmi stumbled on the answer. "I saw a book by this same expert, the Nobel recipient," Carmi said. "When I read this book, it was all about quantum physics and I recognised the equation that Yuri had told me he'd solved and asked me to send to his friends in the West – it was a nuclear equation. I didn't know that at the time, obviously, and I thought that if I'd been stopped in Russia I'd probably still be there!

"I later told some of this to a New Scotland Yard officer, a very personable chap," he added. "When I mentioned this letter, he said I'd better not go back to Russia or else I might be arrested."

~

Jelinek continued enthusiastically working with The 35s on his return to London, even more trusted than he was before. He went on demonstrations with the group but he never joined any activity that could lead to the police being involved. The women chained themselves to a hotel once, but he wasn't there. He didn't want the authorities looking closely at him.

His star was rising in Moscow, and he no longer felt alone in London. Jelinek was on a roll. He was feeding valuable inside information that helped direct Soviet policy, especially regarding human rights issues that had become an international hot potato for the Soviets. As Moscow looked forward to an increasingly uncertain future in early 1986, Gragert's inside intelligence about the Refuseniks would become pivotal in one of the most important spy swaps of the Cold War.

CHAPTER
NINETEEN

Glienicke Bridge, Berlin, 11 February 1986

With an ill-fitting fur hat, bulky black overcoat and baggy trousers held together by safety pins, an unprepossessing figure threaded his way through parked vans on a snow-covered bridge to cross over from East to West. Anatoly Sharansky, the 38-year-old Russian scientist and human rights campaigner, walked uncertainly across the infamous "Bridge of Spies" linking West Berlin to the East German town of Potsdam, hardly daring to believe that every step was one closer to freedom and a reunion with his wife, Avital. A few minutes later, Karl Koecher, a Czech spy convicted of infiltrating the CIA, marched the opposite direction across the bridge with his wife Hana. Along with Sharansky, the Soviets also freed three men accused of being NATO agents. In exchange, they got Koecher and five spies.

It had taken a November 1985 summit meeting between US President Ronald Reagan and Soviet leader Mikhail Gorbachev to make Sharansky's release possible. By then, the Jewish dissident had spent eight years in prisons and labour camps as part of the Kremlin's attempts to silence him. The high-profile swap that icy morning in Berlin made headlines across the country, but Gragert's role in instigating the big political moment remained secret. Everything he learned from his new Jewish 'friends' in North London was being drip-fed across to Prague and on to Moscow. His intel on the Refusenik freedom networks in London had given his Czech masters exceptional insight into their workings in the West and, in his reports, Gragert emphasised just how important Sharansky's case was to the movement.

While the Soviet Jewry groups were lobbying tirelessly on thousands of cases of Jews desperate to escape persecution and emigrate from the USSR, Sharansky was the jewel in the crown, Gragert told his bosses. Born in Ukraine in 1948, Sharansky came from relatively meagre beginnings. His father was a journalist who worked for a Communist Party newspaper. After working in Moscow as a computer scientist at the Institute of Oil and Gas, Sharansky applied in 1973 for permission to emigrate to Israel. He was refused and faced persecution from the authorities, losing his job in 1975.

That same year, 35 countries ratified the controversial Helsinki Accord, leading to international outcry over the Soviet Union's treatment of Jewish people. The agreement focused on four key parts, including finding common ground on political, military and territorial matters, as well as scientific and trade cooperation, between the 35 signatory countries. Critics like Sharansky insisted the Soviets were blatantly ignoring the fourth section, which covered human rights such as freedom of emigration, the reunification of families divided by changing borders and freedom of the press. While the agreement was supposed to ease tensions with the USSR, Europe and North America, Moscow's refusal to address its human rights abuses

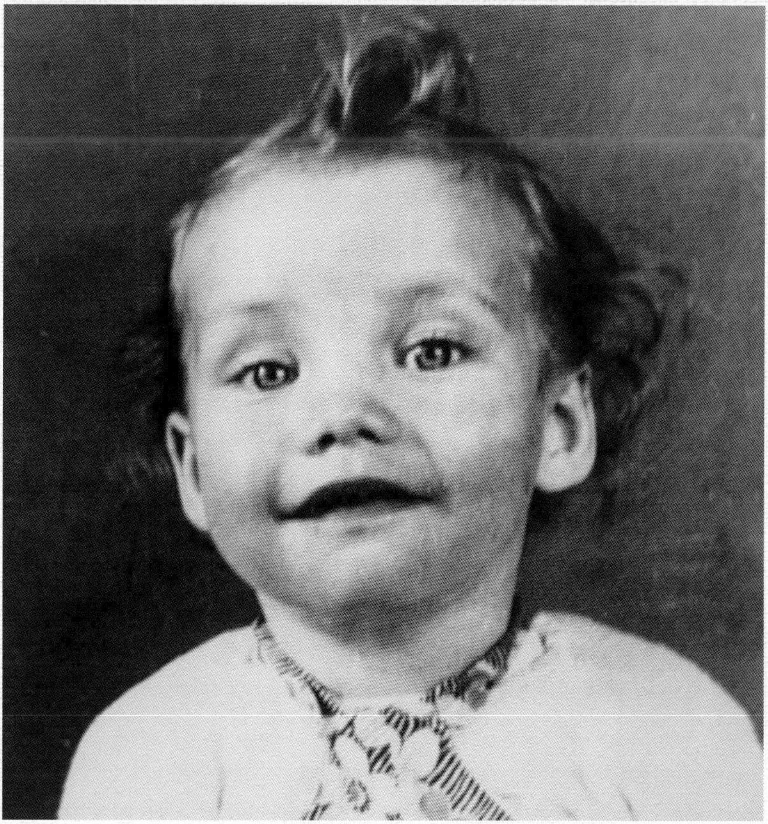

The real Erwin as a baby. Photo provided by his wife Zdenka

Erwin with adopted parents Jan and Marie Radek

Johanna van Haarlem as a young woman

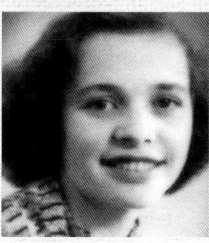

Erwin on the left wearing a pair of big ears

Gregor Kulig in his uniform after being drafted from his farm

Gregor Kulig,
Erwin's father,
suited *(top left)*

Kulig with
his family in
Poland

The spy, Vaclav Jelinek, pictured on the
left with an unidentified girlfriend while
acting as Erwin van Haarlem

Vaclav Jelinek as Erwin van Haarlem

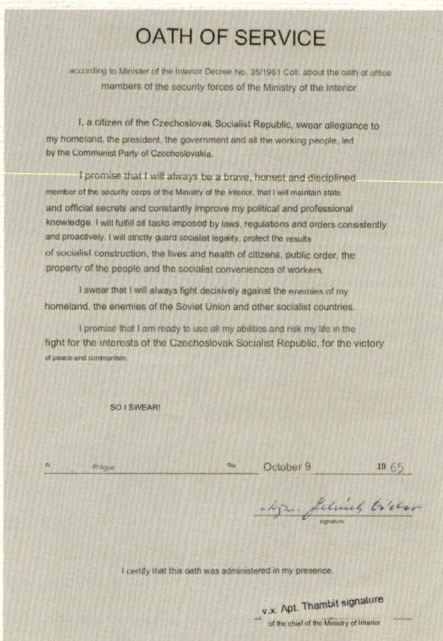

OATH OF SERVICE

according to Minister of the Interior Decree No. 35/1961 Coll. about the oath of office
members of the security forces of the Ministry of the Interior

I, a citizen of the Czechoslovak Socialist Republic, swear allegiance to
my homeland, the president, the government and all the working people, led
by the Communist Party of Czechoslovakia.

I promise that I will always be a brave, honest and disciplined
member of the security corps of the Ministry of the Interior, that I will maintain state
and official secrets and constantly improve my political and professional
knowledge. I will fulfill all tasks imposed by laws, regulations and orders consistently
and proactively. I will strictly guard socialist legality, protect the results
of socialist construction, the lives and health of citizens, public order, the
property of the people and the socialist conveniences of workers.

I swear that I will always fight decisively against the enemies of my
homeland, the enemies of the Soviet Union and other socialist countries.

I promise that I am ready to use all my abilities and risk my life in the
fight for the interests of the Czechoslovak Socialist Republic, for the victory
of peace and communism.

SO I SWEAR!

In   Prague   day   October 9   19 65

signature

I certify that this oath was administered in my presence.

v.x. Apt. Thambit signature
of the chief of the Ministry of Interior

The spy's oath of service to the Czechoslovak Socialist Republic *(translated above left)*

Spy pictured with Refusenik's child

Photo of the spy with The 35s
members wearing prison shirts at a
protest over the jailing of Refuseniks
in Russia taken from Southampton
University archives

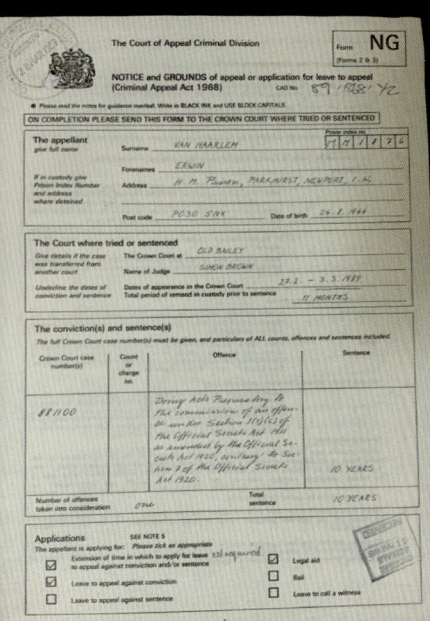

Indictment and appeal documents
taken from the spy's Old Bailey trial

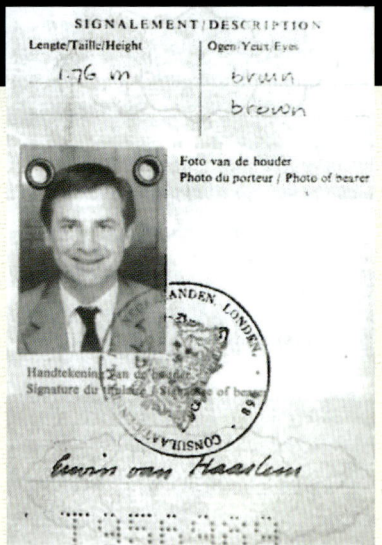

Passport of Erwin Van Haarlem, unveiled
at his trial, along with other spying
equipment, 3 March 1989

Radio used by Jelinek to comunicate
with superiors in Prague

Johanna van Haarlem with the spy
pretending to be her son

residential area of Silver Birch Close, Friern Barnet, Middlesex, where Erwin van Haarlem was living when he was arrested; Van Haarlem, covering himself with his jacket, at Bow Street Magistrates' Court, London; police removing evidence from the spy's home

Olesovice children's home south of Prague where Erwin stayed

Johanna and her real son, Erwin, who became Ivo, at Dutch clinic where he was born

Johanna and Ivo reunited at the Grand Hotel in Brno 1991

Daily Express

MONDAY APRIL 4 1988 *** 22p TODAY'S TV: PAGE 22

MI5 CRACK SUBMARINE SPY PLOT

Mother kills her children

- A MOTHER killed her two children as they unwrapped their Easter eggs yesterday. Then she ran out of the house, still in her dressing gown, cut her own throat, and drowned in a pond.

- Devoted wife Linda Mockford, 34, stabbed her eight-year-old daughter and strangled her four-year old son with his pyjama cord. The tragedy stunned the Cotswold village of Great Haseley.

- Husband Ron Mockford, 38, was said to be in a state of deep shock last night. His wife's body was found near the M40 motorway by a police helicopter.

Full story: Page 7

By OWEN SUMMERS and ALUN REES

BRITAIN'S security services believe they have uncovered a KGB spy ring aimed at crippling Britain's submarine defences.

Czech national Erwin van Haarlem, a suspected agent, was being detained under tight security at a London police station last night.

Other arrests, some of them Britons, are expected shortly.

A six-month surveillance operation targeted 42-year-old van Haarlem after intelligence reached Whitehall of a secrets-busting mission by Soviet agents in Bath, headquarters of the Admiralty's underwater research unit.

Special Branch detectives arrested him at the weekend at his flat in Friern Barnet, Hertfordshire.

They acted on instructions from MI5 chiefs who have been coordinating the investigation which has spread from the West of England to nuclear bases in Scotland.

American CIA men, deployed in Britain, were alerted before van Haarlem's arrest.

U.S. agents have been working closely with British counter-intelligence officers for more than a year on a security screen around underwater warfare operations.

Van Haarlem appeared to be a Dutch-born art dealer. But police suspect him of being an "illegal", the espionage term for an agent dedicated to working for the KGB without the protection of diplomatic cover.

He asked officers to contact the Czech embassy in Kensington. At first the embassy, which has housed several known spies in the past, denied all knowledge of him and his activities.

GCHQ mole mystery as Czech is questioned in secrets probe

SECRETS

But sources last night confirmed that embassy officials had been in touch with the police inquiring about van Haarlem.

Spycatchers have been trying to crack a submarine espionage ring operating in Britain for at least two years.

They fear there has been a leak of vital secrets on allied submarine movements and highly sensitive information on sonar "burglar alarms" which are used to warn NATO over Soviet submarine movements.

The hunt for a mole had centred on the intelligence headquarters at GCHQ in Cheltenham.

Russian spy Geoffrey Prime was caught eight years ago.

Another line of inquiry was the possibility of a mole in the naval hydrographic intelligence centre based at the Empire Hotel in Bath.

But one intelligence source said: "There are deep suspicions that Prime had an agent organised and "sleeping" in GCHQ until his arrest.

"Prime was a clever agent and in the end his activities only came to light because he was a paedophile and was arrested over his obsession with little girls."

The source said there could also be a link with a jailed East German couple who were arrested under the Official Secrets Act in the Hounslow area.

The centre in Bath was formed during the Second World War when vital sections of naval operations were moved out of blitz-torn London.

... key secret is the location and ... stretching

MYSTERY AG... JAILED FOR 10 YEARS—AND HE TAKES HIS SECRETS WITH HIM

Spy with no name

Betrayed by the 'Jew' who came to help

The girl who fell in love

Newspaper coverage of the spy's capture in the UK. *Daily Express* front page story, 4 April 1988 *(above)* and continued story inside a year later after sentencing on 4 March *(right)*

Daily Mail article written by authors Paul Henderson and David Gardner *(above) Daily Mirror* front page and inside spread, 4 March 1989 *(right and top)*

Jelinek's grave, engraved with both his and Erwin van Haarlem's name. Inscription reads: "Life is a book, you can read it just once" *(right)*

Ivo, Johanna's son, hosting a family barbecue *(left)*

Johanna van Haarlem at 98 years old, living in Holland

Paul Henderson, Ivo's daughter Zdena, Ivo's wife Zdenka, Ivo's daughter Iva, family friend and translator Vera Navratilova.
Picture by Pavel Horejsi

instead left an indelible stain. Many Western politicians also felt signing the accord suggested their leaders had ratified the Soviet domination of Eastern Europe, including its annexation of Russia's neighbours, and President Gerald Ford took some heavy flak in Washington for adding his signature.

Sharansky was a founding member of the Helsinki Watch Group launched in Moscow in 1976 to hold the Kremlin to its obligations under the accord. In part due to his fluent English, he took a central role in publicising the Refusenik cause until his arrest by the KGB a year later in 1977. He was the victim of a classic entrapment after his flatmate, unbeknown to him, reached out to US intelligence and passed on information about the Helsinki group. The evidence was twisted to suggest Sharansky was working with the CIA, and he was convicted of trumped-up charges of treason and spying for the United States. Russia sentenced him to 13 years of imprisonment and hard labour. His imprisonment was seen in the West to symbolise the plight of all Jews in the Soviet Union.

After his arrest, Lynn Singer, the president of the Union of Councils for Soviet Jews and the American lobbyist for Soviet Jewry, began a dedicated campaign for Sharansky's release. In doing so, Singer also became an unwitting resource for Jelinek's intelligence gathering through her connections with The 35s, which he was monitoring.

Singer emphasised the importance of the Soviet Jewry issue in Washington DC at a special congressional meeting on Human Rights and International Organizations. On 23 June 1983, she told the House that the state-sanctioned Soviet media was seeking to demonise Jews, rewriting children's books to portray them in a bad light. A favourite game among school children, she told the meeting, was called the 'Concentration Camp

Game'. The rules were simple enough: Jewish children were given a number by which they were referred to that day instead of by name.

"The most frightening aspect of the Soviet antisemitic campaign," Singer continued, "is the emerging parallel which equates Zionism with Fascism." Jews were being accused of having been collaborators with the Hitler regime, the most intolerable and obscene charge of all. "At this moment in Jewish history," Singer told the shocked gathering, "we are witnessing a cultural genocide, an intellectual genocide, and a human genocide. Soviet Jews are deliberately and systematically being stripped of their culture and of their very identity. They are coldly treated as outcasts in a regime that neither allows them to live as a people nor leave."

It was amid this swelling sense of international indignation that Jelinek urged his bosses to act. He knew the British and US governments were under immense pressure to negotiate Sharansky's freedom and, according to Gragert, they would be prepared to give up a lot to make it happen. It was the perfect situation for the Soviets to press a hard bargain for a spy swap. "The time is right," he told his controllers. The successful swap made everyone a winner: Gragert, for his brilliant intelligence harvesting; his Prague bosses, for impressing the kremlin, and the Russian negotiators in tit-for-tat espionage tactics. With it, Gragert's stock rose even higher.

CHAPTER TWENTY

Capital Hilton Hotel, Washington DC,
11-15 June 1986

In 1986, growing in confidence and feeling invincible, Jelinek embarked on his most audacious mission yet, travelling with Rita Eker and other campaigners to Washington to attend America's National Conference for Soviet Jewry. He was heading into the dragon's den. If the Americans got the slightest sniff of a spy in their midst, he was unlikely to be allowed home. While Jelinek was spying in London in 1977, Christopher John Boyce, a former altar boy from California, was sentenced to 40 years in jail for selling US satellite programme secrets to the Soviet Union. News of this would not have passed Jelinek unnoticed. If he had any doubts about his decision to fly into Washington, however, they likely would have faded away as soon as the conference delegates introduced him as an important person from the UK who had been supporting the women's campaign.

Sending the full agenda in a secret message to Prague, he boasted about his chance to get close to President Reagan and former Vice President Walter Mondale, both of whom would be at the conference. Reagan was a huge supporter of Israel, loaning the state billions of dollars during his presidency, and he was critical of Soviet imprisonment of Jewish dissidents and the curtailment of their emigration. In 1980, the former Hollywood actor declared: "The long agony of Jews in the Soviet Union is never far from our minds and hearts. All these suffering people ask is that their families get the chance to work where they choose, in freedom and peace. They will not be forgotten in a Reagan Administration." When he came to power the following year, he kept his word and appointed several Jews to key roles.

Throughout their trip to the US, Gragert skillfully stayed on message. He told the Americans he met at the conference that he felt happy and privileged to be in the presence of the great supporters of the Jewish cause. While Rita and her friends did notice some strange behaviour from their enthusiastic friend on this trip, the moments were easily dismissed. Just before going through customs and passport control at Heathrow, for instance, Gragert said he would rather go through alone, telling Eker, "Officialdom makes me nervous." It seemed out of character to Eker, but it didn't ring any alarm bells. They trusted that their friend had no other motive than to assist their ideals for Jewish freedom and peace.

The Union Council of Soviet Jewry arranged conference sessions between the English groups and the North Americans so each group could learn about the others' work on a greater scale. Gragert and The 35s also met businessmen trading with Russia to see what they could do to get freedom for people through their agreements. Perhaps most importantly, as far as Gragert was concerned, the group also met President Reagan during their few hectic days in the US capital. George Bush and Bill Clinton were big supporters, although neither was present. Throughout the trip, Gragert was feted like a celebrity. He was invited to receptions with senators on Capitol Hill and he chatted with Reagan's Secretary of Defence Frank Carlucci, who thanked him for helping the Soviet Jews.

Soon after his return from DC, Jelinek posted his findings in a dead letter box by Marble Arch at the end of Hyde Park. Their spy was displaying his sense of history in the making by choosing the huge triumphal marble arch built in the 19th century as a grandiose gateway to an expanded Buckingham Palace and celebration of Great Britain's conquests in the Napoleonic Wars. When his intelligence was received by a London agent/courier, Gragert, in turn, received a coded message from Prague, reading: "Receipt of the shipment has been confirmed." By then, the report by Gragert would have been winging its way to the Czech capital in diplomatic bags or decoded in London and sent by radio to Prague, classified 'Top Secret'.

Valuable information in hand, Prague soon deemed the DC trip, with their London sleeper daring to enter the mouth of the beast in the American capital, an enormous success. The spy had taken his Soviet masters into Washington and brought the enemy into Moscow. He felt unbeatable, impregnable – a one-man unit ready to take on and launch any special operation ordered by command from Moscow and Prague. He had penetrated the heart of power in the most powerful country in the world. They'd even thanked him for his service!

Several months after his return from Washington, Jelinek was instructed to return to Prague for a briefing. He took an elaborate route back through four European airports, including Germany and Austria. This time, he used a passport with his old alias of Karel Elsner and other forged documents to enter Czechoslovakia. He was unsure what to expect, but he needn't have worried. After a celebration dinner of champagne, ham and horseradish, the head of the Czech secret service General Karel Sochor told him, "I commend you for your exemplary combat mission."

"I serve the socialist homeland," Jelinek replied, delighted that his work in London was getting him noticed. He was also making a mark at the highest levels in Moscow. His Czech bosses basked in his reflected glory. It was a win-win all-round again. The days when he was being ridiculed for his work prying on the British royals were long over. Moscow lavished praise on his extraordinary abilities to swerve the attention of British intelligence on their home turf, and for his insatiable appetite for finding and sending important secrets and analysis. On the same trip to Prague, he was awarded a medal 'For Services to the Defence of the Fatherland' and Ukraine-born KGB chairman Viktor Mikhailovich Chebrikov, a war hero who had been a battalion commander in World War Two, presented him with a top Soviet award "For the strengthening of combat friendship".

The fact that Moscow's spymaster conferred the honour personally on Gragert spoke volumes for his espionage skills and achievements. His superiors admired his mendacity and his resilience. He'd now been an undercover agent for Chebrikov and, unlike others, he'd never broken down. The presentation was made at a luxury villa in Čtyřkoly, a small village near Prague, where the guests, many of them former KGB 'illegals', drank vodka and plum brandy and congratulated Jelinek on his work in London. He marvelled at paintings by Václav Brožík and Vaclav Spala on the walls and drank out of cut-glass Moser crystal. No expense was spared for the new hero of the hour.

Jelinek even brought along latex dolls of Margaret Thatcher and Ronald Reagan for the guard dog to play with.

Promoted to major, Jelinek was described as "a class-conscious, ideologically advanced party member devoted to the politics of the Communist Party of the Czech Republic" in the justification for the award. The award document continued in excessive communist dogma that he had not succumbed to anti-socialist tendencies. "He stuck to the principles of socialist and proletarian internationalism and firm friendship with the Soviet Union. In the same way, during his long-term work in the environment of the active influence of the enemy's ideology, he correctly orients himself in political issues from the class positions of Marxism-Leninism."

Chebrikov heralded his continuous intelligence reports as being of high operational value for Soviet secret service agents. The KGB chief described him as showing "personal bravery, diligence and honesty" in his spy work. "The award of a gift in kind will be an appreciation of his long-term successful intelligence work abroad."

To Gragert, his promotion to major and the prestigious awards were confirmation of his self-belief as well as his successful intelligence harvesting for Prague and Moscow. He was feeling very proud of himself. Finally he was getting the credit he believed he deserved. Jelinek's parents also benefited from the spy's rising star. His handlers had met regularly with his parents at their home on the outskirts of Prague to reassure them, usually with a carton of strong Aske beer for his father and flowers for his worried mother, that their son was doing a great job for his country. One official visitor reported that he told them Jelinek was "doing well and is perfectly fine and healthy apart from slight diabetes". Vaclav Sr. and Poláková understood the parameters of his mission abroad, they had no idea what their son was doing or where he was going and were unable to see him. To them, the explanation by government officials that he was a patriot making great sacrifices for his country was enough.

However, his bosses were not altogether happy. They noticed that, while he always had a confidence bordering on arrogance, he was becoming more boastful, enjoying the high life a bit too much, in their opinion, and could be prone to exaggeration. He was saved from serious reprimand by his ability to provide intelligence reports that were largely well-considered and detailed. The grey men in their Lubyanka headquarters weren't overly concerned. They wouldn't be the ones risking going to jail for a long time in enemy territory. Such is the cynicism of spying.

~

In the same year he received Soviet accolades, Jelinek met French air hostess Sylvie Lepetre. She was a beautiful, bubbly 36-year-old brunette. Jelinek fancied himself as an artist and sketched Sylvie as she posed in the nude. It was a very happy time for the self-styled art dealer. He spoke to Johanna about his girlfriends, introducing her to Sylvie, and she concluded that his good looks and smart dress sense made him quite the ladies' man.

Like everyone else, Sylvie knew Jelinek as Erwin van Haarlem and their three-year affair was a tempestuous one. Neighbours heard them arguing and laughing and would see them strolling up the street arm in arm after rows. Sylvie was a free soul and worked for Dan Air, flying on charter flights to the continent and short-haul flights to cities in the UK and Europe. At the time it was Britain's biggest independent airline, and the Frenchwoman was well-paid and independent. They had pictures taken of themselves on beach holidays. Jelinek loved to show off his gorgeous girlfriend. Perhaps most importantly, however, Sylvie also showed little interest in politics. There was no reason for his bosses to fret. His success in the field emboldened him to challenge the no-girlfriend rule that had been enforced during his early years in London when he had been forced to drop the doctor girlfriend he'd liked so much because of her left-wing interests. At this point, with his bosses happy, his love life fixed and a circle of friends, he felt he could do anything.

CHAPTER TWENTY-ONE

Friern Barnet, North London,
25 September 1986

As much as he enjoyed his spymasters' praise, Gragert was paying a price for his success in the field. It was exhausting to keep up a false front at work with his contacts in London's Jewish communities, not to mention at home with Sylvie and abroad with Johanna and her extended family back in the Netherlands. His spymasters may have noted his resilience, but the truth was that Gragert had been pretending on so many counts that he did sometimes lose sight of who he really was, Vaclav Jelinek or Erwin van Haarlem?

He'd been in London for more than a decade and his success was a double-edged sword. It had been rewarding to finally win the appreciation from his superiors for all his sacrifices and there was no doubting his value to his country, but the life he had created for himself made him realise just how much he had sacrificed.

He found himself thinking about settling down with a wife, maybe some children. He looked at his Jewish friends and their close families and wanted some of their happiness. And he was weary of his fake relatives.

Forever looking over his shoulder, watching every stranger for the slightest hint of recognition, worrying he could slip up at any moment – it was all getting too much. Besides, his parents back home in Modrany, a suburb of Prague, who he hadn't seen or contacted since being posted to the UK, were getting old. They were unaware of their son having adopted another name and pretending to be another mother's son while on a top secret mission in the West. His father was a good communist, a baker who ran a small business called Durable Pastry, and lived in a spacious ground floor flat with his wife. His parents accepted that their son was doing something important for Czechoslovakia but had no details. They had been conditioned in a communist state to know they would not be able to pry into government affairs. After so many years, his youthful devotion to the cause was being worn down by the desire for a simpler life. For all the cloak-and-dagger adrenalin rush, he was feeling the heat. He had always been aware of the consequences if he was exposed as an 'illegal' foreign agent of a hostile state. It would almost certainly lead to one place only – the Old Bailey, Britain's Central Criminal court, topped with a copper roof dome and proudly displaying from its great height the bronze Lady of Justice arms outstretched with a sword and the scales of justice, a reminder to everyone that crime would not pay. He knew that as an Eastern Bloc agent, his day of reckoning, if it ever came, would happen at the same place where history's most notorious spies had been imprisoned. That list included several notorious traitors, such as British spy George Blake, who had been sent down to the cells for an unprecedented 42 years after betraying dozens of MI6 agents to the KGB before escaping and fleeing to the Soviet Union; Geoffrey Prime, jailed for 38 years for passing British national security secrets to the KGB while working for the RAF and GCHQ; and civil servant John Vassal, blackmailed into passing secrets to the Soviets and sentenced to 18 years in prison.

Jelinek, as an illegal on his own, had no diplomatic immunity. As the years marched on, he worried more and more about what that might one day mean.

~

With every success Gragert was becoming more paranoid and exhausted. He was having trouble sleeping and was more irritable with Johanna. He started travelling outside London to look for quieter spots for his 'dead letter boxes,' having become convinced that he was being watched. He began using spots on the eastern outskirts of the Hainault Forest, close to suburban council estates and nouveau-riche Chigwell, where legit businessmen and East End criminals mixed with top-level football players in their mansions. One of his favourite new places for drops was Sandy Heath at Hampstead Heath. Apart from its beautiful undulating terrain, it was boggy with precipitous hollows providing natural areas of seclusion for concealing messages. He used his once-regular drops, such as a 150ft black poplar tree located close to his home by the North Middlesex Golf Club in North London, less and less.

The club's head greenkeeper Trevor Uxterby remembered mysterious messages pinned to the tree about missing cats. "Every month a cat was said to have gone missing," he recalled. "Each one was different, with different descriptions and phone numbers." Jelinek was telling case agents the times for his pick-ups and the coordinates of where the packages were hidden on the course.

~

After Gragert took up the cover story of an antique dealer, he often disappeared on long trips, telling acquaintances he was taking holidays to Hong Kong, Singapore, Malaysia, and Thailand. This was all a pattern to convince people he was successful in his work and a carefree bachelor able to travel freely anywhere with the money he was earning. The trips would also enable him to meet up with his superiors in more relaxed settings. But while he'd once delighted in his jet-setting, Gragert was now growing tired. At about this point, worn out from the unrelenting pressure of juggling stories and living under someone else's identity, he tried hard to return to Prague for good.

He couldn't shake the feeling that he had pushed his luck far enough and it could soon run out. He told the StB he was done. He was no longer able to keep up the 24 hours-a-day, seven days-a-week charade. He wanted a wife, he wanted children, he wanted a normal life. He wanted an exit – one that would be covert but easily done with his Dutch passport. However, the answer came quickly and definitively. "Your conduct is a gross violation of discipline. You will not be returning home now or later. Your task is to fight the enemy on the front line. Don't even think it might be otherwise."

Too much time and effort had already been spent getting him into position in London. He would have to stay. A classified StB memo declared that he had provided 33 pieces of information over the course of a single year, between 1985 and 1986, including documents with an average rating of 1, the highest classification of intelligence. "He continues to have access to information that represents the interests of our intelligence and, in particular, the interests of the intelligence of our Soviet friends," the note stressed. Another Czech intelligence memo described Gragert as "one of the most productive developers of information that we have in our network."

Jelinek was a victim of his own success.

Faced with his bosses' refusal to give him what he really wanted, Gragert did what many disgruntled workers do when their employers want them to stay – he asked for a raise. He told the StB his work "physically exhausts him and practically makes intelligence work impossible".

He wasn't going to be allowed to return to Prague, but he had been given a cash payment of thousands of pounds. They approved a raise to help him "maintain balance and calmness, but only if he agreed to stay". They also offered him the opportunity of a transfer to the United States, running a team of agents, if he continued to do well in London. They would even provide him with a 'wife' to keep him onside.

~

During one of his trips to Hainault Forest, he started to believe more strongly that there was some foundation for his paranoia. He'd gone to pick some mushrooms as part of his cover and couldn't help noticing two men, apparently strangers, smartly dressed and wearing ties. One ventured so close he looked inside his bag of mushrooms and smiled.

Driving home to North London, he spotted two cars following a few spaces behind. Using his evasion training he tried to lose his tail, but not so hard it would reveal he was suspicious of his shadows. Several miles later, they were both still there.

Now he was certain of it: he was being followed. What is more, it seemed they wanted him to know. Jelinek was convinced he was being sent a message. Give up and go home now – or else! Or perhaps they were trying to signal something else, he thought. They may have wanted him to know that he could change sides and become a double agent. It was an MI5 specialty. They showed their hand just enough for the foreign spy to know the game was up. Then they would wait for him to come to them. If the game really was up, he would have to make a decision on what to do next. And the clock was ticking.

CHAPTER TWENTY-TWO

Prague, Czechoslovakia, 7 January 1987

Jelinek wasted no time in putting his extraction plan into action. The mushroom picking incident had spooked him and this time he didn't ask if he could return to Prague – he just went. He told his spymasters that this time it wasn't about the money. He wasn't simply posturing to get a raise. This time he really meant it. He wanted to retire Gragert and Erwin van Haarlem.

He needn't have bothered with the trip. His bosses ordered him to get right back to London.

"You're imagining things," his superiors told him when he met with them in the Czech capital. "You can't go home. We need you outside. Getting to England is not easy. In addition, the Russians are pushing us. You have excellent news, they need it in the disarmament negotiations, we are gaining solid ground."

It was clear that Moscow was now pulling Gragert's strings. Prague's power was waning, and his handlers had another big reason for him not being allowed to return anytime soon. "Do you know how many illegal people there are in England?" they asked him. "Two. Rather, there were two of you. The other betrayed us. "

His bosses told Gragert that the other illegal had fallen in love with an English girl whose father just happened to work for MI5. The father didn't feel right about his daughter's suitor and had him checked out. Discovering he was a Soviet bloc agent, MI5 tried to turn him in the hope he would work as a double agent. Luckily for Gragert, Czech intelligence found out before he was able to betray anybody and dragged him back to Prague. "He doesn't know you exist," the StB told Jelinek. "Or if he does, he certainly doesn't know your identity."

Jelinek wasn't altogether reassured but had little choice. He reasoned that disobeying his order to return to the UK would probably end up with him behind bars in Prague. Even if it all went pear-shaped in London, an English prison was preferable to a Czech one. He managed to win one more concession – to be allowed a visit home once a year – and then he flew back to London knowing he would now need to keep a watchful eye over both shoulders.

~

Johanna continued to have no idea that her 'Erwin' was a spy and a fraud. He showed no signs to her of distress or pressure as their mother-son relationship built over many years. They spent many intimate occasions catching up on their lives, but by Gragert's design the conversations were one-sided and mainly delved into Johanna's past trials and tribulations, beginning with being an unmarried mother during the war in Holland. Johanna no longer questioned his reticence about discussing the past. She accepted it would be too painful for him to roll back the years that must have given him an identity crisis. She worried that he never had the confidence-building security and love of his own biological parents, but he insisted to her that he had a happy childhood and that his adopted parents were good to him. He hardly talked about them, however, and when she pushed him for more details about his formative years, he went quiet.

~

The Cold War was given its name by British author and journalist George Orwell in an article published in 1945, in which he stated a world living in the shadow of nuclear war was "a peace that is no peace. It was a cold war". Orwell's description grew in resonance as the years unfolded. The nuclear arms race raised worldwide tensions and political superpowers funded wars by proxy, probing to find weaknesses around the globe while seeking dominance. If the West was equally capable of obliterating countries as the Russians were of launching Armageddon then the balance of probabilities stood at no leader pushing the button. It was a false peace, but it was a nuclear peace.

The stakes couldn't be higher and it soon became clear why Jelinek's superiors were so determined to keep him in place. Up to this point, the Russians had been happy to let the Czechs dictate their spy's mission. Now they had some demands of their own. They wanted him to find them classified military secrets in addition to keeping in communication with the Jewish groups. There were plans for him to take on top secret operations that could put the Soviets in a stronger position militarily as they tried to catch up with the West, led by the Americans, in the arms race.

CHAPTER TWENTY-TWO

Jelinek had been a good student at spy school and knew the history. The Americans had tested the first atomic weapon at Los Alamos, New Mexico on 16 July 1945. US nuclear armed war planes launched attacks on Hiroshima and Nagasaki on August 6 and 9 the same year, killing more than 200,000 Japanese people. Thousands more died from radiation sickness in the following weeks, months, and years in the horrifying aftermath. This unimaginable human cost in the incineration of two large cities compelled the Japanese to surrender unconditionally, bringing an end to the war in Asia. But the use of the atom bombs was criticised, not only for the monstrous death toll and countless injuries, both physical and psychological, but also many conflict experts believed the Japanese were on the verge of surrendering anyway.

The mushroom clouds that formed over the cities would become forever symbolic of the terrifying new class of weapons able to decide the outcome of war in just a couple of detonations on targets anywhere around the world. Gragert was keenly aware that the Soviets were determined to keep up with the American ability to unleash weapons of mass destruction. In 1949, Russia detonated its first nuclear weapon at a test site in Kazakhstan. Britain came next, testing its first atomic device in 1952 in "Operation Hurricane" on the Monte Bello Islands, off the west coast of Australia. In the same year, American scientists who had developed the hydrogen bomb were given permission to detonate one on Eniwetok, in the Marshall Islands, halfway between Hawaii and Australia in the western Pacific, an explosion hundreds of times more powerful than the bomb dropped on Hiroshima. It was hard to imagine. The world looked on in horror. If World War Three ever happened, would it be the end of the planet?

In 1958, the Soviet Union, Great Britain and the United States detonated more than a hundred bombs in nuclear tests. In his training, Jelinek learned how there had been discussions about a permanent testing ban with the three nuclear powers, eventually signing the Test Ban Treaty in Moscow in 1963, prohibiting nuclear weapons tests "or any other nuclear explosion" in the atmosphere, in outer space, and under water. Such was the concern about global obliteration, or at least a large part of the Earth being destroyed with millions being killed in retaliation attacks, that a high-speed telephone hotline was set up between Washington and Moscow to prevent the risk of accidental warfare. Russia and the West remained deeply suspicious of each other's intentions, nevertheless.

~

Jelinek's masters were operating with their own set of rules and the big prize would be to dig a mole deep into the UK and US weapons systems to work as a double agent for the Czechs and Russians. This work was classified at the highest levels, with only a small number of trusted operatives in the know.

Political doctrines were at stake. The US democratic constitution guaranteed citizens freedom to travel, to express their views, to democratic elections, to a forthright and investigative press, to protest against government and practice any religion. Meanwhile, the Soviet system had one political party and that was communist. The party appointed all its leaders in government and controlled every aspect of life. Both sides feared domination by the other; an outright winner would mean the end of democracy or the end of communism.

Jelinek's spymasters wanted him to bag what was potentially

the biggest weapons prize of all. He received a communication to go all out for anything he could gather on the Strategic Defence Initiative (SDI), nicknamed 'Star Wars' after the blockbuster science fiction movies first released in 1977. He had been aware of Reagan's signature defence system for years. On 23 March 1983, Gragert joined the rest of the world as they watched President Reagan address his nation live on TV, stressing the importance of the project. With the Kremlin very much on his presidential radar, Reagan boasted that he planned to use a space-based shield to prevent the Soviet Union's potential nuclear attacks. Arms domination would be tilted in Washington's favour to such a degree Moscow would be rendered toothless. Concerned Americans remembered that two decades before, President John F. Kennedy's administration had been brought to the brink of nuclear war when a US spy plane discovered Soviet nuclear sites on Cuba, right in America's backyard, just 329 miles from Key West in Florida.

According to Reagan, the successful development of SDI would provide a space-based defence system able to destroy Soviet ballistic missiles by interception at various stages, preventing catastrophic attacks on US cities. Sensors on the ground, in the air, and in space would use radar, optical and infrared detection to negate threats. There would be space and earth-based laser stations directing multi-formed beams to destroy any Soviet large-scale nuclear attack targeting US cities. This system could make Soviet nuclear missiles obsolete.

The reason Gragert was now becoming involved was because there was a new link with Britain. Gragert's spymasters suspected the Americans shared their technology with the UK, or asked them for help, so Jelinek's first penetration of the Star Wars system would be in Britain. He had already shown he could get results. His masters were hungry for more. If he hit a rich seam of intelligence gold, it would be a game changer in military supremacy. He would become a Soviet hero.

The increased demands and the added pressure of having Moscow on his case only made Gragert more anxious. His spymasters were demanding more and more, sending him on increasingly dangerous missions. He could sense the creeping danger, weighing heavier and heavier. In his worst moments of paranoia he wondered if he was considered expendable. The Russians had the world's most dominant chess players. They were only interested in delivering checkmate. Pawns were sacrificed.

~

Jelinek had also been given orders to probe the UK's Polaris programme, which if launched could cause cataclysmic results from launch pads under the sea. The British Naval Ballistic System, its official name, had been providing submarines outfitted with ballistic missiles carrying nuclear warheads to the British Navy since 1968. Jelinek began scoping out how he could get classified information about four Resolution-class ballistic missile submarines, each carrying 16 Polaris A-3 ballistic missiles, at the Clyde Naval Base on Scotland's west coast at Faslane, near Glasgow, home to the navy's nuclear sub fleet. The thermonuclear warheads were highly sophisticated, second-generation nuclear weapons capable of the most terrifying destructive force. Beyond launching their own attack, the Soviets would pay anything and do anything to get the manual for Polaris.

They wanted Jelinek to find out for them and they would rather his cover was blown trying, than not trying at all. All this on top of his concerns that he had been compromised. There was one bright side to Gragert's growing danger. The high-risk situation in which the prized Czech spy was operating for Prague and Moscow – the UK having unmatched counterespionage forces – meant that Gragert's spymasters had finally decided to craft a real exit plan.

So far, Czech intelligence was convinced that Gragert was "clean" – his clandestine work had been impeccable as far as his masters in Prague could gather. Nevertheless, cover stories for even the best of agents can quickly unravel. Their legends can be blown by double agents, suspicious neighbours or a slip by the spy. Gragert was to go to one of his dead letter drops in Broomfield Park in London's Palmers Green where he often went for an early morning jog through the ancient woodlands. He could raise the alarm by leaving an enciphered message if he didn't want to risk a radio signal. He was assured there were plans to have him pulled out by land and sea when it was deemed necessary. But they didn't want him to leave. Not yet.

~

Still, Jelinek kept at it. He sent back intelligence about the processing of uranium at a company called Springfields, near Preston. Springfields had been making nuclear fuels for power stations since the 1940s. Gragert probed its work in case there was a connection to nuclear weapons that could be used by the Polaris system. He reported that "nuclear fuel is packaged in fuel rods which are distributed to power plants and reactors". He explained that rods were sent to Sellafield nuclear power station in Cumbria and that there were storage facilities in

Aldermaston, the atomic weapons research establishment in Berkshire. He pointed out that nuclear warheads were being transported in military convoys to high-security warehouses in Suffolk.

His high-risk work on the nuclear agenda didn't stop Gragert flying to America in the autumn of 1987 to attend a Jewish-organised New York conference entitled 'The New Political Agenda: Making It Relevant'. As Erwin Van Haarlem he sailed through immigration at the John F. Kennedy International Airport (JFK). Once again, he passed through an enemy border, clutching his Dutch passport, greatly relieved that his legend was holding firm and allowing him to go deeper into hostile territory for the cause. He was looking over his shoulder all the time now, worried his fabricated life was about to unravel around him at any moment.

However, he took some succour in sending a message to Prague informing his eagerly waiting controllers that the conference had provided ample intelligence, giving Gragert more opportunities to widen his web of deceit and to entangle Jewish activists with political connections. He reported that the conference chairman Rabbi David Goldstein from New Orleans introduced him by saying, "We have among us a distinguished guest from London. Allow me to welcome Mr Van Haarlem. Erwin, please stand up." Jelinek reported that once he did so, someone started clapping and then others joined him in the applause. In the coded message, his old arrogance seemed to have returned. He told Prague: "One idiot got up and the others started getting up too and they clapped." He clearly got a high from his deception, describing his feelings to Prague about the delegates unknowingly praising a "Czechoslovakian intelligence officer". All he could think of to say in response at the conference applause was, "Comrades, thank you for allowing me to perform so excitingly and satisfyingly." Nobody appeared to notice the irony of an American audience being described as "comrades".

To celebrate his latest intelligence coup, he went to a fancy Manhattan restaurant for dinner and enjoyed a bottle of fine wine, thanking his bosses in advance for paying the substantial bill. While he was in New York, for the first time in a while, he felt he could breathe. His relief was, in part, because he was away from London and the suffocating feeling that he was being watched. There hadn't been anything obvious since the approach in Hainault Forest. But he could feel them out there in London. He could feel the walls closing in. If the UK knew he had flown to New York then he knew that he was being watched, but there were no signs of US agents following him and he wasn't going to tip them off by communicating with anyone from a hotel phone.

He also informed Prague that Rabbi Efry Spectre from Detroit included in a roll call of Soviet Union Refuseniks a man named Yuli Edelstein, and he passed on Edelstein's address in Moscow to his Prague handlers. Undoubtedly this information would have been passed to Soviet intelligence in more coded messages or by couriers travelling east. Yuli Edelstein was arrested in 1984 aged 26 and sent to Siberian labour camps on charges including teaching Hebrew. The date of Gragert's individual intelligence reports are sometimes unclear, but the Soviets would have been interested in any information about a Jewish Refusenik who would also be seen as a dangerous subversive. Eventually, Edelstein was released from prison and was allowed to leave for Israel where he became a Knesset speaker.

In the same communication, Jelinek's ego ran riot as he heaped derision on his opponents. He poked fun at the world's most powerful man, describing President Reagan as a "strange actor, definitely a cowboy". He wrote that Israel's best brains would be joining the US "in research and development of strategic weapons" and pointed out that Israel was the "only country in the world" with a free trade agreement with the Americans.

Without naming sources of material and informants, possibly to protect them and possibly because he got some information from published sources available in the West but wanted to pass it off as exceptional spywork, Jelinek emphasised the Americans enormous firepower by describing the MX (Intercontinental Ballistic Missile – ICBM) as representing "a huge increase in the ability" of Reagan's military might to "hit and destroy Soviet missiles". His message said, "each MX carries 10 independently aimed warheads, they compare with an accuracy of 300 feet" (two times more than the best rockets in existence now!).

Moscow would have been devouring Gragert's informed MX analysis, seen as America's most highly developed ICBM in the Cold War against the Soviets. Its accuracy could be updated in flight by signalling from navigation satellites following its 7,000-mile range. Its 300-kiloton thermonuclear warheads had the potential to destroy fortified underground missile silos and command bunkers in the Soviet empire. Officials at the highest levels would have been shown the reports to initiate projects and finance new programmes to find ways to counter US firepower. They were doing all they could to compete on all levels in the arms race with Washington.

With his sights still on the Jewish question, in the same report he underlined Israel's nuclear capabilities. He wrote, "I came to the conclusion that it is possible Israel would use atomic weapons in a dire emergency." He continued, "Israel is convinced that its military superiority did not deter the Arabs from attacking on Yom Kippur in 1973… if the Arab countries would briefly unite to attack Israel, it has no possibility to stop the attack with conventional weapons."

~

The New York trip was deemed another success, but that only drove Moscow to demand more. By this time, his Prague handlers were operating almost entirely for their Russian KGB colleagues. Jelinek returned to London just before Joanna's latest planned visit. Their relationship had gone through many phases in the decade they'd now known each other. For a while in the early days, he had even considered her a surrogate mother. But he was tired of her now. She was nothing like his real mother and her personality was grating on him. He was beginning to dread their calls and her visits. The charade was becoming too exhausting.

CHAPTER
TWENTY-THREE

London, England, 25 May 1987

It turned out that Gragert was right to be worried about his cover being blown after more than a decade. It was easy for his bosses to tell him to continue as an illegal. They were making decisions in the safety of their secretive bunkers thousands of miles away. Their spy was operating as an illegal amongst the enemy. His presence in London was discovered by chance when a member of the Soviet Trade Delegation who was suspected of being an officer in the GRU, Russia's military intelligence, was followed to Hampstead Heath where he behaved in a "generally furtive manner" before going into the Old Bull and Bush pub.

Gragert turned up 30 minutes later and appeared to be searching around outside before he, too, went into the pub. Agents followed him to his home in Friern Barnet. Initially, MI5 thought he was a GRU "legal" agent, but they soon identified him as a Dutch art dealer named Erwin van Haarlem. They later found out he was working as an 'illegal' for the Czechs. British counterintelligence deployed a team to watch his every move. He could be an important player for Moscow. For a year, no amount of money, time and expertise was spared as MI5 and MI6 worked hand in glove to try and discover Van Haarlem's real reason for being in the UK. British secret services knew that if he was a serious player, the ultimate secrets to steal from the West would be nuclear secrets and that the Soviets would be telling their agents to go to any lengths to get them. No risk would be too big. British agents needed to answer some vital questions before they could figure out how to act. What was his real identity? Who was controlling him? What intelligence had he gathered? How damaging could his work be to the UK and its allies? The only way to find out was to watch his behaviour and to investigate connections from a distance.

Surveillance teams sometimes spend months, even years, watching a single suspect. If the suspect is a big enough threat, agents will monitor them night and day, for however long it takes to prevent a threat to the state. Teams mount observation from a distance using electronic equipment, including closed-circuit television (CCTV). Listening devices are planted. Postal interception takes place. Tracking equipment is attached to cars to follow persons of interest. Sophisticated techniques are employed to avoid alerting targets who are tailed in unmarked cars. If there's any suspicion the target could have rumbled the operation, the agents will withdraw immediately, taking a wrong turn to make the targeted spy or terrorist feel they'd got it wrong; that it was all just paranoia fuelling unfounded suspicions. On foot, men and women will change over constantly.

There is just one prerogative for the watchers – to not be seen. (The only exception was when an obvious attempt was made to turn an agent to work for the other side). For the most part, the agents trailing Gragert were successful. Their big problem wasn't that Gragert was suspicious, but that they could not figure out what he was up to. They were convinced of his importance; they just didn't know exactly why. They suspected Erwin van Haarlem was a fake identity, but they didn't have a clue what his real name was.

One thing his MI5 watchers had no doubt about was that the Czech spy could be dangerous. There was the persistent concern that Jelinek would have no hesitation in killing any of his Refusenik activist friends, or indeed his intelligence service watchers, if he thought they were onto him.

Moscow's iron-grip control of satellite countries meant that its dark arts were practiced from capital cities throughout eastern Europe. It didn't just pull the strings on its puppet states, it trained puppet masters and their spies, and sent out assassination directives along with detailed plans for taking down an opponent. The KGB spymasters were noted for their long memories and ingenious and brutal methods of execution. The best operatives received awards and promotion from the Kremlin. There was no shortage of trained killers willing to act.

The British agents might have been thinking about Bulgarian dissident and writer Georgi Markov who was crossing Waterloo Bridge in London in 1978 when a hitman from his home-country used a poison-tipped umbrella to inject one of his legs with a pellet of deadly ricin in murderous repayment for his defection in 1969. Markov died four days later. The truth of Moscow's involvement in Markov's demise was only revealed with the fall, in 1989, of the Berlin Wall, 96-miles long and 13 feet high to stop people escaping from Soviet-controlled East Berlin for West Berlin during the Cold War. One of the many secrets that seeped through the demolition cracks of the wall was how the KGB assisted the Bulgarians in Markov's revenge killing, probably by an illegal agent who had been "sleeping" in the UK for many years waiting for orders to liquidate the "traitor".

Even long before the wall's collapse, Soviet lone assassins and death gangs scoured the world to eliminate their perceived enemies. As far back as 21 August 1940, the Soviet-born political activist Leon Trotsky was sent to his death in his study in Mexico City at the axe-wielding hands of Spanish communist Ramon Mercader. Twenty years later Mercader was awarded the Soviets' highest civilian honour, the Order of Lenin, for his grisly work in the name of Trotsky's mother country.

MI5 remained convinced that Jelinek's ultimate role, perhaps the most important reason for his mission, was that he was in place and ready to carry out whatever was required of him by his Soviet masters at a moment's notice. That could well have included murder. They were perhaps lucky then that Jelinek, for all his spy craft, did not truly know he was under surveillance. Sure, he had suspicions at times, and had taken some counterintelligence measures, but was unable to prove anything, not even to himself. And he kept being told by Prague not to be paranoid. Ever the good communist he tried to listen and agree for his motherland.

CHAPTER
TWENTY-FOUR

Prague, Czechoslovakia, 20 June 1987

For months Jelinek had see-sawed through periods of heightened paranoia believing his every movement was under scrutiny, then shaking it off by convincing himself he had imagined the worst. Truthfully, he'd felt his British watchers' presence for a long time; he'd noticed something unusual, something small, then convinced himself he was paranoid, until the next time he'd sensed them out there without ever being certain. Now Jelinek knew for certain that he was being watched. From the windows of his flat in Silver Birch Close, Friern Barnet, he saw painters paint fences that didn't need painting, he saw a young couple walking with an empty pram, and he saw watchers-cum-joggers starting their shifts with a daily run around his block. He was so convinced his little Renault 18 GTS was bugged that he crashed it on purpose so he could buy a new car.

What he did not know was how he'd been detected and what the British intelligence knew about him. The thought kept him up at night. He was supposed to be working incognito, his identity a secret even from his country's own consular staff.

CHAPTER TWENTY-FOUR

Only his immediate StB superiors in Prague and top Soviet security officials knew his true identity.

He raised concerns with Prague but was once more told not to be concerned. There had been no leaks. His identity was safe. Still, he now remained in the UK and refused to travel elsewhere – not to visit Johanna, not to keep up his appearances as a successful art dealer, and certainly not for other spywork. As long as the Russians were calling the shots he wasn't going anywhere. His best course of action would be to redouble his efforts to avoid being caught red-handed. The Brits could suspect him as much as they liked, he thought, and they could watch him around the clock, but this was London not Moscow and he couldn't be arrested unless the authorities believed they could prove he had done something wrong. If he was caught, then his training dictated he keep his mouth shut and that his superiors would have him out of prison as quietly and as soon as possible. Five years tops.

His feeling that he was on borrowed time now dominated his every thought and the arrival of a new neighbour only added to his fears. Keith Edmundson was a friendly sort. He asked Jelinek to help lift a fridge for his girlfriend from his flat into his car and then invited him over for a glass of wine. He had a beard and never mentioned to his neighbour that he was a policeman, but Jelinek had spotted him coming out of a police station before walking up to the first floor just days after he moved in.

The spy assumed he must have been a plant. His suspicions appeared to be confirmed when his new friend took his wine glass away, saying it was dirty and returned with a clean one. In a reflection on the window, Jelinek saw the young cop carefully putting the fingerprinted glass into a plastic bag and putting it away in a drawer.

"So that's what a whore disguised as a friend looks like," Jelinek said to himself. "That's what I'm really like. That is how I act."

His shame was only fleeting. As a professional, Jelinek was insulted at the poor methodology of his counterparts. His post had been steamed open and resealed with glue, changing the feel and structure of the paper to a seasoned eye. His phone also stopped working, a chestnut of a tactic in the intelligence business. Gragert knew that if he called for the line to be fixed, an MI5 operator would be sent in to install a wiretap. As expected, a telephone worker turned up at the flat three days later to 'fix' the problem. He became so used to the changing cast of postmen, construction workers and dog walkers outside his home that he took delight in obtrusively taunting them, losing their tail when he went to the shops to buy milk. When Keith asked for a lift to the station, complaining his car had broken down, Jelinek assumed the bugs inside his home were malfunctioning and MI5 needed him out of the way to get them back on track.

If he was honest, he was a little insulted that they had sent a rookie like Keith to befriend him. Surely an agent of his experience was worthy of a more assured adversary. This was just too easy. Still, he remained on guard for weeks, expecting a knock on the door at any time. When it never came, he started to believe that perhaps he'd outwitted them, after all. If Keith was anything to go by, they weren't that good.

He just had to be careful.

CHAPTER
TWENTY-FIVE

New Delhi, India, August 1987

Lt. Col. Vlastimil Ludvik couldn't cultivate an intelligence source to save his life. He was the exact opposite of Jelinek, who prided himself on his professionalism. Gragert learned various languages, avoided commitments that could compromise his work and took time and care to impress his controllers in Prague and in Moscow. Ludvik did no such thing. His most impressive piece of spy work during his posting in London was to fabricate an approach from MI5 to try and get himself sent back home to Czechoslovakia. And he was the very worst kind of spy. He was a double agent and defector who had betrayed and placed many colleagues in danger. He didn't know Gragert's real name or details about his operations, but he was drip-feeding British agents pieces of intelligence that, together with other intel from London sources, led to Erwin van Haarlem. Although both men were in London at the same time and their clandestine tasks were not altogether dissimilar, they would not have met, and Gragert was unaware of his existence until it was too late. As an 'illegal' he kept a wary distance from his colleagues on the official side of the StB-controlled intelligence network. Ludvik, on the other hand, probably would have made it his business to know what Jelinek was up to, since he worked firstly as an economist in the Czech Embassy's commercial department and later as a senior clerk.

The two spies could not have come from more different backgrounds. Born in Zlín, Czechoslovakia on 16 March 1943, Ludvik's father, Vladimir, served as ambassador to Belgium, Italy and Pakistan before retiring in 1982. Given such a pedigree, it was hardly surprising that his son received an offer to join the Czech intelligence service in 1968 following his graduation from the University of Prague. He accepted the job and spent 10 months at spy school learning skills such as secret writing and photography, plus how to make transmissions and lose a tracker.

Yet, Ludvik was hardly spy material – and it showed. He had been an average student with a duodenal ulcer because he was so stressed by his studies. Beyond that, he didn't feel suited to the profession of espionage. Worse still, he worried it would be difficult to leave the Czech secret service because of his inside knowledge of targets, informants and methods used to plunder state secrets from the enemy in the West.

Nevertheless, he started his spy work just weeks after Soviet troops crushed the brief 'Prague Spring' of reforms and was packed off to London in 1975 to spy under the guise of a diplomatic official. A mediocre report suggested his personality veered towards "reservedness bordering on reclusiveness" and "little boldness and decisiveness" Not exactly a glowing recommendation for a budding international spy.

Once in London, he moaned about it being impossible to carry out espionage in Britain. "It was difficult for us to establish personal friendly contacts on any level. We had several intimate contacts, but no real agent. The only friendly faces around the embassy were well-known firms working for the British counter."

Ludvik may have been a competent penpusher, but he regularly got flak for his lack of intelligence activity. "The contact base consists only of official contacts, and this is insufficient, his two registered contacts are non-recruitable," read his personnel file. A year later, in 1977, he was told that he didn't have a single contact worth developing.

Yet, three years later, he was still in London – only now he was desperate to get out "with a healthy skin". But the Czechs refused to release him.

In response, he put his cloak-and-dagger skills, questionable as they were, into action to try and prove he had been compromised by the British and therefore of little use. He complained to his bosses of an attempt by MI5 to turn him during a 27 January 1981 meeting with one of his contacts, a British Department of Trade executive, at the Duke of York pub in Victoria Street. The attempt was entirely fabricated. Like most of his efforts, it didn't work. He later blamed the faked double agent approach on not feeling well.

Rather surprisingly, the StB believed Ludvik's account of the MI5 intervention but it didn't do him any good. They determined that the British should know they weren't going to be forced to withdraw their agents just because of their provocative actions. Ludvik would stay another year.

He finally returned to Prague in March 1982, hoping no doubt to settle into bureaucratic anonymity. But there was another surprise in store. Despite his lacklustre performance – or because of it – his spymasters decided to send him to a one-year KGB course in Russia. He found the camp, based in a bunch of wooden huts in the hamlet of Nemÿinovka, about one hour's train ride from Moscow, to be a jarring experience. He observed that the centre of the village was the local pub, which survived off the sale of vodka. "What impressed me the most was the terrible appearance of the local alcoholics. Yes, we also met drunkards in Moscow, but there were not as many of them as here in the countryside."

Once back in Prague, his wary bosses gave him the job of specialist clerk in charge of managing the residencies in London, Athens, Nicosia and Helsinki. London was a particular problem, with the government there weeding out potential operatives and refusing to grant them visas. Again, Ludvik wasn't lighting up the place. "He gave the impression that he was not very interested in operative work and was not necessarily passionate about it, on the other hand he was quite active in discussions at member meetings and other party meetings," read his file.

It was more Austin Powers than James Bond. In one case, a potential recruit left a dinner meeting laughing after he was offered a £10 bribe by Ludvik to work with the Czechs thanks to a typo. The instruction from Prague should have read £1,000 but the the slapdash spy stuck to his orders. In another debacle, Ludvik posed as an Italian journalist at a peace movement conference in London during the World Cup, which was taking place in Spain. When a foreign journalist asked about the result of a match the previous night, he became suspicious when the "Italian" knew nothing about it and found out he worked at the Czech embassy. A proposed posting to Paris – a promotion – was nixed because of Ludvik's "failure" and he was instead shipped out to the intelligence backwater of New Delhi.

If he wasn't keen on London, where an illegal called Gragert was impressing the Soviets, Ludvik definitely wasn't a fan of India.

CHAPTER TWENTY-FIVE

He had been assured the life of a diplomat in New Delhi was like being in paradise. For Ludvik it was "hellish, heat, dust, dirt, the smell of human and animal excrement everywhere, beggars and their children with their hands constantly outstretched, the danger of infectious diseases from the non-existent level of hygiene. All this, despite the impressive impression of the historical monuments, struck me as a great disappointment".

He was also a continuing disappointment to his bosses, who complained about his inability to recruit any worthwhile intelligence contacts. The last months of his residency in New Delhi in 1988 were full of nervous tension and deep suspicion about his work by senior people in the "rezidentura", the base for operations in India.

He decided his only solution was to defect to the West. Without telling his colleagues, his wife or his son or daughter, Ludvik left the Czech Embassy in New Delhi on Friday, 16 December 1988 in his car with diplomatic number plates bound for a meeting with one of his contacts. He never arrived. Instead, he parked his car under the Sheraton Hotel, where he was met by members of MI6 who drove him straight to the airport and onto a waiting plane to London.

There was some confusion and worry about his whereabouts for a couple of weeks, not least from his wife and family. His disappearance was explained with a message from the British Foreign Ministry on 4 January 1989, declaring that Ludvik had applied for political asylum in Britain. His panicked bosses in Prague immediately sought to assess the damage. A preliminary analysis put more than 50 intelligence "assets" at risk and exposed at least 30 agents at residences in the UK, France, Belgium, Holland, Greece, Italy and other countries.

One of these agents – the most hidden and consequently the

most valuable – had been Gragert. Another reason for the intense MI5 surveillance of the sleeper spy was finally revealed – Ludvik had been working as a double agent with its sister service, MI6, since 1986 and the information he had fed British intelligence had been sufficient for Gragert's cover to be blown completely. Ludvik didn't know Jelinek's real name, nor his alias, but he knew enough to support MI5's suspicion that he was a big fish.

Dozens of StB operations were terminated in the aftermath of Ludvik's defection, and on 25 May 1989, four Czech diplomats would be expelled by Britain for "activity incompatible with their mission".

Gragert may have expected with reason that his identity as Van Haarlem was kept from the embassy staff, even those involved in intelligence work. Had his controllers taken note of their sleeper spy's instincts that he was being watched, maybe his secrets would have been preserved and he would have lived to spy another day.

But Jelinek's spymasters decided there was no way Ludvik would have known Gragert's true identity. He was a useless agent, they reasoned, so he was the last person likely to track him down.

Jelinek was sent back to London from Prague and ordered to carry on as if nothing had happened. But MI5 was already watching, acting on information from its sister service. Ludvik had known many of the details, without being able to identify him by name. As a result of Ludvik's warning about a rogue 'illegal' in London, the British intelligence monitoring of suspicious transmissions at GCHQ in Cheltenham was on high alert. Jelinek had also made the mistake of opening a bank account in Israel, opening himself up to the scrutiny of Mossad, the Jewish state's notoriously watchful secret service.

CHAPTER TWENTY-FIVE

Slowly, laboriously, MI5 had connected the dots, and they led to the nondescript art dealer and straight to Silver Birch Court.

CHAPTER TWENTY-SIX

London, December 1987

Nothing had happened with British intelligence since Gragert first felt sure he had been followed to Hainault Forest in 1986. No approach. No arrest. No raid. Jelinek began to think they'd given up. He'd put a halt to his spying activities after Prague ignored his latest requests to leave.

Though he worried about being caught, he could admit to himself that he would miss many aspects of London when he returned to Prague. He had started a drawing class and had met women with similar interests. Gone were the days of strobe lights and sweaty dancing in discotheques. He'd even allowed himself a serious relationship with Sylvie, even if she didn't know his real name. And his job as an art dealer, real or not, was more in keeping with his image of himself as a sophisticated man about town.

But he wouldn't miss Johanna. After nearly 10 years, the pretense of being her son was becoming unbearable to him. From its awkward beginnings, their relationship had settled into a comfortable rhythm, and then he'd started to pull back. It was too much effort to keep reassuring her about her past. They would still talk regularly on the phone but he was less keen to meet up in person. She would confide in him and he, consumed with his own worries, barely listened. After all, he reminded himself, Johanna wasn't his mother.

No matter how hard Johanna promised herself that she'd try to make peace with the scant information she had about his past, she couldn't let it go. She decided to fly to Prague in May 1987, to try and find out for herself, infuriating Jelinek. She found the ancient city very much to her liking. So much so that she sent a letter with a photo to Erwin gushing about how wonderful she found it.

In his 20 June 1987 reply, Jelinek said he still considered Prague "my city" but went on to tell her a story with a sinister edge about the Czech capital. It illustrates the kind of enmity he was starting to feel toward her. It was hardly the kind of letter anyone would send to their mother.

> *Dear mother,*
>
> *There was a good gentleman. He didn't drink much, he stole only little and he beat his wife only occasionally to keep his self-respect. And because he was so good, one day, God invited him and said: 'You are going to die soon, but because of your pious life, you may go and visit the heaven and the hell and see which you like best and after your death, you will have the choice where to go.'*
>
> *So, the good man visited the hell first.*
>
> *The devils played a guitar and shared bottles with the sinners and the sinners danced with pretty girls with only little clothes on.*
>
> *There was also plenty of food and you didn't have to wash at that.*

Well, our man saw enough to know that this was the place to go after his death.

And so it happened, after he died, he decided to go to hell.

But the moment he was there, the devils, previously so friendly, put him into a kettle with hot oil and pulled his ears and pricked him with forks. And the man cried out: 'Here, what's all this? When I was here last time, you were friendly and there was drink and girls and now all that!'

And then Lucifer told him: 'Yes, but last time you were a tourist.'

So, mother, even if you liked Czechoslovakia so well, don't forget you were a tourist.

The strain was clearly getting to Jelinek, and there were other clues that his relationship with Johanna wasn't all plain sailing. She once called him at 3am complaining about comments her ex-husband's family had made about her obsession with finding Erwin.

"I will come to London, and we will live together," Johanna told him. "I will sell the house and come to London. We will live together."

"I fully understand your anger, Mum," Jelinek told her. "They shouldn't have told you that. Such things are not said in jest or anger. Of course, it would be nice for us to be able to live together if fate made that possible. I'm just sorry."

When she pressed him about moving to London, he tried to console her. "Mum, you know what, let's go to sleep now. I will call you tomorrow," Jelinek replied, but he was left wide awake. He knew that if Johanna moved to be close to him, living a lie to her on a daily basis would be more than he could cope with. And, she was likely to become even more inquisitive about his life in Czechoslovakia. She would demand answers to questions he would never be able to answer for fear of ruining his legend. Johanna had already become more demanding even while living hundreds of miles away in Holland.

On another occasion when they were out for a drive together near Golders Green, Jelinek apologised to a motorist after failing to give way.

Johanna ranted at him. "Who are you apologising to? Why are you apologising? You are so pliable! A typical Slav!" Johanna had no idea she was sitting next to a man who could become far more threatening if he wanted to.

Still, shocked at the outburst, Van Haarlem defended himself, saying: "He had priority."

She mocked him and, pulling to the side of the road, incensed, Jelinek told her, "What you call pliability is called decency in my culture. Why did you call me a typical Slav? I'm not Slav. Because I lived in Czechoslovakia?"

She didn't answer him, and they spent the rest of the journey in silence, but Jelinek remembered thinking: "I will return the pliable Slav to you with all the interest. I don't know when or where, but I know it will come and that I will be ruthless… and maybe it will pay you back for little Erwin."

Johanna and Jelinek had contrasting ideas on how their relationship was progressing. As much as she tried to cherish him, he kept pulling away. With MI5 on his case, he was thinking that he may not have need of her much longer.

After one sharp phone conversation, Erwin sent her a letter saying he wouldn't be travelling to see her in the Netherlands that year.

Dear mother,

I think the time has come for me to sit down and write you a letter and at the same time thank you for both writings, telegrams and phone calls. I would like to express my heartfelt thanks for your kindness and interest in everything I do. So I'm leaving for the USA knowing that I owe it to you. I am surprised that people from your immediate surroundings doubt my love for You. What do they really expect from me? That I will act like a dog that has found its lost master again?

That I will bark a lot and wag my tail? They forget that I am thirty-four years old and that I have only now met you through no fault of my own. The woman I called mother and who helped me overcome the weight of bones I encountered in my life has been dead for eight years. She didn't teach me Dutch because my mother tongue is Czech. True, I was born in Amsterdam, but then I lived in Czechoslovakia for thirty years. Is it really so strange that I find the Netherlands a beautiful country, but that's where it ends for me?

What do your loved ones have to say about love? I think we have a beautiful relationship. Dignity comes from respecting one another. You take note of my current situation, I take note of what you had to go through. Happiness is the result of being together. I am happy that I can finally say that I have found my real mother. In other words, I didn't just have someone in my life who raised me and took care of me, but with whom I have no blood ties. I know that you are an honest person, and you have earned a certain status and recognition in society. Your life was not always all milk and curds, as the Czechs say, but you still kept faith in life and a sense of humor.

I had no intention of breaking up our relationship. I thought you knew intuitively how I feel about you. But now I feel that it needs to be said. I really like you. Moreover, I admire you. But you don't have to tell your friends and relatives that. These words are not addressed to them, but only to you. And speaking of you, I can't think of one thing. I have the feeling that you are ashamed of what happened, and so you want to help me as much as possible with all your heart. Please don't do it. You've already done more than enough for me. You made me feel like someone was thinking about me. You mustn't forget how old I am. Don't be surprised that I consider everything to be an intrusion into my private life. This applies even to any offer of help. I have decided that I will not come to Holland this year. There's no point in you asking why. I have told you this several times, but you refuse to hear it. You don't listen to me with your ears, but with your heart. I have nothing against visiting you from time to time, but I definitely don't want to go to see you month after month. At the same time, please believe me that I will always be happy to see you here in London. I mean it, you are my mother after all.

Yours with love

Erwin

He did visit Johanna out of the blue, however, following a trip to Austria and she remembered him looking more prosperous, with neater hair and cultured, business clothes.

Johanna brought out some family photos, including one of her father's mother, who moved in with the family after her husband's death. "She was a very nice Jewess," Johanna remembered telling Erwin, who was surprised to learn of the Jewish connection. His sometimes-stand-offish nature still upset Johanna and when he was short with her, her guilt at abandoning her son would return. But families weren't always easy. She knew that better than most.

Back home in Schaijk, a small town about one-and-a-half hours' drive south from Amsterdam, Johanna couldn't hold the aggressive attitude of "Erwin" against him. She understood how difficult it must be for him. She had won him back against all the odds and was doing her best to make up for the years they were apart. If her ex-husband hadn't been able to understand why she needed so desperately to right her historic wrong, then that was his problem. It was the Christmas season and she would get a card from her son in England.

CHAPTER
TWENTY-SEVEN

Leicester Crown Court, England,
22 January 1988

While Vaclav Jelinek was dodging his MI5 watchers around London, it's quite possible his interest may have been piqued by a story making headlines in the rapacious British media involving a repellent double murderer by the name of Colin Pitchfork.

Pitchfork, a married cake decorator with two young boys, was a psychopathic sex attacker whose crimes against young schoolgirls were becoming inexorably worse by the year as he evaded any consequences of his perverted obsessions. What began as indecent exposure progressed to rape and murder. Had it not been for a striking new scientific development called DNA, an innocent man could have been convicted of at least one of his crimes. Instead, DNA profiling nailed Pitchfork and helped to sentence him to 30 years behind bars.

The first of Pitchfork's known victims, Lynda Mann, 15, never made it back to her Narborough, Leicestershire home after taking a shortcut back from a babysitting job on 21 November

1983. Her body was discovered by a country footpath the next morning. She had been raped and strangled. Three years later, Dawn Ashworth, also 15, was raped, beaten and killed by Pitchfork after he grabbed the teenager on her way home to Narborough in the middle of the afternoon from a friend's house in the nearby village of Enderby. Semen samples suggested the assailant had the same type A blood type, but with little other evidence, detectives were unable to solve either case, despite the clamour for results from the community and the press.

A local 17-year-old with learning disabilities, Richard Buckland, admitted to the second murder under police questioning. Although the evidence pointed to the likelihood that the same man was responsible for both murders, which took place within a few hundred yards of one another, Buckland said he was only responsible for the one. The police didn't believe him and charged him with killing both girls.

However, just five miles away at the University of Leicester, geneticist Alec Jeffreys had stumbled on a dramatic discovery that would change the face of criminal science. Though his experiment to discover how illnesses were inherited through families did not come up with the findings he had hoped for, the process revealed a much bigger and far-reaching discovery. His discovery identified that short DNA sequences varied from person to person, and could be used to identify individuals.

Identical twins, for example, would be an almost perfect match, while total strangers would have almost completely different gene patterns. In simple terms, the experiment could be used to prove kinship, a breakthrough that became better known as genetic fingerprinting or DNA profiling.

DNA had never been used in a criminal investigation but

CHAPTER TWENTY-SEVEN

Jeffreys said that it could be an extremely useful tool to help solve cases that had long gone cold. Still, likely for reasons of geography – the murders happened close to Leicester where Jeffreys worked – he got a call out of the blue from detectives hoping he may be able to help them prove that Buckland had killed both Dawn and Lynda.

After carrying out tests of Buckland's blood and matching it with semen obtained from the victims' bodies, the scientist told the police that, while their hypothesis that one man probably committed both murders was correct, that man was not Buckland. His tests showed that not only did Buckland not kill Lynda, he didn't murder Dawn either. The murder squad officers weren't overjoyed at the findings. "One minute we got the guy," said the senior investigating officer, according to the Guardian, "and the next we've got Jack shit."

Buckland was released after three months in custody and the search for a double killer was back at square one. Rather than write off the new technology, the detectives, desperate for a new breakthrough, asked Jeffreys if he would help provide a test screening of every male living around the area of the murders. DNA would be collected from blood samples taken from every man born between 1953 and 1970 who lived or worked in Narborough and the surrounding villages. The community, appalled at the savagery of the crimes, rallied behind the voluntary scheme and, apart from a few grumbles, turned up in numbers, providing more than 1,000 samples in the first month.

The case received international attention, with the *Los Angeles Times* reporting: "Police investigating the murders of two teenage girls near this small Midlands village are applying a new scientific technique. Some predict it could be the most significant breakthrough in resolving serious crime since fingerprinting was invented." Referencing opposition from some groups, including the National Council for Civil Liberties, *The Times* continued: "A strong sense of community outrage among close-knit villagers and an effective police public relations campaign effectively overcame apprehensions among some residents that the tests were an invasion of their personal rights."

A total of 5,511 men gave their DNA after eight months, with just one man refusing to provide a sample. Colin Pitchfork was among those listed as cooperating, but the test results revealed that none of the men matched the semen samples taken from the victims. The reason for this anomaly wasn't revealed until September 1987, when a colleague of Pitchfork named Ian Kelly told some mates in a Leicester pub that he had been persuaded to impersonate Pitchfork and take the test in his name. Pitchfork had told him that he couldn't give a sample because he'd pretended to be a friend who had a sex offender conviction and was worried that he'd come under suspicion for the killings.

One of the men in the pub reported the conversation to police and Pitchfork was arrested and charged with Dawn and Lynda's murders. When asked why he attacked Dawn, the baker is said to have replied, "Opportunity. She was there and I was there."

He also told police that when he raped and murdered Lynda, his baby son was asleep in his car parked nearby.

Without the genetic fingerprinting, police said Pitchfork may have never been caught and may have been free to strike again. He pleaded guilty to the two murders and was jailed for life on 22 January 1988, with a minimum recommendation of 30 years behind bars. His plea meant that the genetic evidence wasn't tested at the Leicester Crown Court hearing. "But the case had proved the potential usefulness of the then new discovery and the following year, DNA profiling would be front and centre at a high-profile trial at the Old Bailey – one of the first times Alec Jeffreys' discovery was ever used in a case at London's Central Criminal Court.

Jelinek would not have thought the case in Leicestershire had anything remotely to do with him, but it would turn out to have a significant impact on his future as a spy.

CHAPTER
TWENTY-EIGHT

Scotland Yard, London, 10 March 1988

Dame Stella Rimington was said to be the inspiration for Dame Judi Dench's portrayal of "M", the ruthlessly matriarchal intelligence agency boss in the James Bond movies. No doubt "M" would have come up with a successful plan if she was tasked with stopping a mysterious enemy spy hiding in plain sight in the middle of London. But Rimington, then head of MI5's counter espionage unit, had thrown the not inconsiderable might of the UK's secret service behind finding out what Jelinek was up to and had still drawn a blank. Worse than that, the combined forces of the domestic intelligence service, MI5, the foreign intelligence service, MI6 and Scotland Yard's Special Branch hadn't even been able to find out Erwin van Haarlem's real name.

As the months of surveillance went on and the costs mounted, the pressure grew on Rimington to pull the plug. But there was lingering concern that while they were looking and failing to find out what Van Haarlem was doing in London, he could do some real harm to Britain's interests. And nobody wanted that kind of embarrassment, especially not MI5 agents when they had him in their sights.

Agents and Special Branch officers had been following leads up and down the country, learning enough about Van Haarlem to know he was up to no good. They had established he was a spy working for the Czechs and that was never going to be good at a time when East-West relations were on a knife-edge.

Special Branch became aware of Van Haarlem's efforts to infiltrate Keston College, a Christian outreach organisation based in Kent. Keston College (now Institute) was founded in 1969 as the Centre for the Study of Religion and Communism and was seen by the KGB as one of the Cold War's most effective anti-Soviet organisations. It focused on repressed religions behind the Iron Curtain. It was regarded as the "voice of the voiceless" for many religions, Judaism in particular, that the Russians persecuted.

Detective Sergeant Geoff Lloyd, a language specialist attached to the team, had travelled to the college in Bromley after its founder, Michael Bordeaux, called to say he was suspicious about the motives of a new supporter, but the police could find nothing incriminating to further help build the case against Van Haarlem. It was yet another frustrating dead-end and offered no real clues to the spy's mission.

Information about institutions like Keston College was, of course, useful to the Soviets, but Rimington remained suspicious that there was a bigger purpose to Van Haarlem. There was some admiration among the officers in MI5 and MI6 for Van Haarlem's spycraft, his daring and chutzpah honed by the many years he had been in the UK. His professionalism as an old-school, skilled, by-the-book agent was also acknowledged. The big breakthrough that Rimington had hoped for hadn't yet materialised. The evidence on him was circumstantial at best. She didn't have the luxury of sitting back and reading thousands of pages of files, locked away in vaults in Prague, detailing intelligence plundered by Gragert.

After following Gragert around London for close to two years with little to show for it, MI5 was finally forced to act when it became clear the spy had worked out that he was being followed. Fearing Van Haarlem would fly the coop, Rimington finally pulled the trigger on the operation – codenamed Operation Orlando – and briefed the Special Branch officers to move in. The high-flying espionage chief would later usher in a new era of openness in the service when her name was published upon her announcement as the agency's first woman director general and she posed in front of the cameras on the release of a pamphlet detailing MI5's activities. But this mission was planned in absolute secrecy.

The spy's flat was almost certainly bugged, enabling the intelligence service listeners to know when he was transmitting to Prague. The service's last hope was to catch him in the act and give them something to hang a prosecution on. At the very least that would enable them to take him out of circulation and avoid the possibility of an embarrassing foreign spy incident in the English capital, even though nobody knew what that might be. In the end, Rimington made the decision that it was better to be safe than sorry.

CHAPTER
TWENTY-NINE

Friern Barnet, North London, Saturday,
2 April 1988

Inside the pleasant, nondescript flat on the second floor of a block in Friern Barnet, Agent Gragert was busy making himself some strong coffee. Outside, Special Branch Detective Constable Dainis Maris Ozols was silently putting a hydraulic ram into place by the front door. The spy had been up late watching television with a bottle of dark rum and slept in later than usual, so he was still in his pyjamas and barefoot when it was time for his pre-timed 9:10 am radio hook-up with his controllers.

He was sitting on a stool in the kitchen taking down a coded message from Prague when he spotted an unusual movement outside. By the time he heard a harsh whisper it was too late to hide his receiver. He could only crush the paper he was writing on and throw it under the counter when DS Ozols blasted open the front door and the first shouts of "police" filled the flat.

Special Branch officers barreled into Gragert's lair knowing that he could have a gun and would be prepared to use it. They needed to overwhelm the spy in just a few moments.

Special Branch Inspector Richard "Dickie" Bird grabbed Gragert from behind as he desperately tried to push down the antenna in a vain attempt to hide the obvious "Enough! It's over, it's over," shouted Bird.

Gragert reached for the knife drawer, thinking better of it as he saw he was outnumbered by the officers flooding through his front door and a second man, Superintendent Nigel Somers told him, "Erwin van Haarlem, I am arresting you on suspicion of espionage. Do not try anything. I have a gun."

Somers and Bird pinioned Gragert's arms behind his back while the radio continued to crackle. They told him he was being held for spying for a foreign power, or, more formally, for acts preparatory to the commission of an offence under Section One of the Official Secrets Act between 1 May 1975, and 2 April 1988.

All the time, the soft clatter of morse code played as a backdrop to the noisy interlopers. His earphone had dropped out after he jumped to his feet in surprise, knocking over the stool.

"Given how much of a shock this must have been to Van Haarlem at this early hour, I was very impressed by his cool reactions and thought at the time that this betrayed some military training," Ozols said later.

Ozols's 'day job' was in the European Liaison Section of Special Branch, handling enquiries with the Bundeskriminalamt (BKA) – the central German police division liaising over Provisional IRA targeting of British servicemen. He was called in for some weekend overtime for the swoop on an Eastern Bloc spy. He was to spend three days sifting through Gragert's flat in suburbia and thinking to himself it was an unlikely place for a spy to live.

Detectives found six one-time pads, a disposable encryption method then used by spies to decipher messages and then throw them away. Jelinek wasn't sure whether to be flattered by the numbers deployed to arrest him or shocked by the overkill. Uppermost in his mind was the necessity to dispose of a report on Keston College, the anti-Soviet college in Kent, that he was planning to send to his controllers that morning. It wasn't especially interesting, but he knew it would be seen as damning evidence by the police.

Jelinek's report on the college was already encrypted and hidden in a toilet roll in his bathroom. Other than asking the Special Branch officers Bird and Somers to report his arrest to the Czech embassy (not, the officers quickly noted, the Dutch embassy), Jelinek had refused to say anything about espionage accusations. But before he was led out of his flat he had one other request, even simpler than his first. He needed to go to the toilet.

To his surprise, they allowed him to go and, although a detective was assigned to watch him, Jelinek – ever the true professional – defecated loudly and used the secret message to wipe his behind before flushing it down the toilet.

The Keston College report was never found. Investigators did, however, make one discovery in that same bathroom. Knowing the officers would turn his flat upside down, Jelinek tried to put them off the scent by admitting, "I think what you want is in the soap in that drawer." Concealed inside a bar of soap were "one-time pads" used for decoding messages.

There was nothing else unusual about the modern, tidy flat with just a couple of antiques. As hard as the Special Branch officers looked, they couldn't find Gragert's "escape kit," which would have contained false passports and money, as well as other falsified documents and possibly a firearm.

Before he was taken from the flat, Bird had an offer for

Jelinek that would mean his life would go on as normal, on the surface at least. If he agreed to work with MI5 as a double agent, there would be no police station, no trial. It would be as if the raid never happened; he could even attend a friend's Passover celebration he had been invited to that evening. "If you cooperate, nothing has to happen," said Bird. "No court, no jail, an officer rank, a secret identity. But you have to make up your mind now."

The ultimatum came as no surprise to Jelinek. He was very well-versed in counterespionage tactics and acutely aware of the primary goal when an enemy agent is uncovered: try to turn them against their masters. They'd already tried to turn him once and he still wasn't turning. "I already made my mind up a long time ago," he told Bird calmly. "Many years ago."

Jelinek nodded his head, walked out and got into the waiting police car, knowing that any escape plans he had made were now compromised by his arrest. He no longer had the freedom to leave the country under another passport, another name. As a diplomat he would have had immunity from prosecution, but as an illegal he had nothing and nobody. He knew the Czech embassy officials would deny any knowledge of him. They wouldn't be fooling the British or anybody else for that matter, but those were the rules of the game. Lie and deny.

Ozols remembered that the media was quickly on the scene. "Somebody at the local police station must have alerted the press at some stage, as a few reporters turned up outside to watch us loading seized material into our vehicle," he said. "I am guessing that station staff would have rightly considered it unusual that a Special Branch Superintendent had detained a foreigner at Friern Barnet under the Official Secrets Act." It was screaming headlines for news desks and print rooms in

Fleet Street rolling out millions of copies every night. Delivery vans for *The Times, the Daily Mail, Daily Mirror, Daily Express* and many others would soon deliver the papers and news of a MI5 coup countrywide.

~

Gragert was taken first to Rochester Row Police Station and then to Brixton Prison. At both locations, officers attempted to grill him, but he remembered his training well.

When he was asked if he was a spy, he turned to his solicitor, Dennis Lynch, an on-duty free legal adviser, to ask for the definition of the word. Having received the explanation, he said, "I would like to emphasise that I have never intended to damage or create damage to the interests of the United Kingdom Government nor its people." He refused to answer when asked if he had been working against the interests of any other government or group.

To virtually every other question, he answered, "I refuse to answer that question at this stage."

Gragert did not confide in Lynch, believing him to be in league with Scotland Yard. He didn't need legal training to know that the evidence they had against him was largely circumstantial. He had been careful to cover his tracks in the months since he first suspected he was being followed. He would even try to claim that the morse code receiver was a method of staying in touch with the Refuseniks. He felt certain none of his dead letter drops were compromised. He had drawn maps indicating his boxes for his superiors, but that important and incriminating intel was always delivered to one of his dead letter boxes. Very little would remain in his flat. Every message he had sent arrived without a problem. There were no witnesses, no Mata Hari, no compromising wiretaps, or at least none that could be used in court.

Jelinek gave them the answer to just one question at Rochester Row. Bird wanted to know why he kept two identical hammers in his apartment, and what they were for. The spy, a keen jogger, said he used them instead of dumbbells and ran with one in each hand to strengthen his arms. The Yard man didn't believe him for a second.

Jelinek was asked if Erwin van Haarlem was his real name or his cover. He didn't answer. He certainly wasn't going to volunteer the information. It was the one thing he still had control over. When Jelinek arrived at Brixton Prison, officers ordered him to take off his jacket, shirt, trousers and shoes and put on the standard brown prison uniform with a pale blue striped shirt and gave him a numbered metal box to store his clothes. The box was numbered 007. The reference to Ian Fleming's suave secret agent with a licence to kill was obvious, albeit probably coincidental. It was hardly the kind of connection to the spy for which Jelinek had hoped.

An MI5 officer who quizzed Erwin in prison reported, "Van Haarlem claimed to be well aware that his television had been 'fiddled' with, that he had been frequently followed by a silver Mercedes, and that Service personnel 'were in and out of his flat quite often'."

Jelinek was taken from his cell for a meeting with Lynch, his lawyer, and Special Branch Inspector Bird. "I want you to give a blood sample," Bird told him, getting up to leave. "I will leave you to consult with your lawyer."

Jelinek insisted later that Lynch had advised that it would look better for him to throw the police a bone and agree to the request – although according to Gragert he offered nothing to substantiate the advice. It was just the police and intelligence service ticking boxes, he said, and the odds were that this new-fangled DNA testing wouldn't amount to anything.

This wasn't an issue that came up in any of his training sessions. He was a good soldier, although he undoubtedly saw himself as an officer. He was a colonel in rank, after all. He knew what not to say but this was a tricky one. Few people knew about the power of DNA, or how it might be used in court. He couldn't message Prague for instructions from his jail cell, although it is unlikely that they would have any better advice for him. In all Lynch's years working London's courts, this had never come up. What was the harm? So, Jelinek agreed, and the doctor was there in a matter of minutes.

The spy had made a crucial operational mistake.

~

Johanna was in her kitchen in Schaijk preparing lunch when the phone rang at about 2pm on 3 April 1988. It was Scotland Yard calling from London. They wanted to fly out to see her.

CHAPTER THIRTY

Schaijk, Holland, 6 April 1988.

There was a knock on the door of Johanna's family home in Schaijk. The past had come back to haunt her yet again and this time with a terrible vengeance. Two Scotland Yard officers told her that her son had been arrested for espionage. They said he was working for the Czech StB intelligence service and, by inference, for Russia's KGB.

For three days, Johanna had been trying to find out what had happened to Erwin after she heard the BBC's Jennie Bond reporting the arrest. She'd expected a call from her son explaining the whole thing was a mistake, but the call never came. When she asked the Dutch Embassy for help, they said they knew nothing about him.

She was shell-shocked and disbelieving. Her Erwin would never do such things, and she vowed to support him and stand by him whatever their evidence. Her son had gone through enough in his life without the support of his mother. This time it would be different.

The deep sense of guilt that Johanna had spent the past

decade trying to assuage was once again overwhelming her every waking moment. It suited her to believe that Erwin had overcome the circumstances of his childhood to succeed beyond even her wildest dreams.

As much as she'd wanted to know everything about her son, every hardship was like a self-inflicted knife to her heart. She'd pressed him, but not too much. His evasiveness was often an unintended kindness. As hard as it was for Johanna to admit, it was easier not to know. The visceral shock she'd felt at first learning of his alleged secret life had slowly turned to disbelief. The news headlines were sensational, but the more she thought about the accusations the less she decided she really cared. It didn't feel real. The story read like the plot of a Le Carré novel. What difference did it make to her if he was spying on the English for the Czechs, or even for the Russians? He was not hurting anybody, and she had seen much worse. Her family had done much worse…

~

The British police at her door wanted to know everything about her relationship with her son, down to the tiniest detail. He'd stayed in her home, had he not?

Sitting in her kitchen, the spring sunshine fading outside as she spoke, Johanna told her story once again, from her wartime relationship with German soldier Gregor Kulig and her family's fraternisation with the Nazis through her flight and subsequent abandonment of her son in Czechoslovakia to her renewed search for him and their reunion as mother and son.

The officers told her they didn't believe anything Erwin had told them… and that included his name. The police informed her that she might be called as a witness at her son's trial.

For the first time, a terrible question rushed into her mind. Are they telling me he's not my son? The thought had never fully occurred to her before, not even when she noticed the colour of his eyes. She had wanted him to be her son so badly that she had convinced herself the difference in his eye colour was normal. Had she been wrong? Were they lying eyes? The idea of it held her for a moment and then she shook her head. That's preposterous, she thought. Of course, he's my son.

The detectives were polite, but they had a job to do. They asked if the man charged with serious espionage offences had given her any photos of himself as a boy with his adoptive parents and she told them he'd spoken sparingly about his past. No, that didn't surprise her, she told them. She had discovered Erwin had experienced a difficult childhood, and he didn't want to cause more pain for his mother by talking about it. Their attitude annoyed her, and she quickly made her loyalties clear to her visitors. She had let her son down once; she wasn't about to do it again.

"I can't believe what you are telling me," she told her questioners. "I know my Erwin is a good man. I believe in him – and I'll do everything I can to prove his innocence."

Even if he did the things they claimed, she told herself, she would stand by his side. It had taken so long to find him; she wasn't going to lose him again.

When they finally got up to leave, their notebooks full, it was pitch-black outside in the countryside with no street lights, and Johanna was exhausted.

"One last thing," one of the men said to her as she showed him out. "Would you mind giving us a blood sample? It's just routine. And it may help support his story." Johanna agreed to give her blood to a doctor who would be booked by the detectives.

As soon as the English detectives left, Johanna called the number she had been given for Erwin's lawyer and offered her help in clearing his name. She also wrote a letter to her son and begged the lawyer to pass it on. It read:

> Dear Erwin,
>
> *I do not know what to say. What can I do? Everything is full of questions. But no one (including you) can take away how I feel about you or how I long to see you again. Remember that no matter what happens, my heart is always with you.*
>
> *Your loving*
>
> *Mother*

She still believed in him. Just.

CHAPTER
THIRTY-ONE

Metropolitan Police Laboratory, London,
19 April 1988

Erwin van Haarlem's letter arrived three days after Johanna received the results of the blood tests from John Edward Bark at the Metropolitan Police Laboratory. She had barely spoken to anybody during that time. Her mind was a cauldron of anger and despair and the absolute agony of knowing that her past had caught up with her once again to punish her.

She asked herself repeatedly what she had done to deserve this. She tried so hard and for so long to atone for the sins she had been told she committed as a young girl in a time of turbulence. As much as she regretted giving up her baby son to the Czech Red Cross, she knew there was very little choice. She'd had a domineering father and few resources beyond whatever he deigned to give her.

And yet, against all the odds, she had found her son again. But now, it seemed, she had not.

The 19 April 1988 report was on the table in front of her and she had read it over and over in the hope of discovering a different meaning. But the findings were devastatingly clear. Science cared nothing for the feelings of a mother.

She read the report one more time. It was saying that almost certainly, Erwin – this Erwin – was not her son. It wasn't even close. He was, essentially, a stranger. Up until a few moments before, she thought he was her son. Now she didn't know who he was. According to Scotland Yard, this mystery man had another biological mother, a mother of his own who wasn't her.

She stood up to clear her head and sat back down again. Not again, she thought. Please don't let me lose him again.

"These samples were examined using a DNA profiling technique to determine whether Erwin van HAARLEM was the son of Mrs. van HAARLEM," the report read with capital letters blaring out the Van Haarlem name like some sort of highly infectious plague.

It continued to explain this new science: "DNA is a substance found in most body cells, including certain cells in the blood. The chemical structure of DNA determines the expression of inherited characteristics, and differences between individuals are therefore shown in the chemical structure of their DNA.

"DNA profiling is a technique that analyses differences in the chemical structure of DNA between individuals. Therefore, this method can be used to determine the likelihood that an individual is the parent of a child.

"The profiles received show that it is 1,800 times more likely that Ms van Haarlem is not the mother of Erwin van Haarlem."

In case it wasn't clear enough, Bark explained in simple terms, "That is why I conclude that it is extremely unlikely that Erwin van Haarlem is Mrs van Haarlem's son."

Johanna kept coming back to his eyes. His brown eyes. Her eyes were blue and so were Gregor Kulig's. She remembered that much about him. When he was born, Erwin's eyes were also a pure, piercing blue. Everybody noticed that about him as a baby. But the man who claimed to be the adult Erwin had dull brown irises. Was that, along with the letter before her, enough proof that the man she thought was Erwin was truly an impostor? She didn't know. She'd read that some children's eye colour could change right up until they were six years old and sometimes even older. Some babies hardly had any pigment in their irises when they were born. More melanin – the pigment that colours the skin – tends to accumulate in the iris in the baby's first few months and it wasn't unusual for the eye colour to change from blue to brown in the first six months. It was less common for blue eyes to turn to brown after that, but not unheard of.

When she was reunited with the man who claimed to be Erwin, there was so much lost time to make up that Johanna didn't dwell on the issue. It was a miracle that she had found him, and it wasn't such a stretch, she thought, to believe that some smaller miracles played into that life-changing event.

Now she couldn't escape from his eyes. They haunted her.

But Johanna wasn't a person who was easily moved. She had committed so many years to finding Erwin and loving the man she believed to be her son that she wasn't going to allow a fledgling scientist to throw her off course, even if Erwin did have the wrong-coloured eyes.

After two days with her curtains drawn, unable to face the possibility that she could have been so wrong, Johanna called Superintendent Nigel Somers, the Special Branch officer in charge of the investigation. Johanna didn't do self-pity for long. Her strongest traits were resilience and the will to fight against all the odds. She told Somers she would not be giving evidence for the prosecution. She didn't care what the police said, Erwin was her son, and she would stand by him through everything they threw at him. If they wanted her to take sides, then she had chosen. She was on his.

With that, Johanna put down the phone and decided her only option was to fly to London as soon as possible and visit Erwin in prison. She would ask him straight. She didn't care whether he was a spy or who he was spying for. She would ask him to his face if he was her son. That was what truly mattered to her. If he said that he was, then she wouldn't ask again.

She opened the blinds and picked up her pen to write him a letter to let him know she supported him no matter what.

Dear Erwin,

I sent you a postcard yesterday, but I had no idea how the blood tests turned out. Did the news hit you as hard as it did me? And what consequences will it have for your defence? The fifty pounds still hasn't arrived. I still don't understand why you're giving it back to me right away. Of course, I understand that you have money, and you are enough, but you understand that I am not in need either. I understand from the information from your legal representative that you will be very busy when he receives the relevant materials. So I will leave the date of my next visit to London to him. I think he has every right to request the collection of new samples and their independent examination. What do you think? If you agree, I will come to London when you say. But the tests will take a while. I'd rather you were free already. Is there a way to speed up your dismissal or justify it in another way? Please, write to me how you view this "blood feud". It is a terrible blow to me.

Your loving Mother

It was several months before Johanna received a reply. The

tone was distant and formal. It was as if she had received a letter from a stranger. She felt like she'd been hit over the head with a hammer.

I can well imagine your surprise and disappointment after receiving the results of the blood test. I myself had to come to terms with it, however we must accept the facts, even if our minds and hearts refuse to believe it. The results say that it is possible you are my biological mother, but the probability is low.

The letter dated 29 July 1988, was from Erwin. If he appeared nonplussed by the results, he continued in a more perfunctory, accusatory tone, writing:

Perhaps you should contact the home in Czechoslovakia where you deposited your child.

They might try to contact the persons who were at that time together with me as children in that home. Alternatively, you could contact the maternity hospital in Amsterdam where you gave birth. Maybe similar blood tests could be arranged. But even so, you could never be sure, because as you can see the present blood tests are not reliable. They can stipulate the probability but do not eliminate for sure and as a matter of fact they leave quite a big margin.

As for the accuracy of the test, I don't see any reason why the test should be repeated. Even so that the MI5 officers are not my favourites at present, we can safely credit them that they didn't falsify the result. Not that they wouldn't be able to twist the result, oh yes, they would, but in my particular case, they wouldn't gain anything from that. I was raised as Erwin van Haarlem and they are trying to solve a case of espionage and not that of a mistaken identity.

I would be very sorry to lose you as a mother because I grew to like you through the years and if you can't be my mother perhaps I can keep you as my friend. I certainly would like to see you again but if you don't feel like travelling to London I will understand.

I hope that you appreciate that under prevailing circumstances, I am unable to visit you in Holland.

The present case is really my problem only and shouldn't involve you anymore.

I wished I could help you in the difficult times you are going through but there is very little I could do for you. I am facing the same dilemma as you do.

The letter finishes formally, with...

Yours sincerely

Erwin van Haarlem.

But the real hammer blow came right at the beginning. In every previous letter he had written to her he had started with the endearment, Dear Mother.

This one began, *Dear Mrs van Haarlem.*

CHAPTER THIRTY-TWO

Brixton Prison, South London, 31 July 1988

In the waiting room at Brixton Prison, Johanna once again felt the past crushing her. Her father had suffered the shame of imprisonment for his collaboration with the Nazis during the war. Now she was visiting the sins of the man she had believed to be her son. Imprisonment and shame again.

She had barely slept for months since getting the blood results. Erwin's cold letters had shaken her absolute resolve to stand by him. She paced around her small house in Schaijk through the nights, trying to marshal her fractured thoughts, running sepia scenes of family life during the past decade through her mind, seeking some light from the projector memories.

Why was she so ready to accept a man who looked nothing much like herself or the doomed soldier she knew so fleetingly? Was everything he told her a lie? If not, then how would she ever know? If this Erwin was not her son, then who was he? And where was her real son? It was easier for her to believe in him than to contemplate the fact that he had made a lie of her life.

Initially, he refused to see her, but she insisted and he relented.

When she was finally allowed in to see him, he looked thin and pale in his brown prison suit. They hugged and she clutched him even closer to her than usual, desperate for him to know that whatever happened in the past, he could count on her now. Her younger son, Hans, was with her. He looked bemused at being taken to see a big brother who, in some ways, had overshadowed his own life. It's never easy to have a sibling who commands so much of the spotlight. It wasn't just that Johanna was losing a son; Hans was losing a brother, too.

Johanna and Jelinek sat down facing one another in the cramped room and, for the first time since they had met, Johanna didn't know what to say. For his part, Jelinek sat staring straight ahead, making no attempt at conversation. There was more at play than hurt feelings. Special Branch would not have cared too much about the spy's relationship to Johanna; they needed evidence of his double life and exposing this one big lie would help persuade a jury that he was also lying about everything else.

"I just wanted to let you know that I'm there for you," Johanna said finally, looking around to see if the guard could hear. "Even if you are a spy."

It was Jelinek's turn for a wry smile, but he seemed indifferent to Johanna's evident discomfort. It may have been prudent for him to keep Johanna believing in him for his defence case, but he no longer had any appetite for the deception.

As much as she wanted to offer her support, she also wanted him to confide in her and say if he was, indeed, a Czech intelligence agent. She begged him to tell her the truth. Or at least a truth she could believe in. "Tell me, I'm hearing all these strange stories," she said. "You're not really a spy, are you?"

"We have a saying that where you see the smoke, there will be a fire," he said quietly and stood up, gesturing to the guard that he was ready to leave. "But this time it is not true. Too much of the smoke and no fire. I did absolutely nothing that could harm England."

But what about me? she thought. Did you do anything to harm me? She had read his letter. His half-hearted attempt to deny the blood test results and to suggest they were faked. She didn't really know who to believe, but she was still prepared to believe in Erwin.

All he had to do was to look at her with those brown eyes and tell her he was her son.

Johanna looked up and into his eyes without flinching. She had seen too much misery in her life to look away now. But she saw neither the blue eyes of her baby son nor the soft brown eyes of the man she spent much of her adult life searching for.

She saw the cold, hard eyes of a professional liar.

And he was the one to look away first.

"When we finally made eye contact, I felt hurt," Johanna said later. "I didn't see any sign of remorse, not a wink, no warmth, nothing. He showed me coldness and looked at me like this was the end."

~

Back in Prague, Jelinek's handlers were busy covering the tracks of their failed agent. Country first, agent second, had been drilled into them. His painstakingly and expensively created legend was blown. There would be no viable rescue operation from behind the walls of Brixton Prison. It was time to deceive and confuse as British counterintelligence, through GCHQ, locked onto their radio wavelengths, hoping to discover something about Van Haarlem's activities. Jelinek always knew it could happen but now he truly understood what his spymasters had always told him. He'd been caught. And now he was on his own.

~

In the waiting room at Brixton jail there were no hugs as Johanna and Hans left. He was not her son; she knew that now. His eyes had finally given him away. She resolved right then and there that she would make him pay for the humiliation he caused her. Worse, much worse than that, he had wasted more than 10 years of her life, and she was now no closer to finding the real Erwin than she was when her father banned her from bringing him home. She left Brixton Prison and took out a business card that Special Branch Superintendent Nigel Somers had given her. As soon as she arrived back at her hotel room, she picked up the phone and dialled Somers' number. She had changed her mind, she told him. Having met face-to-face the man calling himself Erwin, she no longer believed he was her flesh and blood. She would testify against him in court.

From that moment on, Johanna would no longer call him Erwin or her son. She would refer to him simply as "The Liar".

CHAPTER
THIRTY-THREE

Court 1, The Old Bailey, London,
27 February 1989

Erwin van Haarlem finally got his name mentioned in the same sentence as royalty, but it wasn't the kind of recognition he was hoping for, and it certainly wasn't the kind of privileged address he was instructed to infiltrate when he first arrived in London. On 27 February 1989, indictment number 881100 appeared on the docket at London's Central Criminal Court, better known as the Old Bailey, as The Queen v Erwin van Haarlem.

The particulars of the charge were that on diverse days between the 1st day of May 1975 and the 2nd day of April 1988 for a purpose prejudicial to the safety or interests of the State he did acts preparatory to communicating to another person information which was calculated to be or might have been or was intended to be directly or indirectly useful to an enemy.

(i) By residing in the United Kingdom.

(ii) By having in his possession equipment for the receipt of secret information.

(iii) By receiving secret radio transmissions from a person or persons in Czechoslovakia.

(iv) By having in his possession materials for the communication of secret/information to others.

(v) By having in his possession a list of places in the United Kingdom at which secret information could be left or collected.

(vi) By using a false identity.

The final "particular" was only added in handwriting to the official charge sheet after the results of the DNA tests became clear. The Director of Public Prosecutions at the time believed the new genetic science was ready to be tested in court. It would prove crucial when the case eventually went to the jury.

On Monday, 27 February 1989, Van Haarlem – for that was the name he was charged under – took his seat in the wood-panelled dock at the Old Bailey minutes before the jury was led into the courtroom. Gragert was smartly dressed in a navy pin-striped suit and tie. At 43, his healthy good looks had gone, replaced by a prison pallor. While some of The 35s were in court to give evidence for the prosecution, no friends appeared to support Gragert in court. After all, he didn't have any. By contrast, the press benches were full, as was the public gallery. Publicity over the arrest had sparked widespread interest in the case, especially as it was rare for such a prosecution to go to trial.

He was sitting in the same dock at London's Central Criminal Court where notorious poisoner Dr Crippen, the murderous Kray gangster twins, serial killer Peter Sutcliffe, better known as the "Yorkshire Ripper" for killing so many women, and many more blood-curdling characters had finally met justice. Now it was his turn.

Erwin van Haarlem pleaded not guilty to the charges brought against him in the name of The Queen. And during the course of the week-long trial, the prosecution ripped away the fabricated tissues that he had created until he had just one lie left that nobody could crack.

His name.

It was the first time in British legal history that a defendant had appeared in the dock at the Old Bailey with his identity a mystery. Of course, it wasn't his only secret. He faced charges of espionage so serious that parts of his case would be heard in private on grounds of protecting the national interest. The spy is not the only one to jealously guard their secrets; governments also have much to hide when the nation's intelligence services are discussed in open court.

The judge, Simon-Brown, had already agreed to an application by Van Haarlem's barrister Nigel Salts for Jewish people to be excluded from the jury panel on the grounds they may be biased against him because of his betrayal of the Soviet Jewry groups. When Gragert faced the jury of his peers there were no Jews among the five men and seven women selected.

After the defendant officially lodged his not guilty plea, it was time for Roy Amlot, the prosecutor, to lay out his case against the man calling himself Van Haarlem, who sat, impassionate, watching the proceedings going on around him with a wry smile. He was amused by the "black theatrical costumes" and white wigs of the lawyers and thought of the prosecutor as a "vain flute". He was doing what he had been trained to do. To never show weakness, say nothing.

Amlot was an experienced criminal barrister who took the biggest Crown cases of the time and threw everything he had at the man facing him in the dock.

"You will be shown evidence that he has been receiving secret messages on a regular basis from the Prague area since 1975. The Crown alleges he is a secret agent working in this country for the Czech secret service.

"We say he is what is known as an 'illegal', an officer of a hostile agency operating abroad under a false identity and using clandestine methods. He would be given many years of training before being assigned to the West. Although the Crown can point to the evidence of his communicating information to Czechoslovakia, we cannot establish what he was sending or what he intended in the future to send."

Although Amlot claimed Van Haarlem had sent more than 200 coded messages to his spymasters, all written in a series of five-figure numbers on one-time pads of the kind found hidden in the soap bar, he admitted British intelligence experts had only managed to crack the last one. The one message found for Gragert read, according to Amlot: "Prepared the report for handover in Vienna, repeat Vienna. Indicate how you use the micro-file. Regarding immigration, use your initiative."

Amlot went on to claim that authorities had also found information about companies involved in the Star Wars defence project at Gragert's flat, along with details about how to obtain British citizenship. A piece of paper found in Van Haarlem's wallet had a list of supposed dead letter boxes around London, one of them the Minstrel Boy pub in Colney Hatch, which had the suitably Soviet codeword "Marx".

It was hardly George Smiley and the jury, while engaged, wasn't transfixed. Van Haarlem's claims to MI5 and to his own lawyers that the evidence against him was flimsy at best didn't seem so far off the mark. The spy in the dock felt empowered by the famed British secret services' failure to discover all of what he had been doing in their country for more than a decade. The gathered evidence seemed especially miniscule compared to the fat file about his intelligence successes stored in a top-secret building in Prague.

Undeterred, Amlot continued to present the ordinary looking man in the dock as an important spy. Amlot detailed the 10 to 12 bank accounts in Van Haarlem's name and the sums of money he received that were unaccounted for by his "charade" of working as an art dealer specialising in miniatures. He talked about the defendant pretending to be pro-Jewish to pass on secrets about The 35s work helping Jewish dissidents in Russia.

In the dock, Van Haarlem doodled on a piece of paper, drawing the courtroom, until it was grabbed by his lawyers who were worried the impromptu artwork could incriminate him in some way. It wasn't just the would-be spy whose future was on the line who seemed bored by the proceedings; the jury was also dulled by the lack of fireworks in the evidence.

But the atmosphere in Court One of the Old Bailey changed with a jolt when Amlot told the jury about Johanna van Haarlem's heartbreaking search to find her son.

"Hers is a tragic story," he told the court. "She is Dutch and in her early 60s. In the war she had a child by a German soldier who was killed in 1944 at the Battle of Caen. Her father would not tolerate an association with a German and threw her out."

Jelinek looked on impassively as Amlot described the story of Johanna's long-sought after reunion with the man she believed to be her son. She couldn't be in the courtroom to hear her story because, keeping her word to Somers, she'd been called to give evidence for the prosecution and was sitting outside on a court bench. Amlot had finally captured the jury's full attention and they were hanging on every word.

After DNA exposed his deception, Amlot said, the spy wrote "what can only be described as a cold letter addressing her for the first time as Mrs Van Haarlem, not his mother, and expressing the hope that they could be friends.

"The Crown says as an agent he has been given a false identity of someone else and cynically persisted in that identity after Mrs Van Haarlem's independent investigations led to him. If she is not his mother, then the whole basis of his account to police is false.

"You may think that if he knew all along that he was not her son it was a cruel thing to do to her."

The jury suddenly looked at Gragert in a new way. They may not have especially cared about the nature of his spying; they may not have been convinced he was really doing too much harm. That was the message his calm confidence in the dock was meant to impart; what's all this fuss about? But they understood a son being cruel to his mother and this was much worse than that. This was the cruelest of deceits.

The jury and the press were still caught up in the heartbreaking story of a Dutch mother who wasn't in court for the opening. But Johanna van Haarlem was still in a corridor outside the court waiting patiently to give her testimony against the man she no longer believed to be her son. And she was up next.

CHAPTER THIRTY-FOUR

Court 1, The Old Bailey, London,
27 February 1989

Johanna could feel the 12 jurors watching her intently from the silence at the side of the high-ceilinged, wood-beamed Court No. 1 at the Old Bailey. A man in the public gallery coughed relentlessly but otherwise all the attention was on her. She felt like a late middle-aged woman who was foolish enough to believe there could be a happy ending when everything she had seen in her life pointed to the opposite.

She glanced up at the only eyes she was interested in, but he was looking away. He knew her story and had no interest in her now. The stranger she had known as Erwin van Haarlem sat in the dock as if he was in a Parisian café with an air of disdain for his surroundings and especially for her.

When she heard he had been arrested in West London, she flew in from Holland hoping to help him, but now she was there to bury him, even if that meant being judged herself. She had been judged before and judged harshly. Nothing could ever be as bad.

Amlot, his rosy cheeks at odds with the dirty grey of his horsehair wig, tried to catch her attention as she settled her mind back into the past. It was 4:45pm, towards the end of the first day's session, and the jury's attention had once more been wavering.

"Mrs Van Haarlem, can you please tell the court your full name?"

"Johanna Hendrika van Haarlem."

"And Mrs Van Haarlem, do you see the accused in this court?"

She nodded.

"Would you point him out, please?"

She pointed to the small, dapper man with a Beatles haircut and a sharp face who was sitting across the room in the vast wooden dock. He showed no sign of recognition.

"Mrs Van Haarlem," said the prosecutor, leading her eyes back to his, "can you tell the court, in your own words, about your relationship with the defendant and how that came about?"

She wanted to run, to escape, to be anywhere else but she stayed, just as she did at home as a young girl in The Hague when the Germans rolled in with their tanks and their certainty. Whatever happened there would be a price to be paid for telling her story. There always was.

Johanna looked across the court and this time he met her eyes. There was no love there. It wasn't that he hadn't heard her story before – they had pored over it together countless times – but as she recounted it again, she thought she detected the slightest sign of guilt. It was so hard to tell. His eyes were now such a mystery to her; she searched them once more for the slightest tint of blue. She'd looked so many times, hoping against hope, but now she couldn't get close enough to him to see. He was displaying that blank look she always took to be a protection from the past. Now she wasn't so sure, it may have been more practised than pained. It was only when he looked away that she recognised his expression for what it really was – contempt.

She told her story. Their story. After all that she'd been through, all they had been through, she still couldn't believe that it had come to this.

The coughing had stopped in the public gallery and a woman in the jury with a kind face smiled at her. It was the first time Johanna realised her own face was wet with tears.

"Would you like a break, Mrs Van Haarlem?" The judge spoke quietly, as if they were alone in his chambers, and she shook her head. She knew that if she left the court she would never return.

Johanna became lost in her thoughts again, this time at the happy memories, the happiest in her life, all given to her by the man in the dock. He was looking down and studying his hands, hiding his expression. She knew there would be no shame but hoped at least for a little understanding.

The sensibly dressed Dutch mother in her 60s took a deep breath. She still couldn't believe that she was there, the star witness for the prosecution against the man she thought had finally made her life complete. Erwin van Haarlem, the lost son she thought she had found.

Johanna had believed in him, she had trusted him and loved him.

Johanna's entrance had caused a shift in the courtroom that couldn't be described in a stenographer's notebook. As hard as the prosecutor tried to portray Gragert to the jury in a bad light, he had charmed them into having reasonable doubt over the espionage accusations. Could such an ordinary, pleasant man really be a spy? The film noir subterfuge of dead letter drops, one-time pads, ciphers, and codes the prosecutor described him as using in his work spying for the StB seemed more mundane in real time. What kind of secrets would a Hilton waiter really have to send over on a radio from his kitchen in Friern Barnet?

But the defendant had lost his bluster since Johanna took her oath vowing to tell nothing but the truth and stood across from the dock to accuse him. Watching a mother's heart breaking in front of them had changed the mood among the five men and seven women who would decide Gragert's fate.

The prosecutor was hesitant to break the spell, but Johanna had once again become lost in the past. He coughed politely and she got the message and carried on.

Johanna could feel the spy's eyes boring into the back of her head as she walked slowly out of the courtroom. Everyone could sense that he had lost the room, even the judge. It was no longer a farcical circus with Jelinek rolling his eyes at the evidence and mocking the prosecution case with a tight sneer of a smile and a raised eyebrow. He had searched for Joanna's eyes from the dock as she stood to leave, but this time it was her who looked away. She couldn't bear to waste another moment on him.

~

Next in the witness box was Rita Eker, who had trusted Erwin and showed him only kindness. Now she was terrified. She told the jury how he had used her and her organisation to betray Jews in Russia, but it was obvious the jury's thoughts were still with Johanna. So were Eker's. She looked over at him once and swore she could see the evil in him. She was so frightened she didn't look at him again.

Afterwards, outside the court, she sat on a bench that backed onto another bench. Johanna was sitting behind her. She leaned around to ask if she was Mrs Van Haarlem and how she was coping.

"Yes," Johanna told her. "I was supposed to be his mother."

Eker sensed that Johanna, too, was frightened and felt a barrier around her. She didn't want to talk any further.

Michael Carmi, the doctor who had travelled across the Soviet Union with the man he thought was his friend, was also called to give evidence. He'd been driving home from a family celebration with wife, Louise, when he heard of Erwin's arrest on the car radio.

Later, a Special Branch officer called, asking to talk to them about Erwin van Haarlem. When they agreed, he was at their house within minutes. He spent eight hours at their kitchen table asking questions about their relationship with the spy. He was especially interested to hear that they'd been for dinner with Erwin at his flat not long before the arrest and that he'd cooked them wild mushroom soup. His choice of vegetable wasn't a coincidence.

"We were gutted to learn that he had been lying to us all that time," said Michael. "We had to assume that everything we did to help the Refuseniks was being passed onto his controllers. Once we found out what Erwin was doing, we obviously worried about who else we put in jeopardy. What did he report back to his masters about them?"

"Absolutely we could have put people's lives in danger in Russia without realising it," said Louise later.

Jelinek hadn't just been lying to Johanna – he'd been lying to everybody.

And everyone in Court One at the Old Bailey knew it.

CHAPTER THIRTY-FIVE

Court 1, The Old Bailey, London,
1 March 1989

MI5 was keenly aware it needed to build on the emotional impact of Johanna's story to convince the jury that Erwin van Haarlem – or whoever he was – was, indeed, a spy.

Johanna's testimony had gone even better than the prosecution had dared to hope, but they needed to button down the importance of the spy's espionage and make the jury understand how much of a threat he posed to the security of the country. Being a liar wasn't enough to guarantee a conviction.

Rimington made the difficult decision to take the stand. In the 1980s – as it is to this day – it was virtually unheard of for Security Service personnel to give evidence in court. Such a path to conviction was extreme for a service that relied so completely on its cloak of anonymity. Nevertheless, the prosecution considered it crucial to the success of the prosecution case that the jury be given a credible motive for Van Haarlem's presence in London as a spy.

After hearing the evidence of prosecution witnesses, few

doubted that the man claiming to be Erwin van Haarlem was a spy, despite his lawyer's early attempts to convince the courtroom that the prosecution was something of a farce. The judge, prosecution, probably defence lawyers, the public watching in the court who had been reading about the case in their newspapers, and even the jury – they all knew. But there was a very real fear at MI5 and the Crown Prosecution Service that the jurors would not be convinced that the evidence of his crimes was worthy of a weighty conviction.

Apart from his deception of Johanna van Haarlem, which was powerfully damning, did he really harm anybody? As he had gone to great pains to insist to his interrogators, he had not intended any harm to Britain. Had he? He was a spy who knew how to cover his tracks. He was confident, bordering on arrogant, and his courtroom demeanour suggested he had few fears about the jury's ultimate decision. Johanna's testimony may have shaken him, but he gave no outward sign that he was overly concerned. His only reaction had been to shake his head and look down when she got to the part where she learned of his betrayal.

Stella Rimington would tell the jury in person what it needed to know – the threat Van Haarlem posed to the security of the nation. And so it was that the press and public were cleared from the Old Bailey on the third day of the trial for a witness known only at the time as "Miss J" to give evidence. The judge described Rimington only as a "very senior and experienced person involved in intelligence". To help shield her identity, Rimington also wore a disguise involving a curly wig and heavy make-up that made her look 10 years older. Her clothing was very unlike her usual elegant style. She found it to be a disorienting experience and thought she looked rather like

Agatha Christie's Miss Marple. It all felt faintly ridiculous for such a serious matter. But it worked. The costume was so good that when Rimington met the judge at a dinner party several months later, he didn't recognise her.

"It was all terribly hush-hush," remembered Sir David Calvert-Smith, who was junior treasury counsel on the case. As expected, Rimington's testimony painted Van Haarlem as a bigger player than the evidence had suggested. She argued that he wasn't in London simply to report on the Jewish Refusenik groups. Illegals were expensive to train, expensive to run and prized by enemy intelligence services. She portrayed him as a "sleeper" ready and waiting for the call to take a frontline role should war break out with the Soviet Bloc, or should the Cold War escalate to such an extent that Russian diplomats and their "legal" spies were unable to operate. He was, in short, a big fish and a catch and release could simply not be countenanced if the jury was serious about protecting the security of their country.

Recognising the importance of Johanna's testimony, Rimington also detailed how foreign agents used the technique of stealing another person's identity to allow them to move freely in the West without suspicion. "This man had been successfully identified and investigated by our staff acting in close collaboration with the police," she said. "We were able to arrest him in flagrante as he was sitting in the kitchen of his flat listening to his regular shortwave radio broadcast from his controllers at home."

Van Haarlem considered her evidence to be respectful and dignified. He could respect a fellow professional. (He was less impressed with the disguise and would later describe her as looking like a prostitute who had just been to the hairdresser.)

~

With the defence offering no witnesses and Jelinek keeping his silence, there were no witnesses left to call. The prosecution was done with their questioning and, with Gragert keeping his silence, the defence had nobody to call. Judge Simon-Brown began his summing up on the evening of Thursday, 2 March.

He started out with the questions at the heart of the case: "What was it all about? What was he doing here? What was he interested in? Whose side was he on?

"Those and similar questions you will be wanting to ask yourselves when, at some stage tomorrow morning, this man is placed in your hands and in your hands alone, to decide yea or nay, is he a spy?"

The judge appreciated the cloak and dagger nature of the case and offered a nuanced warning to the jurors to take their responsibilities seriously.

"It is really very easy to smile from time to time in a case like this, and I suspect I have been as guilty as anybody. One can almost mock some of the features of the case, sneer at parts of the evidence."

The judge knew that Gragert's strategy had been effective, at least to a degree. While Johanna's story had appeared to horrify the jury, Gragert had also at times charmed the jury by poking fun at the seriousness of the allegations against him. The judge's job was to sum up both sides of the case, but he wanted to be sure the jury understood that they were being asked to decide on a serious matter.

"To those of us – and I suspect that really this is to most of us – who live what are no doubt somewhat humdrum, ordinary lives, there is perhaps an air of unreality, almost sometimes of fantasy, about something of the story that has unfolded before us," he continued. "Evidence here of dead letter drops, all the paraphernalia of secret message writing, one-time pads for coding and decoding, false identities. These usually are the stuff, are they not, of novels that you take on trains, and television programmes. As I think one of the barristers said, they smack of John Le Carré and Len Deighton, but make no mistake about it, members of the jury, states do have intelligence services.

"Spies really do exist. People are trained to gather and communicate information to powers abroad who are not always concerned in the same interests as another state, and those things can matter.

"National security is no joke. One day, our freedom may depend upon it. So, by all means allow yourself a wry smile from time to time and see the amusing side of the case, but do not lose sight of its importance."

It didn't take long for the judge to come around to the question of Van Haarlem's identity. He knew instinctively that this was the crux of the case for the jury.

He told the jury they had three options regarding the spy's story as they weighed their decision. "One is that he is not who he says he is, that he has, in fact, assumed the identity of that baby as it was originally put into the children's home back in the war years by Mrs. Van Haarlem." Judge Brown explained that the DNA evidence was stacked against the defendant. "Then there is a second possibility, that he is who he says he is, he is that baby, grown up, but perhaps because that was actually quite a suitable background for a Czech spy, he was trained and employed as such. So, he really is who he says he is, but he is still a Czech spy.

"Then there is the third possibility, that he is who he says he is, he is that baby, but he is innocent as the day is long.

"Those are the three basic possibilities, are they not?"

The hallowed chamber was silent in rapt attention. Everyone had their eyes locked on the judge, except Jelinek, who was staring down at his hands. Judge Brown broke the spell, telling the court he would resume his summing up in the morning. Johanna wasn't there; she'd flown home to Holland after giving evidence.

~

On Friday morning, the judge reminded the jury of how Mrs Van Haarlem had suffered from bigotry and degradation when she became pregnant during World War Two and was forced to leave her son Erwin in an orphanage. He said the prosecution case before them claimed she was terribly deceived by the man in the dock, who had claimed to be her son but was a Czech spy.

Judge Brown didn't spend long trying to explain the emerging science of DNA and the human genome but asked the jury to consider the experience of the profiler in determining the huge odds against the spy being Johanna's biological son.

"What does the blood test show?" he asked. "You will remember the forensic scientist, the gentleman who specialised for two years in this new – you may well have read about it – dramatic invention, the DNA profiling that is so much in the news now. He takes blood samples. There is no issue about this. He gets the blood samples taken from both the mother and the defendant and subjects them to the analysis and the profiling system.

"We are not going to spend a couple of years mastering that technique, obviously, and I do not suppose any of us followed it with precision, but what are his conclusions upon it, with his scientific training and experience? They calculated the likely ratio, and it is this; that the chances are 1 in 1,800 against this gentleman being Mrs. Van Haarlem's son; it is 1,800 times more likely that he is not than that he is; and Mr. Bird (Det Insp Richard Bird), at one stage, said: "Extremely unlikely", and you may think that is the very lowest it can be put.

"So that is perhaps the central evidence on it, but one must not forget two other aspects of the evidence."

The judge emphasised the importance of Gragert's letter to Johanna following his arrest, calling her "Mrs Van Haarlem" rather than "mother". It had been the arrow through the mother's heart. It was a strategic error by Jelinek; he must have known it would hurt his defence. But it also showed just how tired he'd become in pretending to be a son to someone else's mother.

"There is the letter that he wrote – well, he now calls her not mother as before, but Mrs. Van Haarlem. You perhaps do not need to turn it up. It is page 297 of the exhibit bundle if you want and need it – and appearing to recognise what, indeed, is, you may think, irresistible to be recognised, that in fact he is not her son," said Judge Brown, who then moved on to Rimington's evidence, although he still referred to her as "Miss J" as her identity was kept secret from the jury and from the public at the time.

"Then there is the evidence of the very senior intelligence officer, 'Miss J', who told you that that would be wholly consistent with all the other indications in this case of him being a spy, because these people, trained up in the Soviet Bloc and sent over here, she says always do have a false identity. It may well be impossible to recruit those with the sort of background that enabled this man to get a Dutch passport, and so Miss 'J' told us what happens, in effect, is that you get one of your native-born Czechs who will do the job nicely and you provide him with an identity which will enable him to travel freely, to come here and not to have the suspicion concentrated on him that would be concentrated on somebody if he came, as indeed one can come, with a Czech passport."

~

The case didn't rest on Van Haarlem's actions, the judge explained, but the information he provided to the Soviet Bloc. The faces of the jurors, so engaged when listening once again to how Johanna was duped, looked more studious, like they were trying to work out a tricky equation.

"Really, what the Crown says on this part of the case is surely this, that as perhaps we all know, human rights, civil rights, the interests of Refuseniks and this sort of thing, loom large, do they not, nowadays at summit meetings?" said the judge.

"They are on the agenda of the international armament talks and the like; people trade off human rights for weapons and so forth. And the delicate balance of negotiation about these things could, suggest the Crown, be affected by one of the negotiating parties, the Soviet Bloc, having a very specific, a very detailed, a very acute knowledge, of the actual level of interest in organisation behind the Refusenik movement in the West. To be forewarned is to be forearmed, and the more you know the better placed, suggest the Crown, you are to deal with that particular item on the agenda of these international meetings."

The judge also drew the jury's minds back to Miss J's evidence about the work of an illegal agent who is not attached to a foreign embassy, but operates in deep cover.

"The basic task of such a person, she told you, is to be what is known as a 'sleeper': that is to establish oneself in the foreign country securely, to build up one's identity, to have one's communications worked out so that if some crisis arises there is that agent ready to do whatever is necessary: and the sort of crisis that she understands that can arise obviously relies on detail; I hope this one will not get to the point of war breaking out, but that is the sort of possibility."

The mention of war woke everybody up. It doesn't get more serious than that.

"Sometimes the regular mission spies, if I can so term them, are sent home," explained Judge Brown. "Sometimes diplomatic relations end and the embassy or whatever it may be, the mission, is closed down. Sometimes a number of them are expelled. We read about it from time to time and as and when necessary, the illegals, the agents in the field, stop in the field and do whatever they are bidden to do, whatever they are tasked to do, whatever task is given to them by the foreign agency. They collect, she told you, information, whatever it may be, of value and advantage to the country that sent them here.

"She told you that it was inconceivable that an agent would be sent over here and required solely to report back on organisations concerned with dissidents and Refuseniks.

"She told you that there was a very close connection within the Soviet Bloc between the various intelligence services, between the Czech and the Russian services, and they will share any significant intelligence either of them has."

With that, Judge Brown sent the jury away to decide on Erwin van Haarlem's fate.

They may not, by then, have been sure exactly who the defendant was, if, indeed, he was Erwin van Haarlem at all, but they didn't take long to make up their minds.

CHAPTER THIRTY-SIX

Court 1, The Old Bailey, 3 March 1989

The Old Bailey jury retired at 2.40pm on Friday, 3 March 1989 and was back after just 50 minutes at 3.30pm with a verdict.

"Would the foreman please stand?" said the clerk of the court in a firm voice from his desk in the shadow of the judge's bench. There was a last-minute kerfuffle of reporters and members of the public rustling into their seats, surprised at the brevity of the jury's deliberations. A quick verdict was generally seen as a positive sign for the prosecution; if jurors voted to deny the Crown, they tended to give the impression of taking more care with the decision by spending longer making it. If jurors were split, they would spend hours and sometimes days reaching a solution, if a decision was possible at all.

Jelinek's sardonic smile was gone as he sat, stone still, in the dock. He knew it didn't look good.

The court had settled into a deafening silence as the clerk continued: "Madam Foreman, would you please confine yourself to answering my next question either yes or no.

"Members of the jury, have you reached a verdict upon which you are all agreed?

"Yes," replied the smartly dressed, middle-aged woman.

"Members of the jury, do you find the defendant, Erwin van Haarlem, guilty or not guilty of doing acts preparatory to the commission of an offence under Section 1(1) (C) of the Official Secrets Act, 1911?"

The air went out of the room.

"Guilty."

The clerk took a moment for the verdict to settle in and asked the foreman. "You find him guilty, and that is the verdict of you all?

"Yes," she replied, and sat down.

All eyes were on the blue-suited man in the dock, who suddenly looked small and vulnerable.

"Erwin van Haarlem," said Mr Justice Brown. "Stand up."

It took the defendant a moment to collect himself and he stood facing the bench, determined to maintain his air of nonchalance.

"I use this name, even though I am convinced it was not yours at birth," the judge continued. "You have been convicted by this jury on the basis of what can really be shown to be the most convincing evidence of a truly serious crime.

"I have no doubt that you are a devoted, disciplined and resourceful spy.

"I also have no doubt that had you not been caught, you would have done whatever your Czech controllers required of you in the years to come, however harmful it could be to our national interests. These interests and our freedoms, we must jealously guard.

"The decision of this court is that you will go to prison for ten years, and I recommend that you be deported from this country after serving this sentence. You can go."

With a curt nod to the jury, the spy without a name was led out of the courtroom and down to the cells. Home Secretary Douglas Hurd had already signed a deportation order for "Van Haarlem" to be forcibly returned to Czechoslovakia. But first, he must serve his decade behind bars.

As he was driven in an armed convoy to HMP Parkhurst on the Isle of Wight in a minibus, the spy held tight to a small victory. Jelinek may have lost the trial but he took some solace in winning the fight to keep his identity a secret. In the world of spies, there was some honour in that. Still, nobody knew his real identity and no British investigator knew fully what coded secrets he had sent to his spymasters in Prague and Moscow. Doubling down on his small victory, he continued to use the name of Johanna van Haarlem's lost son.

"Who is he judging?" thought Jelinek. "He convicted Erwin van Haarlem, born on 24 August 1944, therefore someone else, a real living person. The judge should have said correctly, 'A person who pretends to be Erwin van Haarlem and whose real name we do not know is being sentenced to ten years in prison'."

During his first few weeks in Parkhurst, "Van Haarlem" kept up the pretence of innocence, launching a handwritten appeal against the conviction with an application filed on 23 March 1989. He was, no doubt, hoping to make up for the fact that he had passed on the opportunity to defend himself in person at the Old Bailey.

He argued that the prosecution came up with no evidence of him spying during the two years he was under MI5 surveillance and that nothing that he did during his 13 years in the country could be considered harmful to Great Britain. Instead, he said the judge "directed the jury to consider whether they would be sure that in the future if I came across some information which would be damaging to Great Britain, I would not hesitate to send it to my 'masters.'

"But the law does not cover future information," he added. "The judge must not invent a new 'catch them all' explanation. The law speaks clearly only about information which was already available."

He also questioned whether the Soviet Union and Czechoslovakia should be regarded as "enemies" in law and asserted that the judge's explanation that they were "potential enemies" was misleading. "England, the Soviet Union, and the Czechs and the Slovaks fought together against the Germans in the past. There were five squadrons of Czech pilots fighting for England in the Second World War. It remains to be decided whether under prevailing circumstances, with the friendly visit of Mr Gorbachev on the invitation of Mrs Thatcher to London next month imminent, the Soviet Union and Czechoslovakia should be referred to as enemy, potential enemy or potential friends and future business partners. It is vital to establish it, because if the countries in question are not enemies, I could not have committed the crime I was accused of."

"Van Haarlem" continued to insist that he had helped rather than harmed the Soviet Jewry cause, writing: "The Soviet Jewry leaders evaluated immediately after my arrest the situation and didn't find any evidence which would suggest that my activities were damaging to the movement... Mrs Eker confirmed that from the twelve Refuseniks I visited and 'betrayed' in the USSR, ten already emigrated, one received a permission, and one received a permission but changed his mind and decided to stay."

Despite the DNA tests – which he claimed Mr Justice Brown didn't understand – he said that "one of the biggest flaws in the performance of the judge was that he overemphasised the importance of whether Mrs Van Haarlem was my biological mother or not".

He continued: "He failed to comprehend and subsequently mention that not being the biological son of Mrs van Haarlem didn't mean that I wasn't Erwin van Haarlem. I have always been Erwin van Haarlem, there are my school friends, teachers, neighbours, employers, etc., who could testify to it. I have got documents given to me by my parents and issued to me by authorities to prove my identity. Nothing of it was mentioned by the judge to the jury in his permit to convict me as a spy." His deception continued.

He signed the application as Erwin van Haarlem. It never went anywhere, but the spy probably enjoyed asking for Legal Aid from the Crown to cover his costs.

~

While he was sticking to the identity created for him by his Czech spymasters, his neighbours in Parkhurst Prison had a new name for him: Boris. In Prague there was no time for jovial names for their man jailed in Britain. His controllers were contacting Russian and Eastern German secret services to find a way to pull off a prisoner swap. They wanted assistance in finding British, American or Israeli detainees who could be handed over to free Gragert. They described him as a patriot who had been "defending the interests of the Czechoslovak state" and added that "active steps were being taken from our side and the Soviets to free him." Importantly, Czech officers had decided there was no point in keeping up his legend. It didn't matter how much Gragert wanted to protect his real name. The cat was out of the bag. British intelligence services knew he was either a Czech or Soviet agent.

As they worked to free him, Czech authorities were also honouring Gragert's request to look after his elderly parents. His parents would continue to have access to the best medicines, even from the West, and be supported financially. They had no idea what their son had been doing but understood and accepted it was for the betterment of Czechoslovakia. If one parent died, a good retirement home would be found in Prague for the survivor. There were also plans to ensure the development of a plot of land for Gragert to build a home on his return. Gragert may have been caught, but he'd served his country well. As long as the Soviet Bloc was in place, "Erwin" would be guaranteed a hero's welcome on his return to Prague. But, unfortunately for Gragert, Moscow's empire was already crumbling, and the spy's life work was rapidly becoming irrelevant.

PART THREE

HER SON

CHAPTER THIRTY-SEVEN

Olešovice, Bohemia, Czechoslovakia,
17 October 1991

Orphans are the forgotten victims of war and orphanages are always busy in the aftermath of the bloody conflicts of men. To these children, all that's left of their parents is often a line in a ledger with the names of mothers and fathers they can no longer remember. It was to the orphanages of Bohemia that Johanna now looked to try once more to fill the hole in her heart. For more than a decade she had thought she could look forward. Now she had no choice but to go back to the beginning.

~

I first met Johanna in Holland where she had returned while the Old Bailey trial was still in progress. At the time, my co-author, David Gardner, was the *Daily Mail*'s Crime Correspondent and he was at the Old Bailey covering the Van Haarlem court case for the British newspaper. After Johanna's moving testimony in the witness box, I was sent by the *Daily Mail*'s News Editor Ian

Monk to find and interview the Dutchwoman who had made headlines from the witness box about her ordeal.

By now Johanna was fearful of any stranger turning up on her doorstep unannounced but she eventually agreed to speak. My exclusive story, detailing her wartime plight and her long, painful search for her son, threw a tragic new light on the spy's cruel deception. Knowing how important it was to Johanna to find the real Erwin, I stayed in touch with her as she came to terms with Gragert's betrayal in the weeks and months after the trial.

With the trail long gone cold many decades earlier, Johanna eventually sought my help to return to the country where she had left Erwin behind, a country that was going through its own transition once more with the end of the Cold War.

With *Daily Mail* photographer Clive Limpkin, I met Johanna in Prague in the last week of October 1991 and, together with her younger son, Hans, we decided to make enquiries in the capital before driving to Bohemia. There, we planned to try to get on the trail of Erwin, who we knew had spent his early years in an orphanage in the region. Bohemia formed a large section of the central and western parts of the country, but there were few other clues about where to start. Translator Vera Vitvarova, a hardworking single mother of three children from Prague, joined us to tour a series of orphanages and social services offices.

The days were grim with low clouds and mists shrouding the hills, the forests and the grey buildings. It was foreboding weather. Even so, Johanna's spirit remained undimmed. We soon discovered that each home had kept perfect records of the children that had been cared for. I called those records "Ledgers of Despair". Names were carefully and clearly written in ink in thick record books. Dates were given for arrivals and departures. Sometimes the name appeared more than once, possibly because an adoption had not worked out and the child was returned. The ledgers told countless tales of tragedy in black and white, often with no endings, happy or sad, recorded. The children were just passing through. The one thing they did discover in Czech orphanages was love. For many, it was the first time in their lives they had ever experienced it.

In these orphanages, there had been an influx of children from 1939-1945 and for several years afterwards, caused by the turmoil and bloodletting that came with World War Two. Jewish orphans arrived from concentration camps, German orphans from families now despised and often imprisoned or dead, and other stateless orphans fathered by invading soldiers from Nazi Germany with mothers from occupied countries. Of course, Czechoslovakia also had its own orphans. We couldn't help worrying about the innocent girls and boys who had suffered. We imagined that many of the children, like Erwin, who were told they were given away must have felt deep wounds of rejection. They didn't know why their parents were not with them. For many of the orphans, there wasn't a choice; their parents were dead. But what about those with mothers or fathers who had rebuilt their lives after the war without their children. What of them?

Johanna's thoughts inevitably harked back to the brutality that had led to some of the poor souls being taken to the children's homes. Those in the early years of World War Two who had been orphaned when their parents were killed in raids by air and land, others with a father lost on the front line and a mother who couldn't cope. How many other mothers were forced to give up their children like she had against their wishes?

CHAPTER THIRTY-SEVEN

It was a hard grind searching for a clue from so long ago and the disappointment was compounded with each list of names with no sign of Erwin. As determined as she was, the spectre of failure sat heavily with Johanna. She began to worry that the journey was at yet another dead end.

~

After visiting several homes across the country, we found ourselves in front of a rambling old building in Bohemia where, according to a local woman, abandoned war babies had been taken. As Johanna walked through the wooded grounds of the large, once grand house in Olesovice, she grimaced at the sound of the autumn leaves being crushed beneath her feet.

"It is deafening," she said. "My senses are so heightened." Suddenly, her face lit up. "This is where Erwin came when he was one year old," she told me. "Don't ask me how I know, I just do."

Her step quickening, she made her way between two grand entrance pillars. The white-coated orphanage director, Jiri Dousa, greeted her at a large and impressive wooden door and politely invited us inside. He had helped mothers like Joanna before and presented us with a few yellowing "Ledgers of Despair" that were left.

"I am shivering," Johanna said to me in a hushed voice. "I feel Erwin lived here, laughing and crying in these corridors. I am going over his footsteps."

She explained to the sympathetic director how she had brought her baby boy to the Czech Red Cross in 1944, and she did not know the name of the children's home where Erwin would have lived in his early formative years. The decades since had clouded her memories – memories which were also formed in the fog of war. It was understandable. Dousa said he had other similar inquiries over the years and had done his best to help mothers and fathers desperate to be reunited with their children. Johanna told him how in 1945 and through all of the years that followed, she had been overwhelmed with a strange grief. Her child was very much alive when she left him, but she feared he would never be found again as Europe was torn apart. She explained how Erwin's identity had been stolen by a Czech spy.

The orphanage staff listened intently as she told her story. Once again, she worried she would be judged, but there was only kindness in the faces of the people who had seen more than their share of heartbreak etched on the little faces in their care. Their work was to give the children some stability, lots of love and kindness, to bring some happiness into their young lives. When a child smiled for the first time in their care it was like a miracle happening; it made the nurses so happy too.

As we waded through the documents Dousa had given us, so many fearful scenarios were racing through our minds. Had Johanna's boy been assassinated by the Czech secret service, the StB, to protect their agent's cover? Surely, they would not have been that brutal. We were letting our imaginations get the better of us. Johanna prayed, and so did all of us, that he had been adopted and given the surname of caring new parents?

One yellowing "Ledger of Despair" contained a type-written list of 933 names, which we began to carefully work down, hoping against hope that we would find the name we were looking for. If it was another dead end, even in the place where she believed Erwin had been left, Johanna would have to steel herself to carry on the search.

Erwin van Haarlem was number 10 on the list.

CHAPTER THIRTY-SEVEN

The entry was brief but definitive. He was born in Amsterdam on 24 August 1944 and arrived in Olesovice in 1945. He left the home on 2 April 1949, aged four.

But there was an alarming comment written in Czech next to his name. It read: 'Chybi Pred. MV'. It was an abbreviation which meant, said Vera, the interpreter: "Missing. Hand-over. Home Office."

"What does this mean?" asked Johanna in a trembling voice. "Was my son handed over to the authorities so that his identity could be taken from him (to be given to a spy)? Could they even have murdered him? Or does it mean he was given to adoptive parents?"

There were no explanations in this book. Nobody knew. That was the purpose of the cold phrase used by an official of the government representing the secret service. There would be no clues to his whereabouts. It was supposed to remain hidden. From what we understood, Erwin's identity had been earmarked from the start as potential cover for a spy. It was hard to believe in such a long, long game but Erwin the toddler had something of high value. His birth in Holland meant he could get Dutch citizenship and along with it a passport allowing travel anywhere in the West.

Clive asked if there were any photos of the children from the time Erwin had been in the home. Johanna's worried expression changed dramatically as a worn leather photo album was produced. Inside were many pictures of children who had stayed at the home just after the war. Excitedly, Johanna flicked through the pictures, which had been captioned by staff over many years. We were afraid the StB may have also got to the album and removed any photos to protect their agent's legend. But we needn't have worried. There was one beautiful, blond child aged about two in the arms of a nurse. Clive, with the trained eye of a brilliant photographer, pointed to it as he could see likenesses with Johanna. Written on the back were the words, 'Erwin van Haarlem, 1947'.

"Oh, yes. Oh yes!" exclaimed Johanna. The StB had not covered all the tracks. They had left a beautiful clue to be found four decades later by a mother desperate to discover the fate of her first born. The child's long hair was almost white. His features were round and Western European. The spy selected to take his place had black hair and a strikingly dark complexion. That didn't matter as his spymasters never in their wildest dreams thought that Erwin's mother would turn up one day to discover the truth. But she had. They had not wiped out his memory altogether.

Dousa told us of an elderly woman called Helena Klapova in a nearby village who was a nurse in the home in 1947, when Erwin was three. Joahnna felt her luck was finally changing. Maybe this woman knew what happened to her son after 2 April 1949.

CHAPTER
THIRTY-EIGHT

Olešovice, Bohemia, Czechoslovakia,
18 October 1991

While the rest of the world was in upheaval in the bloody aftermath of World War Two, Přemysl Pitter and Olga Fierz were intent on saving the innocent victims of this and every conflict – the children.

They were primarily involved in caring for the Jewish children who returned from concentration camps. These children had lost their parents and everyone they knew in the Holocaust. They were alone in the world and to compound that, they had seen the worst that man can do to man. But Pitter, a Czech, and Swiss-born, English-educated Fierz did not restrict their care to Jewish children; they also helped German children of families left in Czechoslovakia after the war. In time, the "Nazi children" and the Jews grew to live together in loving homes the couple created for them in chateaux around Prague. One of these stately houses was in Olešovice.

Pitter was already well known for his work with children in Prague's poorer communities. At Christmas in 1933, he opened Milíč House, a centre providing food and hope for children in the working class Žižkov and the surrounding areas. The house welcomed children of German emigrants fleeing Nazi Germany along with the local children. Later, during the German occupation of Czechoslovakia, it became a secret refuge from persecution for Jewish families. The couple hid and fed Jewish families from the Nazis and continued to do so even after Pitter was hauled away and interrogated by the Gestapo.

But it was after the war that Pitter and Fierz made perhaps their greatest contribution when they were instructed by government officials to use the confiscated castles of Štiřín, Olešovice, Kamenice and Lojovice to care only for orphans born in Czechoslovakia. Ignoring the order, they opened the buildings to about 800 homeless, malnourished Jewish, German and Czech children aged between three and 14. Jewish and German children were housed in orphanages together. In Pitter and Fierz's view, no blame should ever be attributed to children.

As was the case in Holland, Czechoslovakia reacted with wrath and retribution after the country was liberated in 1945 following seven years of brutal German occupation. German families who had lived in the country for generations took the brunt of the animosity. Many were imprisoned in the same concentration camps the Nazis built and young children were again the most vulnerable victims.

It was against this background that the chateau orphanages sought to first heal and comfort the children of war and then to seek foster or adoptive parents for them.

It had been Přemysl Pitter, then working as director of the children's homes outside Prague, who had discovered Johanna's documentation in 1946 and set in motion the attempts to find her through the Dutch Embassy that ultimately resulted in her father's ultimatum that she must turn her back on her son. When his attempts to contact Johanna were rebuffed, Pitter ensured that Erwin was loved and cared for at the orphanage in Olešovice for as long as he needed or as long as it took to find him a safe and happy home.

However, Pitter's support for the displaced German children put him at odds with the Czech authorities and both he and Fierz were eventually forced to leave Czechoslovakia and settled in Switzerland where they continued their work. Both were declared Righteous Among the Nations, a title given by Israel to non-Jews who risked their lives to help Jewish people in the Holocaust.

We decided not to go to Switzerland to find Pitter and Fierz and went looking for Helena Klapova, the former Olešovice nurse who had cared for Erwin so lovingly and was still living in the area, working as a schoolteacher.

~

When I arrived with Johanna, Clive and our interpreter Vera at the old apartment block where Helena lived, Johanna felt overwhelmed. She hesitated outside to collect her thoughts and emotions in the dusk descending on the building. The glow of lights escaping through curtains into the winter chill outside felt warm and welcoming. It was a good omen, Johanna told me. A long time ago she had knocked on another door praying for refuge denied to her and baby Erwin by her own father. She prayed the knock on this door would reveal happier recollections of her Erwin.

The door creaked open and a lady who appeared to be in her late 60s looked at us in the darkened hallway. She was initially puzzled at the sight of the huddle of people – Johanna, me, a photographer and our interpreter – at the door. Vera, a loving mother with masses of empathy for everyone, soon put Helena at ease. She explained that Johanna was Erwin's mother and had been looking for Erwin for many, many years since leaving him with the Red Cross and the Olešovice children's home. She was with journalists from England who were helping her in the search, Vera told the former nurse, and soon Helena's cheery round face began to relax. Her smile gave Johanna real hope that this was a caring person who would have looked after Erwin and all his friends in the home as if they were her own children.

"You really are the mother of Erwin?" Helena asked Johanna as she invited us into her home. "I must help you. He was cute. He made us all laugh so much. We all spoiled him."

The delight in Johanna smoothed away the lines of anxiety that had dug deep into her face in the years she had obsessed over Erwin's fate. Her misplaced trust in the spy had shaken her. Finally, she could breathe a little.

"It was a difficult time for the children," recalled Helena. "There was so much hatred between the so-called 'Nazi' kids and the Jewish ones who came from the concentration camps. The 10 Germans at Olešovice were kept together. They slept in one big room, bathed and had their meals with each other." The Jewish children would have seen at first hand the horrors of the Nazi persecution of their loved ones; some would have endured the evils of the concentration camps themselves. They had lost mums and dads there.

"Eventually they were all happy together," said Helena. Their good fortune was to have Přemysl Pitter and Olga Fierz, to help persuade the children to overcome their differences and to be happy together.

Dousa had given Johanna one of the photographs of Erwin taken at the orphanage. She now produced the treasured memento to show Helena, who told her that the pretty young girl hugging her son in the picture was Eva Kvapilova, who now lived in nearby Zbraslav. Someone else to look for. When I showed her a photo of the spy, Helena immediately noticed his eyes and cried out: "No! That is not Erwin. He was like you, Johanna."

Her memory was refreshed by documents acquired by Johanna. She remembered that Erwin was sent to the luxurious apartment of National Theatre actor Vladimir Repa soon after his third birthday in the hope that he would be adopted.

Erwin had loved his life in the children's home in Olešovice, with his many friends and the ladies who all seemed like his mother. He wasn't keen to leave the home where he was cherished to the uncertainty of a future with a couple of strangers. Didn't every orphan want a family of their own?

Initially, Erwin saw his transfer from the institution to a luxuriously furnished apartment where he had his own bedroom as an adventure. It was hoped that the childless couple would fall in love with the handsome blond boy who was so popular with staff and other children at the home. He was considered great fun, caring and intelligent, always asking questions about anything new.

As popular as he was at the children's home, Erwin was too much of a handful for the flamboyant couple in their 50s with a busy work and social life and little experience of children. For a boy used to the rough and tumble chaos of a busy orphanage, life in such rarified surroundings as the Repas' elegant Prague home was stifling. The adventure was to be a short one. Erwin was lonely and the silence in his new home was deafening. He couldn't settle and quickly made it clear to the Repas that he wanted to return to his friends in the orphanage. The feeling was mutual. As good an actor as Repa may have been, he couldn't pretend that the new addition made for a happy family. Money and comfort were never as important to the little boy as love. Erwin returned to the children's home after just one month.

While the nurses were sad the rehoming didn't work out, they were nevertheless pleased the curious and affectionate little boy who had returned their deep love for him was back. Later that year, another set of parents came looking for Erwin to fill a void in their lives. This time, the adventure would become a nightmare.

The adoptive parents were a Jewish paediatrician and his wife. They had survived Dachau, Germany's first concentration camp, which opened on 22 March 1933. Dachau was an early warning of the Nazis' Final Solution policy to destroy the Jewish race and it was to become the SS model for Hitler's death camps. Constructed in southern Germany for the incarceration of Hitler's political opponents, it became the longest-running concentration camp, where countless thousands of Jews died from malnutrition, disease, and overwork. Many were executed after suffering torture and unspeakably inhumane experiments.

The couple were traumatised by the appalling atrocities carried out in the camp and they reacted in very different ways – ways that would impact Erwin once he came into their care.

The husband witnessed the worst of man's inhumanity to man. His first wife and child had died in Dachau. Any husband and father who had lost loved ones in such horrific circumstances could be forgiven for harbouring everlasting hatred for Germans and their offspring. But he still wanted to do good for the children of the world without prejudice. Any child deserves a chance in life was his philosophy. He wanted to give Erwin a future and an education that would bring the boy a good life with a family of his own. He felt it was more than just his duty. As a paediatrician, he had been trained to care for children, whether it be a broken bone or a brutalised mind. He met his second wife in Dachau and lived in Kolyn, about 15 miles east of Prague.

On paper, it was a fortuitous opportunity to mend three broken lives and create a happy ending for innocent victims of some of the war's worst excesses. But behind closed doors life was not rosy for Erwin.

~

With Johanna, I followed the trail of adoptions. It wasn't an easy journey.

In Kolyn, we were taken to the house where the couple had lived with Erwin. There were no neighbours to remember Erwin, but in a nearby neighbourhood, the Passer family, who lived close to them, vividly recalled the little boy.

Josef Passer, an 87-year-old retired Jewish dentist, still had a Mauthausen camp number tattooed on his left forearm. He told us that he was a friend of the couple, but he warned Johanna it wasn't a happy story he had to tell. He hadn't expected to live to see the world at peace and had seen enough suffering at Mauthausen to last a lifetime. More than 90,000 people died within Mauthausen's terrible walls, and in adjoining camps. The SS had slaughtered Dutch Jews, mainly from Amsterdam, along with other prisoners considered to be racial and political enemies of the Nazi state. But he never expected to see cruelty towards a child from one of his Jewish neighbours once he returned home.

Passer was deeply troubled by the way Erwin's vengeful foster mother would lock him in the cellar, screaming at him and calling him a "little Nazi". Rather than find solace in the child, it appeared his German parentage only reminded the tormented wife of her suffering at the hands of her captors. "He met his wife in the camp, and (afterwards) she had lost two pregnancies because of bad health caused by her sufferings," recalled Passer. "She was a moody and dominant woman who seemed to love her dogs more than Erwin. People said they could hear Erwin screaming when she locked him in the cellar. It was even said that she poured water on his head as a torture like she had seen in the camps. And yet he was well-dressed and well-fed. He was afraid of her. When we were in their home he would timidly go into a corner."

For a second time, Erwin returned to the safety and security of the children's home.

Upon hearing this story, Johanna froze, the worries that had filled her nightmares since parting with her son now confirmed. We were all deeply affected. "My blood feels like it is running cold. I feel such a bad mother," she told me in her Dutch accented English. "I wish I had had the strength to stand up to my father and look for Erwin when he was a baby."

~

The next step was to find Erwin's other nursemaid Eva Kvapilova in Zbraslav, a colourfully historic place founded in 1118 on the Vitava River. In the 13th century King Wenceslaus the Second built a Cistercian monastery in the town for the Catholic faithful. It became the last resting place for Bohemian kings. We found Eva's address in a small side street in Zbraslav, which had merged through the years to become Prague's southernmost suburb.

Another knock on a door, full of trepidation and faltering hope, and Eva appeared. She wasn't daunted by the gathering of foreigners and strangers on her doorstep. Eva was a confident woman, still very much believing the best from humankind even though she had seen such suffering through the war years and then during the Soviet yoke of occupation. People were more good than bad in Eva's book. At the age of 63, she was still sprightly and caring for children in a creche while parents worked to feed, house and clothe their young. If only, Johanna thought, she had met Eva in the war when she had to leave Erwin behind.

Vera gave a brief explanation of our quest to find Johanna's son and Eva invited us into her comfortable living room. Everyone took off their shoes at the door, a respectful custom in Czechoslovakia for hygiene and the practical reality that what little families could afford they needed to take care of. Immediately, Eva warmed Johanna's heart a little more, and helped alleviate, if only a little, some of the awful stories she had just heard about Erwin's treatment.

Eva hugged Johanna just as she did the young Erwin in the children's home where she treated him as her own. And there was another precious photo album. This time there were 20 photographs of Erwin in the leather-bound book of long-ago memories. "Eva had loved my child," Johanna whispered to me. Erwin is pictured kissing a little girlfriend, drinking broth from a cup and playing in the woods. He is even featured in the arms of a teenage girl on the cover of a Czech women's magazine called Vlasta which was stored, along with other memorabilia from the children's home, in the album.

Johanna found comfort as she flicked through the pictures. "He looks so well and happy," she said. "He looks just like any ordinary child who has a family of his own. It's hard to say that he doesn't seem to be missing a mother. I'm so grateful for that. Erwin looks like one of the family." She turned to us, saying: "The nurses seem to be treating the children like their own. Eva and the others were the ones that cared for him, the ones who bathed him and tucked him up in bed."

Staring at the photo of Erwin holding a cup and spoon, she continued, "I feel so warm about this picture. I envy the nurses, but at least I know he was in the right place. Look at the cheerful surroundings: this was his home, the place he lived in. I can see the love inside him, although I hadn't been able to give it to him."

Johanna looked up at Eva, desperate for a miracle. "Do you know what happened to Erwin when he left Olešovice?" she pleaded.

The Czech woman shook her head. All she remembered was that a couple from Moravia came for him. As far as she knew, they adopted Erwin, or he went on to another home if that adoption attempt failed.

The trail had gone cold again.

"But you must know that Erwin was a happy child," Eva insisted. "He was the darling of all the children. We let his blond hair grow because among the German children there was only one girl. We were told that Erwin's grandfather did not want him, and the nurses could not understand that. Not only was he the star, but he was also very brave.

"Whenever he went to couples for adoption, I asked him if he was upset. He never said he was and didn't cry when he left. He was curious and wanted to see what the people at the next place would be like." Little Erwin seemed to have inherited his mother's psychological strength.

Overcome with emotion, Johanna wiped a tear from her cheek. "I am so pleased to be with the woman who kissed and cuddled my son, who cherished him," she said. "But I am also jealous of her because she was with him."

Clive copied the photos from the album for Johanna so that she could take Erwin, even if only in black and white pictures, back to Holland.

CHAPTER THIRTY-NINE

Prague, Czechoslovakia, 20 October 1991

The next move was to the Ministry of Foreign Affairs in Prague where a statement had been made confirming that the Czech spy in Parkhurst Prison was not Erwin van Haarlem.

After days of being sent from one official to another, Clive and I took Johanna to a senior consul, Drahomir Kuban, who told us he had news from the Federal Interior Ministry, which controlled the secret service. "Your son was adopted on the decision of a court," Kuban told Johanna. "In the book of births, he has a new name. He has a new identity. He has new parents. He is protected by adoption laws. You cannot know his new name."

The staccato statements stunned Johanna. She fired back, "How can you say this to me? The Czech government has robbed me of my son's identity. It has robbed a Dutchman of his nationality. This is an extraordinary case. Your government owes it to me to tell me where my son is. The spy deceived me, and your government was behind him. They double-crossed me as well. I want to know if my son is happy. If he has a wife and children who are my grandchildren. Or is he a lonely, poor and unhappy man who I could help? More than anything, I want him to know that I did not want to leave him in Czechoslovakia. That I have always thought of him and that I have been actively looking for him for nearly 20 years."

Embarrassed by Johanna's blunt argument, Mr Kuban declared, "We are very sorry for you but there are laws here that must be followed."

Johanna carried on, "But the Czech government has committed a crime in giving a spy my son's identity so that he could get a Dutch passport. Then allowing him to contact me and claim to be my son. I treated him like a son for ten years before he was exposed by the British Special Branch." I could see Kuban squirming. He was probably a parent himself and I imagined he would have liked to do more, but he was only the messenger of a heavily bureaucratised system left over from the authoritarian Soviets. Czechoslovakia was moving towards more freedom and openness but there was still a long way to go.

Concerned about the cynicism of the Czech secret service even under the democratic regime of Vaclav Havel, I interjected, "Do you really believe the Interior Ministry when they say Erwin was adopted? Would they say that to cover up something more sinister?" Like Johanna, I was afraid that the real Erwin had died or been sent to a place unknown.

"I believe it one hundred percent," said Kuban.

His words were of some comfort to Johanna, but under the new regime she had hoped for more. "Could they not make an exception?" she asked. "It's torture. They have given me a little by telling me Erwin was adopted and is still alive, but that is not enough. In some ways it is the worst thing that could happen to me. Just telling me a little but not all. I feel we are still in the brutal, pre-revolution communist regime. The officials, on humanitarian grounds, should take me to my son."

While officials were publicly insisting on following the letter of the law, they were sympathetic to her plight and behind the scenes we were told by a "mole" that they were going through files. If they could trace Erwin then they would make an approach to him before passing on details of his whereabouts to Johanna. There were adoption laws to follow and Erwin would have to agree to a meeting. Nevertheless this was the brightest ray of hope so far.

And if this did not happen, Johanna would not rest until her search revealed what became of the child she lost.

"I need to see my real son for peace of mind," said Johanna as she descended the cold stone steps of the ministry building. "They can steal my heart, but they cannot steal my son," she said. "I will go on searching."

~

Back in Prague, I went with Johanna to see the Dutch ambassador. The ambassador Mr Hans Heinemann was a cultured, elegant man well-versed in English. He was full of understanding for Johanna's quest to find her son. Like with so many others, there were endless kind and understanding words, but little immediate practical assistance. Johanna became convinced that the smooth-talking diplomat knew the name that Erwin was living under and where he was. It seemed yet another dead end for the time being.

Before leaving Czechoslovakia I helped Johanna write identical letters in English to the ministries for Foreign Affairs and the Federal Interior from a small, inexpensive hotel where she had been staying with me and Clive in the Prague suburbs.

It is clear to me now that the Czechoslovakian authorities know where my real son is. It is extremely important to me that my son is told that I have thought of him every day since he was left against my will in your country in 1944.

He must also be made aware of the fact that I have tried to trace him for twenty years.

Once he has the knowledge of this, I do hope my son Erwin will decide to meet me. If that contact is made, it would then be up to him whether or not our relationship should continue.

Please ensure this message is passed on to Erwin.

Nothing was going to stop this small woman with steel-like resolve to get to her real son and the truth. In President Vaclav Havel of Czechoslovakia, she saw some hope. He was a man who knew about human unkindness and hitting the impenetrable walls of rules and regulations erected by a Communist regime. Before becoming President in 1989, Czech-born Havel had been a statesman, author, poet, playwright and dissident.

He was a world-famous leader who courageously fought against state repression. Now he was calling the shots at the president's 9th century castle, once the residence of Bohemian kings, which stands imperiously on a hill overlooking the city of Prague and the Vitava River. In common with Johanna, he knew all about occupation by foreign military forces.

In London, the *Daily Mail* published on Thursday, 24 October 1991, a three-page feature from Prague under the headline: SEARCHING FOR THE CHILD WHO LOST HIS IDENTITY TO A SPY.

She wrote clearly and precisely again in English to Havel from her bungalow in Holland on 26 October 1991:

I am writing again to ask for your help in tracing my son Erwin van Haarlem whom I was forced to leave in Czechoslovakia due to circumstances beyond my control in the Second World War.

Cruelly, officials in your ministries of the Federal Interior and Foreign Affairs have told me that my son was adopted and is alive today, but they have refused to reveal his new identity and address. It was Mr Drahamir Kuban at the Ministry of Foreign Affairs who told me of Erwin's adoption but unfortunately seemed unable to get more information from Federal Ministry officials.

She listed the reasons why Havel should help her, accusing the Czech government's former regime of using her son's identity as cover for their spy, deceiving her for over a decade, and arguing that her son would by then be 47. She insisted there was no need to hide his identity through adoption laws meant to protect children. She also claimed the statement she wrote agreeing to Erwin's adoption in 1947 was signed under duress from her father. She concluded:

Please be aware of the fact that in the 10 years I was deceived, I did not look for my real son. Next month I will be 67 years of age and I will not rest until the Czech government puts right the wrong it has committed against me. On humanitarian grounds, please help me in this matter.

Johanna also sent a letter to Mr Heinemann in Prague thanking him for an hour-long meeting in his embassy office. She attached copies of her letters to the Czech officials to show the stonewalling she was suffering.

The letters worked and her story had stirred up officials behind the scenes in both Dutch and Czech diplomatic circles.

CHAPTER FORTY

Prague, Czechoslovakia, 17 November 1989

Nine days after the collapse of the Berlin Wall, more than 50,000 students filled the streets of Prague on 17 November 1989, protesting against the Communist regime, a demonstration that would have been unthinkable just weeks earlier. Riot police tried to quell the uprising, but the writing was on the wall and 11 days later Prime Minister, Mr Ladislav Adamec, bowed to the inevitable and drew the curtain down on one-party power in Czechoslovakia.

Prisoner MM 1876 – the man still calling himself Erwin van Haarlem – sat quietly in his cell on the Isle of Wight as the Soviet Union crumbled, destroying any reasons he ever had for being a spy. With no Warsaw Pact there was no longer any job. Worse than that, the old school spy detained in a Western prison was an embarrassment to the new regime in Prague. Not so long ago, Jelinek had been a rising star winning awards and plaudits in Moscow. Now he was a dinosaur.

Initially, MI5 pushed to take advantage of the conviction by trying again to persuade him to talk. Still worried about his real reason for being in London, British intelligence insisted that it made sense to cooperate. He had done his duty, tried his best, but the game was up, and he was facing a decade behind bars for a failed ideology and a country that didn't care.

Ever the professional, Jelinek spurned the advances. He held tightly onto his last remaining ace: the Brits didn't know his real identity. By then, he had spent the best part of a year in Brixton Prison in South London among terrorists, killers and drug smugglers awaiting trial and if he continued to refuse to talk to the authorities, he would serve out his sentence at Parkhurst. The alternative was to cooperate and be repatriated quietly to Czechoslovakia. But to reveal his real name would be to admit he had lost. And so, he kept up the pretence, knowing it was costing him his freedom.

The Carmis, Michael and Louise, had written to Gragert in prison. As shocked as they were to discover he was a spy, they believed he had been genuine in his friendship towards their family. He appreciated the gesture and later sent a postcard to Louise, saying: "Thank you for the support you gave me shortly after my arrest." He signed off using his fake name, but there was also a nod to his true identity. He called himself "Col. Erwin van Haarlem".

When a Ministry of Defence official named Emery tried to visit him in prison, Jelinek refused to see him. He even rebuffed approaches by his own embassy representatives. He heard from Johanna who'd reached out saying that she had a "burning" question. She wanted to ask the spy if he had any clues that might help her find her real son and had acquired permission from Parkhurt's director to visit. So desperate was she to find the real Erwin that she was willing to swallow her pride and meet the man who had caused her such pain. She booked the flights for 23 March 1990, but just before Johanna was due to leave for the airport, Gragert changed his mind and would not agree to the meeting, she was told by the prison governor. Johanna cancelled her journey but this disappointment strengthened Johanna's resolve to find her real son. Gragert was convinced that MI5 wanted to recruit him as a double agent to spy on the Russians — a belief that only further spurred his commitment to keeping his real name a secret. He was convinced it was the only way he could walk out of prison — his mystery intact — with his head high. As it turned out, even that was denied to him. In an attempt to win his release on his own terms, Gragert began a hunger strike in 1992. But, after refusing food for more than 40 days, a letter from Col. Radovan Procházka, the new Director of Czechoslovak Intelligence, arrived for him, handed over personally by the warden. It told Gragert he would soon be free, but it also sabotaged his last surviving secret.

The letter was addressed to Lieutenant Colonel Vaclav Jelinek — his real name. To the Czechs, he had become an embarrassment with his Cold War ethics and his insistence on shunning any requests for cooperation, both from his own government and from the British. The use of his real name was a clear message from his old bosses: stop playing the martyr and fall in line. The letter, dated 20 February 1992, began:

> As I am not comfortable thinking that an intelligence officer currently under my command is being held in the UK, I have been looking for options in the last two years that would lead to your early release from prison and your return to Czechoslovakia.

Procházka accused Jelinek of "gross indiscipline" by refusing to speak with him when he first made an approach in August 1991. He said he was making one last attempt to resolve Jelinek's future "without using repressive measures" against him. He wanted to discuss the demands contingent on Jelinek's release, saying:

In this context, I would like to point out that the information concerning your true identity and your activities has been declassified by us for a narrow circle of British counterintelligence at the behest of Czechoslovak political figures.

For some time, both I and the British have highly valued your professional conduct. However, it would be pointless for you to be provocative.

It seemed Procházka didn't hold Jelinek in as high esteem as he might have hoped, saying that he believed the jailed spy was "living completely detached from the present and that the world you have created in isolation has nothing to do with reality".

The spy chief had also included a letter from Jelinek's parents, perhaps as an inducement for him to cooperate. "I will continue to have regular contact with your parents and perhaps I can help them in their situation," he wrote, implying that he could also make life difficult for them if Jelinek refused to step into line.

The intelligence director ended his letter with another threat – one that was not implied but very clear. He wrote:

However, I would like to warn you that in case of your reluctance to meet, I will not be further involved in the issue of your early release. In this context, I must also strongly remind you that, as an officer in the military, you are obliged to obey the orders of your direct superiors. I will evaluate your possible disagreement as a breach of official duties with all the consequences that follow from it, from the degradation and subsequent confiscation of your financial account to the consideration of the necessity of criminal punishment of your person according to Czechoslovakia laws.

Jelinek had misread the changing times. By the early 1990s, some of Russia's closest intelligence service allies – the Czechs among them – were working with Western spymasters after years of working against each other.

The British demands were that Jelinek reveal his true name, admit he was a Czech spy and tell them what he did during his years in the United Kingdom.

"Betrayed! My friends betrayed me!" was Jelinek's response in a letter.

> *All my efforts and sacrifices are for nothing. I could come out of prison with my head held high or horizontal with my feet forward, but as a winner. God! What did they do to me?*

> *I didn't have to go to jail. Suddenly, my superiors felt sorry for my aging parents, words appeared for humanitarian reasons. If I wanted to say my name, reveal my identity, I could have done it myself! I don't need majors or generals for that. Even if I didn't go on a hunger strike, I still had two years left. I would probably overcome them, albeit with poor health, but I overcame them.*

> *The English knew nothing of me, what my name was, what I was doing. I could have come out undefeated or they could have brought me out, but I would have come out as the winner anyway. All my efforts were in vain.*

Deflated, Jelinek agreed to come off the hunger strike and cooperate.

~

The slow wheels of diplomacy began working on Jelinek's early release, even if he wasn't being particularly cooperative. In the end, MI5 was happy to get rid of him and the Czechs wanted to forget he ever existed.

At the request of Jelinek's new superior, Col Procházka, President Václav Havel had a discreet word with Margaret Thatcher, who had been British Prime Minister at the time of the spy's Old Bailey sentencing and asked her to help smooth the way for his release.

On 5 April 1993, the fake Erwin van Haarlem, real name Vaclav Jelinek, flew back to an uncertain welcome on a CSA Czech Airlines flight to Prague.

~

Johanna van Haarlem was informed of Jelinek's release and of his name. "I am not surprised," she said. "He is a deceiver and very good at it. I know he was a model prisoner, painting, writing and always smiling to ensure a release." She knew nothing of the political machinations that had been played out to officially spring him from Parkhurst Prison.

Johanna was already moving on. She had filed a lawsuit against the spy for £13,000 worth of gifts she bought for him during the time she believed him to be her son.

She wanted to make him pay for his deception. "I really believed I had found Erwin. I hugged and kissed this man as if he was my son," she insisted. "I was so glad to find him and to be able to explain that I was forced to leave him as a baby in Czechoslovakia. I wanted him to be very happy too. I wanted to make up for everything.

"I bought him presents on his birthdays and at Christmas. I paid for his hotel accommodation on holidays we had together and even gave him the money for driving lessons so that he could get a British licence.

"He has been jailed for spying, but he has not been punished for what he did to me. I must be compensated. It is not for revenge; it is for justice.

"I also believe he knows what happened to Erwin and he refuses to tell me," she said. "I can't stand that." It was his final cruelty to the woman who had so kindly treated him as her own son. Still the arch manipulator.

Johanna never mounted the case for compensation against Jelinek because she was unable to get legal aid and the fees for a lawyer would cost too much. Hans was concerned a "man of straw" would be unable to compensate his mother.

She was already looking for her real son – without Jelinek's help – and she had some clues to help in her search that had been so cruelly delayed for more than a decade. She was down but she was not out. Her real son was still out there somewhere – and she was determined to track him down.

CHAPTER FORTY-ONE

Prague, November, 1991

Stung by Johanna's criticism, the Dutch used informal contacts in the Czech government to track down the real Erwin.

Less than a month after she'd written her latest letter, Dutch officials informed Johanna that Erwin had been found. He was alive, she was told. It was the breakthrough for which she'd been praying. The only question left was whether he was prepared to meet his mother. Johanna was overwhelmed with joy and apprehension in equal measures. Could this really be happening after all that she'd been through in the last five decades of her life? She hoped for the best outcome: to take her son in her arms and tell him she had always loved him.

The Dutch said that Erwin was no longer known as Erwin. He had changed his name, which, along with the StB's efforts to cover all tracks to him, explained why it had been so hard to find him.

He worked at a metalworks factory not so far away from where Johanna had been searching outside Brno. He was married with two daughters and had no idea that his birth name had been stolen to such devastating effect. Told that his father had died fighting for Germany during the war and that his mother hadn't wanted him, he had taken the name of his loving adoptive parents.

The Dutch authorities promised Johanna they would hand over a message from her within the week, but then she was struck by a chilling thought and called the Dutch Ministry of Foreign Affairs to ask them: "How can anyone be really sure that this man is my son?"

Officials insisted they had done everything possible to check his identity and they were sure this was the real Erwin.

They said he wanted two weeks to think about meeting the woman claiming to be his mother. He, too, was worried whether she was who she claimed to be, and he was concerned about the possible impact on his adoptive parents.

Johanna had no alternative but to wait for word. Her search had been so long but those two weeks seemed to take forever.

Finally, the Dutch officials got back to her. Her son had agreed to a single meeting, to be conducted in Czech.

They also revealed that Erwin was now Ivo Radek. The tragic irony wasn't lost on Johanna. The spy had stolen her son's name. Her real son didn't want it.

~

Johanna had worried herself sick for years that her son's childhood had been miserable. The truth was quite the opposite.

He had a tough start with Johanna and with the first two sets of parents who sent him back to the children's home after failing to give him the love and the home he needed, but little Erwin's life turned around when he was taken from the orphanage by the teachers who had heard his sweet voice singing on the radio all those years ago.

When the four-year-old arrived with his adoptive parents there was a band playing, singing, balloons and welcoming banners. It had been a fairytale start to his new world.

From then on it was a normal childhood. He was officially adopted by Jan and Marie Radek in 1951. They were granted adoption rights at a court after giving a formal declaration to give a home, food, medical care, and education to the young boy.

They never called him Erwin. From the day he arrived in the Radeks' home village of Chrastavec, he had always been known as Ivo. He didn't question Jan and Marie about them not being his real parents. He was much loved and cared for like any other child in a good home. He didn't talk about the orphanage or his friends there. He wanted for nothing so maybe he pushed it deep into his mind to forget the difficult years of trying to find loving parents. This idyll was shattered at the age of 10 when a classmate at the village primary school in Chrastavec told Ivo that Jan and Marie were not his parents. His tormentor had likely heard from their own parents how Ivo Radek had been brought to the village from a children's home.

"You could be the son of a gypsy or circus people," the child taunted. Ivo went home and without saying anything to his mother and father searched for clues in their apartment in the school where Jan was headmaster. He found some official papers that said his mother was Johanna van Haarlem, a Dutch woman.

He then went to his parents and told them, "You are not my father, and you are not my mother." He asked, "If you are not my mother can I not hug you in your bed?"

Jan and Marie, both schoolteachers, drew on all their

experience to help their son get over his doubts. The couple had always planned to tell their son the truth and had been counting the years until Ivo turned 15, the age at which they deemed he'd be mature enough to process everything. They planned to show him his personal ID revealing his mother was, indeed, Johanna van Haarlem from The Hague. Now they told him the truth five years early.

Ivo's insecurity didn't last long. His parents' love for him was unconditional and his worries about his real mother were short-lived. On 21 February 1957, he became a citizen of Czechoslovakia in the name of Ivo Radek. Two years later in Brno, he received his first Czech ID card which stated his Dutch birth mother was Johanna van Haarlem, born on 19 November 1924. There were to be no more secrets.

Ivo's adoptive father was the youngest of five children and grew up on a small farm. He studied hard and became the head teacher at the elementary school in Chrastavec where he taught all grades. His wife was the only daughter of a railway worker who taught handicrafts and cooking at her husband's school for several years.

After hearing the little Erwin van Haarlem singing his Red Riding Hood song on Czech radio, that led to his adoption, Jan and Marie knew nothing of the steps that Czech intelligence took to hide his true identity. Little Erwin cried when he left the orphanage where he felt safe and loved, but this was to be a very different story.

His memories in Chrastavec were happy ones. He remembered going with his father to plant fruit trees in 1953 on the land where he helped Jan build their family home.

Although he wasn't a great student and left school at aged 15, Ivo took metalworking classes in college and became the head of a small workshop in the town of Brněnec. He served two years in the military and married his beautiful bride Zdenka in 1971. The happy couple had two children and Ivo concentrated on providing for his growing family. After Czechoslovakia's Velvet Revolution in 1989, he was promoted to manager of a locksmith workshop in a textile factory in Brněnec. He also produced custom-made security gates and railings. The factory was close to a place where the industrialist and Holocaust hero Oskar Schindler had a plant during World War Two. Risking great personal danger Schindler saved the lives of 1,200 Jews from Nazi executioners.

~

The first clue to anything extraordinary happening in Ivo's life came in November 1991 when he received a mysterious phone call from government officials in Prague asking him to attend a meeting but not telling him what it was about.

Many thoughts raced through his mind until he felt it was likely to be about his early childhood. He had a feeling it could be something about his biological mother. He wondered if she had ever looked for him. Then, protecting his feelings, he asked himself, "Why would she do that if she has clearly distanced herself from me?" He worried that he already had a mother who taught him "diligence, care, willingness and decency and how to deal with people" and fretted that his happy life would be overturned by "a woman coming forward claiming she is my mother". He was unsure about seeing any woman who claimed to be his birth mother. At the end of the day, she was a stranger to him. When he found out that his instincts had been correct and the meeting was about his biological mother, his thoughts turned to his father. Jan had a weak heart and lived with Ivo in his old age. Ivo's adoptive mother, Marie, had died three years before. At the forefront of his emotions was that he knew Jan was concerned that his adopted son would be lost to him forever if he was reunited with his birth mother. Ivo, too, was worried about the devastating effect the reunion might have on his dad and even consulted the family doctor because he was so worried about Jan's health.

There were many tearful conversations about Ivo meeting his birth mother for the first time. Ivo did all he could to reassure Jan that he would never be abandoned. He considered Jan and Marie to be his parents no matter what had happened in the past or what would happen in the future. In the end Jan, who had always put Ivo's welfare and happiness first, told his son that he should go ahead. But even with his father's blessing, Ivo remained deeply conflicted about whether to meet his mother Johanna van Haarlem.

Johanna was also uncertain. Having worked so long and so passionately on the quest to find her son, she was still plagued by doubts and fears that she could be blindsided again. There was only one way she knew all too well that could guarantee that Ivo was her Erwin. She asked the officials if he would agree to a DNA test before they met, but was told that would almost certainly spook him and cause the meeting to be cancelled. She would have to trust him, at least for now. The real Erwin was just as nervous, she was told, especially as he had no idea that his biological mother had been looking for him all these years. When he was a young boy, he was told his father had died in the war and his mother had made no attempts to trace them.

Still shocked at being told his absent mother was desperate to find him, he couldn't help wondering why it had taken her so long. Ivo could not know the answer without meeting his mother. He agreed to the reunion.

Before the meeting, Ivo sent Johanna a photo through the Dutch embassy. It was the first time she had seen him since leaving him behind as a babe in arms. Now 47, he was blond and blue-eyed and sitting at a table with a bottle of beer. She immediately recognised Erwin's father Gregor Kulig's distinctive forehead and his thick, bushy eyebrows.

He couldn't have looked more different than the spy who had pretended to be her son.

CHAPTER FORTY-TWO

Grand Hotel, Brno, Czechoslovakia,
27 November 1991

Johanna returned to Czechoslovakia once more and, on 27 November 1991, she found herself amid the splendour of the Grand Hotel Brno, where the American inventor Thomas Edison and Austro-Hungarian ruler Franz Joseph I had once stayed, waiting to see her son for the first time in nearly half a century.

There were last-minute jitters for Ivo and his devoted wife Zdenka who were giving themselves plenty of time to drive from their home in the tiny forest hamlet of Chrastavec, Moravia to the bustling city of Brno. It was November and bitterly cold. Before they left, Ivo said to his wife, "I'm wearing winter boots and that's not very nice for my first meeting with my mother." He picked up his best shiny shoes and put them in a bag to change into.

In Brno, nerves were overwhelming Zdenka. She told Ivo, "I must go to a cosmetics shop. I'm afraid of the moment and I must look my best." Then, she insisted on going to a flower shop to buy typical Dutch blooms for Johanna. The florist said he had some flowers which were Dutch because they were blue. Zdenka doubted him and suspected he was having a laugh – literally at their expense – but she still bought them.

In the Grand Hotel, Ivo went missing. The Dutch ambassador was worried that he was having second thoughts and wasn't going to walk into the room specially convened for the reunion. But he was in the men's room swapping his boots for shiny shoes and taking far too long to do it. Ivo was still overwhelmed with anxiety about whether his mother would accept him. When he emerged, the Dutch ambassador was hugely relieved.

Johanna was also full of apprehension. She stood in the ladies' room in front of the mirror, studying herself. She decided she was happy with the way her hair looked and the choice of her white blouse underneath a light pink knitted sweater. She was carrying the photos of the young Erwin which had been given to her by his nurses.

Finally, she was shown in to meet her son, who was smartly dressed in a white shirt and brown tie and a newly-pressed grey suit. Zdenka looked beautiful in a blue dress. This was a big moment in all their troubled lives, and everyone had dressed respectfully for the occasion.

But Johanna wasn't taking much notice of what anyone was wearing. She was transfixed by Ivo's eyes – his blue eyes – staring back at her.

"I stared at him and kept staring. I looked into his deep blue eyes and saw kindness, expecting hope," she recalled. "He was staring at me too. I did not dare to hug nor to kiss him. I reached out for him, and he took my hand and kissed it, smiling at me. It was a glorious moment.

"Then I shook hands with his wife, Zdenka. She handed me a

big bunch of flowers wrapped in nice present packing. Turning to Erwin and looking into his eyes, I said slowly, 'Velice jsemrad ze te vidim'."

It was the Czech sentence her friend Vera had taught her. It means: "I am very happy to see you."

Once again, this time through an interpreter, Johanna told her story, starting at the very beginning in those tumultuous times in The Hague, through to the spy's cruel deception and right up to her relentless efforts to find her true son. Seeing the maelstrom of emotions that she was going through, Erwin held out his hand every so often to reassure her.

If she still had any doubt about his identity, he showed her the name Johanna Hendrika van Haarlem as his mother on his ID card. This was an overwhelmingly touching cameo in an extraordinary coming together of son and mother. Johanna was so happy to see both their names on such an important document. He might now be called Ivo Radek, but he was her son.

Johanna told Ivo how terrible she felt about leaving behind such a tiny child, but explained that she could not risk taking him through Germany to the Netherlands. She said she felt he was safer in the home. Johanna looked closely at Ivo's eyes. She was so pleased. She kept saying they were blue.

For his part, Ivo shared that he was always curious about his mother but had never searched for her in case she was happily married and her husband did not know she had another child. He believed it would break up their marriage. Ivo told Johanna that had confided about his childhood to Zdenka even when they were dating. There were no secrets between them, either. Ivo, kind and considerate, could not be more different than the callous man who took his name.

Before Ivo and his wife left the Grand Hotel at about 3pm, he asked if they could all meet again at Christmas. The ice had been broken. "I have been very fortunate," he told Johanna. "People give each other presents mainly at Christmas, but I got it early this year. And to top it all off, the most valuable. Now I have my own mother and brother. What more can I wish for?"

~

Johanna and Hans flew into Prague for Christmas with her newfound "family", including Jan Radek. She celebrated the season of goodwill with her son Ivo, her daughter-in-law Zdenka and her granddaughters Zdena and Iva. They enjoyed turkey cooked at the home of Johanna's Czech friend Vera Navratilova, who also helped translate. Johanna and Ivo also spoke in German and English, so one way or another, they could exchange stories about their lives. Johanna made it a magical time by taking them to a classical music concert where Mozart had played in the 18th century and they enjoyed meals in nice restaurants during a three-day visit to the newly democratic Czech capital. Johanna and Hans were enjoying themselves so much they extended their visit to take up Ivo's offer to stay at his home for another two days of celebrations.

Bit by bit, Johanna opened up fully to her son with more details about what had happened in the Netherlands before he was born. Ivo listened intently as Johanna described how her father Izaak – his grandfather – had banished her and her newborn son from the family home. How she was forced to take a train East with her sister and her babe in arms Erwin. She told how the train had stopped in Verden, Germany where her son was christened in the Protestant faith. Ivo told her that Jan and Marie had been unaware of this and had Erwin christened in a Catholic church under his new name Ivo Radek. He was a Christian twice over. They laughed and sometimes tears welled up in their eyes. Johanna went on to say that she hated leaving her baby behind in Bohemia but had no choice. She believed it would be best for his survival in such hazardous times while she had to return home to The Hague as Russian forces moved in.

Ivo, a kind and sensitive husband and father, found it hard knowing that his grandfather had thrown out his mother in such desperate circumstances. It was so much for him to take in. At least he now knew that his mother did want to find him all those years ago.

Zdenka felt very sorry for Johanna and her daughters Zdena and Iva thanked their "grandmother" for giving them a "wonderful husband and father".

Later, Ivo would write to Johanna to describe the trepidation he had experienced in meeting her, writing that he felt "great joy and fear at the same time".

But he continued:

> All the inner tension and anxiety began to disappear from me when you talked about the painful journey to my rescue.

Johanna was quick to reply as the New Year celebrations neared. She told her son about her journey home with Hans from their meeting in the Czech Republic and sent him an article she had read by Olga Fierz, his saviour from the post war children's home. She continued:

> And now I sit behind the typewriter and write to you. I took a glass of your fruit juice, and it tastes so good, and I think about you

so much! I don't have the words to express how I feel. I have been welcomed into your home as a beloved grandmother and mother and that is more than I could ever have hoped for. My passionate wishes for the New Year have all come true: I have found my beloved son and he enclosed me in his arms. Ivo, thank you from the bottom of my heart. You only gave me gold and diamonds!! So much of me has fallen; no worries about you, none. Looking for you. You have a loving and caring wife and two beautiful daughters. I feel so liberated!! I am happy and bless the day that we will meet again. At exactly midnight, Hans and I raised our glasses and toast you and us, wishing ALL of us happiness and health. Then we went outside, and Hans fired two rockets, one for you and one for us, symbolically our problems exploded into the air and ushered in the New Year.

I send my best regards to Zdena and Iva and my love to both of you,

Mother

There would be more meetings. Ivo invited Johanna and Hans to visit his family home in Chrastavec. And as they grew closer, Ivo opened up further about his initial reticence in agreeing to their meeting. In a letter to Johanna in January 1992, Ivo told his mother about his adoptive father's fears and how he shared them. He wrote:

Although I told father about your life and how you found me, he thought he would lose me because of this meeting. For his part, it is understandable that he had his doubts. He was afraid for me.

I am in constant contact with my father, and I prove that to him every step of the way. After this meeting, nothing has changed between us, and nothing will change. Just as father used to take care of me and share all my joys and sorrows with me, together with mother they raised me. They gave me the opportunity to study and gave me everything that I enjoy today with my family. And so, together with my wife, I will ensure his good old age and that his life in old age is guaranteed and that he will live in security and safety in the circle of his family.

I think that after this meeting father became calm and that he found further security in himself.

I do not regret our meeting and I am satisfied and calm, especially about the way you told me about your whole fate in life. Above all. I am moved by your enormous longing for the meeting with me.

Every year for most of her life on the 24 August, the date of her son's birth in wartime Holland, Johanna agonised over thoughts of the boy she left behind. Now, finally, she was able to celebrate Ivo's birthday with a full heart.

CHAPTER
FORTY-THREE

Prague, Czechoslovakia, 4 April 1993

In Prague, life hadn't worked out quite how Vaclav Jelinek expected. American soldiers serving in Vietnam in the late 60s and early 70s suffered a similar kind of fate. Returning home from duty after serving their country, they were treated with derision and, in some cases, contempt.

The times had changed while they were away, the nation had moved on, and, through no fault of their own, they got left behind. Jelinek, too, returned to a very different country from the one he'd left as an intelligence agent in the early 1970s.

He had served his Communist masters well, but he'd sacrificed his family life, his conscience and his freedom for a system that no longer existed. The Soviet Union leaders who showered him with praise and awards were gone.

Once he left England on a flight to Prague, Jelinek could truly leave behind Erwin van Haarlem and everything that entailed, including Johanna. Having served time behind bars in England as Erwin van Haarlem, he fully expected to be welcomed in his homeland as a hero. At the very least, Lt Col Jelinek thought current intelligence chiefs would be grateful to him as a faithful soldier to Czechoslovakia.

He was wrong on both counts. He was picked up by Czech secret service agents in a government car from the airport on 4 April 1993 and was looking forward to finally being reunited with his loyal parents. Instead, the agents drove him in the opposite direction to Čtyřkol, the same village where he had been feted by the Russians years earlier. He wasn't being honoured this time. He was being interrogated in a safe house. His interrogators said that his money had all been withdrawn by the Czech authorities from his bank accounts.

After three days of questioning, during which time he was guarded by four men around the clock, he was pressured to sign a document agreeing that he was expelled from the Czech military from 31 January 1990, effectively meaning that he was on his own while he was serving his time as a spy in Parkhurst. Only then was he allowed to go home.

Over some months following his release from detainment Jelinek revealed to his parents the full scale of his career as an illegal spy for the Communist regime. They had heard nothing from their son for six years. Learning the truth about Jelinek took a terrible toll on them both. Jelinek's mother died of cancer three months after his return and his father died less than a year later. Jelinek was convinced that the stress of the deception was to blame for their deaths.

Jelinek was certain his phone was bugged, and he was being tailed by his old colleagues. He had crippling sciatica but no job and subsequently no health insurance. He was broke; he had to pay back his salary from 31 January 1990 to comply with the interrogation agreement he signed. His old friends never called. He was persona non grata.

Increasingly desperate, Jelinek wrote to Czech President Václav Havel for help in getting his back pay for the time he served in a British prison returned to him.

The letter he received in reply on 23 April 1993 left him in no doubt that whatever he may have done for his country, he was on his own. It was a new regime in charge.

> *We appreciate the trust you have in the President and your gratitude for his successful initiative in your matter. However, you will certainly realise the diversity of your destinies in the past, which has treated each of you differently.*
>
> *We therefore believe that you understand the position of the management and staff of the Ministry of the Interior, who cannot identify with your illegal mission abroad and cannot bear legal, moral and political responsibility for this activity.*
>
> *We have been informed that your employment ended with an agreement on the date of termination of the service that prepared you for this activity and used your services, and the relevant financial matters were paid to you on that date. We consider this procedure to be moral and correct.*
>
> *We would very much like you to understand the changes in our country in all contexts.*
>
> *I personally wish you good luck.*

Jelinek was left questioning the years he spent as a spy, but, as we have already seen, he was not one to roll over. He decided to write to Prime Minister Vaclav Klaus.

> *For seventeen years, I worked abroad, mostly in England, as an illegal intelligence officer. I am the holder of the award for excellent work, which was awarded to me by the President of the Czechoslo-*

vak Socialist Republic. I was arrested in England and sentenced to ten years in prison.

He complained that when he arrived back in Czechoslovakia, he was tricked while being held at a "conspiracy apartment" into signing a document that meant he had to pay back any salaries he'd earned since 31 January 1990.

While waiting for a resolution, Jelinek found a job as an interpreter for a bank, translating English into Czech, and met his future wife who was a college lecturer. Three days before he turned 50, Jelinek, having told his bride to be that he had little time left, got married and later had a daughter. He retired when he was 55 and lived quietly in Prague. His offers to give insights as an illegal spy to the Czech Republic's rebuilt secret services were rebuffed. This hurt Jelinek who saw his work as honourable. He was trained to be an illegal agent and considered that he risked everything to carry out orders.

Vaclav Jelinek died on 8 February 2022 aged 77, without feeling any remorse for the ordeal he put Johanna van Haarlem through by pretending to be her son for more than a decade. He believed, without reservation, that his deception was necessary in pursuing the interests of his country. His lack of sympathy stemmed from his unwavering belief that such a deception was necessary to maintain his "legend" as Erwin van Haarlem.

Vaclav Jelinek's grave is in a Prague cemetery with an imposing grey granite headstone. The large stone is shaped like an open book with a gold crucifix running down the spine. Running across the top are the words: "Zivot je kniha, kterou muzes cist jen-jednou." Translated in English it means "Life is a book, you can read it just once."

On one page written in gold is his name "Vaclav Jelinek 23.8.1944 – 8.2.2022."

On the other page in gold is "Erwin van Haarlem."

It was the final, cruel act of a man whose only legacy was the identity of a stranger.

Jelinek's loyal widow still declares her husband to be "a hero, a brave patriot of Czechoslovakia". But he died in anonymity. Few mourned his passing.

The real Erwin, who lived happily as Ivo Radek, outlived his impostor by two years. Ivo Radek died suddenly on 21 June 2024 from heart complications, leaving his wife Zdenka and their two daughters shattered by his sudden death. Ivo's ashes were interred by a Catholic priest in a cemetery near Chrastavec where he had lived a happy family life. He left behind a family who loved him for who he was – a good and caring man who put the happiness of his loved ones above his own and welcomed the mother who gave him away back into his heart without a second thought.

In my meeting with the Radek family in Moravia in September 2024 I was deeply moved by their dignity, warm hospitality and openness even though they were very much still grieving for Ivo. I carefully shared details they were hearing for the first time. They encouraged me to be truthful and some must have been difficult to bear. They also shared new information for this book. I left feeling concerned for these wonderful people and I was much relieved when Zdena wrote to me:

> *Dear Mr Henderson, We wish you and all your loved ones a blessed and beautiful Christmas!*
>
> *You came into our lives unexpectedly and meeting you was very important for us, actually only now is our father's life journey*

coming to an end and everything is meaningful… May God continue to accompany you on your life's journey.

Warmly, Zdena with her family

Johanna looked long and hard for her happy ending and finally found the son she loved and lost. It's a small comfort to Johanna but Jelinek's complete downfall began with her brave testimony from the witness box at the Old Bailey when she revealed the devastating human cost of his inhuman deception.

EPILOGUE

Schaijk, The Netherlands,
19 November 2024

Johanna van Haarlem is a force of nature. She celebrated her 100th birthday on 19 November 2024. She has outlived her son and the spy.

She made it to this grand old age against all the odds, her courage and resilience seeing her through so many trials and tribulations. It's not so hard to fathom how her mind and body could make it to become a centenarian.

Hindsight is an extraordinary thing, and it is difficult for Johanna to understand now how she could ever have believed that the spy was the son she left behind. He didn't look like her or her German soldier and his secrecy around her screamed of deception. She wasn't the only woman to be deceived by such a powerful need and she won't be the last. She needed this man to be who he said he was so badly she was prepared to ignore the obvious. His eyes, his face, his mannerisms were all alien to her.

He was a highly trained deceiver. He had convinced the Red Cross who introduced him to Johanna, the Dutch who gave him a passport, the Jewish Refusenik campaigners, the UK authorities who allowed him into Parliament and US security who welcomed him to a Washington conference attended by President Reagan.

It was only when Johanna was given no choice but to see through his lie that she could finally see the truth.

Getting to know Ivo finally laid all those ghosts to bed.

Jelinek's legacy, if there is one, is in the lengths he went to deceive a vulnerable mother seeking redemption from her own troubled past. His cruelty in the name of espionage made Johanna a victim twice over. We may never know the full impact of Jelinek's decade-long spy mission in the UK – a career that once brought accolades from Moscow and promotions from Prague. What we do know is that after an incredible life spanning 100 years, Johanna van Haarlem defied wars and patriarchies, liars and bullies, massive odds and terrible luck, in a lifelong personal rebellion to mend her broken heart.

Johanna lost Erwin twice: the first time to war and the second time to fraud. Few would have blamed her for giving up her baby in such difficult circumstances; nobody would have blamed her for giving up her search after losing her son a second time.

But she persevered.

And along the way, she reclaimed her life. She is a victim no more, but an inspiration, not just to mothers but to anyone who refuses to give up until they discover the truth.

The sun is setting now over southern Holland and Johanna van Haarlem has found the peace she spent so long searching for.

When she closes her eyes for a nap as the light dims behind her favourite comfortable chair at her Schaijk bungalow, she no longer sees the baby she gave away... but the son she found.

ACKNOWLEDGMENTS

First, we must thank Johanna van Haarlem. To have lived through so much and retain such a lust for life is inspiring and she has always been gracious and generous in her dealings with Paul. We are immensely grateful to her for telling us in her own words and through documents, photos and a memoir, her side of an extraordinary spy story beginning in WW2 and stretching beyond the Cold War. Her son Hans Duffhues has also been very supportive in providing sources for our research.

We are grateful, too, for the help and kindness shown by Zdenka Radkova, the widow of Ivo Radek (formerly Erwin van Haarlem) and her daughters Zdena and Iva, along with their friend Vera Navratilova, all of whom gave us a unique insight into the life and times of their beloved Ivo. Prague-based Pavel Horejsi, journalist/photographer, helped us secure thousands of pages of documents from the Czech intelligence archives lifting the lid on a treasure trove of information about the spy Vaclav Jelinek and his Cold War controllers' espionage tactics.

In The Hague, historian Aline Pennewaard joined us to probe wartime collaboration files in the National Archives of the Netherlands. At the UK's National Archives in Kew we accessed Erwin van Haarlem's arrest and charge papers, Central Criminal Court witness lists, trial transcripts, including the judge's summing up and Van Haarlem's handwritten appeal. Sabine Braun, Diptesh Kanojia and Girish Koushik of the University of Surrey provided invaluable assistance in

ACKNOWLEDGMENTS

navigating the huge amount of research material retrieved from the Czech secret service archives.

Among so many people we have interviewed are the wonderfully helpful and caring Rita Eker and Michael and Louise Carmi.

We also want to thank former Old Bailey Judge Simon-Brown, prosecuting barrister Roy Amlot, Sir David Calvert-Smith, junior treasury counsel who became Director of Public Prosecutions, and former Special Branch officers Dainis Maris Ozol and Geoff Lloyd.

Brilliant photographer and companion Clive Limpkin travelled with Paul to Czechoslovakia in 1991, accompanied by our interpreter Vera Vitvarova, to find Jiri Dousa, Olešovice orphanage director and Erwin's nurses Helena Klapova and Eva Kvapilova, who opened their hearts to put us on the final trail to the real Erwin van Haarlem.

Publications: Open Secret, Dame Stella Rimington, 2002; Cesky Spion Erwin van Haarlem, Jaroslav Kmenta, published in Czech 2018; *Dvakrát jsem ztratila syna (I lost My Son Twice)*, Johanna Van Haarlem memoir published in Czech, 2010.

We are especially grateful to our agent, Andrew Lownie for having faith in us and the project, and to editors Clare Fitzsimons and Christine Costello at Reach and Lauren McKeon at HarperCollins Canada. It would be remiss of us not to remember all the great friends both of us made during our time together at the *Daily Mail* – and the other newspapers we worked at – many of whom remain friends to this day.

ABOUT THE AUTHORS

PAUL HENDERSON is an award-winning investigative journalist. While Editor of the UK's Sunday Mirror and Sunday People, he received the London Press Club Sunday Newspaper of the Year for campaigning journalism in 2018. As the Daily Mail's Chief Investigative Reporter and the Mail on Sunday's Investigations Editor he was highly commended in the British Press Awards for filing revelatory despatches from China, Albania and Libya.

DAVID GARDNER is an author and journalist and currently in Washington DC as Chief National Correspondent for the Daily Beast. He also worked for the Daily Mail as a crime writer and senior foreign correspondent, filing dispatches from war-torn Beirut, covering the first Gulf War – where he was the first British print journalist into Baghdad – and travelling around the world on assignments for the award-winning newspaper. His book, 9/11: The Conspiracy Theories was a Sunday Times bestseller.